AS VEGAS &
Laughlin, Nevada

Automobile Club of Southern California

ISBN: 1-56413-659-0
Printed in the United States of America

© 2003, 2004, 2005 by the Automobile Club of Southern California
Travel Information Products A327
3333 Fairview Road, Costa Mesa, California 92626

Table of Contents

Glitter and glamour adorn an iconic welcome sign.

Las Vegas & Laughlin, Nevada

Southern Nevada is a land of extremes and contrasts: mega-resorts and massive dams, bizarre rock formations and noisy gambling halls, bespangled showgirls and fuzzy burros, thrill rides and wedding chapels.... People love it and hate it, sometimes both at once. But from the barren desert to the most elaborate casinos and hotels, Southern Nevada and all its offerings cannot be ignored.

Las Vegas remains one of the nation's favorite vacation destinations. It's a non-stop, 24-hour city where dreams of striking it rich sometimes become reality. But Las Vegas has many facets, and casino action is just one of them. It also offers luxurious resort lodgings, top-name entertainment, fine dining, world-class golf courses, scenic desert treks, nearby water recreation, and numerous activities for children, though fewer than in recent years. Las Vegas is home to 18 of the 20 largest resort hotels in the U.S. (Topping the list is the 5034-room MGM Grand Hotel & Casino.) Not surprisingly, there are also more hotel rooms in Las Vegas than any other city in the world: more than 130,000, with still more on the way. In 2002, Las Vegas attracted approximately 35 million visitors, despite the worldwide decline in travel.

Laughlin, by contrast, offers a more relaxed atmosphere than its flashy northern counterpart. It is an oasis along the Colorado River, where the state lines of California, Nevada and Arizona merge. Like Las Vegas, Laughlin offers plenty of gaming action, but the river remains one of its strongest assets. The area, which includes neighboring **Bullhead City, Arizona**, has long been known as a haven for "snowbirds" in winter (travelers from cold climes who migrate during the winter to sunbelt states) and the river crowd in summer. Boating, fishing, water skiing and swimming in the river's surprisingly frigid waters are favorite pursuits of vacationers, especially during the sizzling heat of summer. Combine the lure of the river with reasonably priced rooms, countless buffets and even an international airport, and it should be no surprise that Laughlin has gained such a foothold in the West. Some 5 million tourists visit this small desert community each year.

Another town that has made a name for itself in the region is **Primm**, located along I-15, 40 miles south of Las Vegas at the California-Nevada border. Once just a mere drive-through known as State Line, the settlement now boasts one of the world's tallest and fastest roller coasters, and is the site of three large resort-style hotels, a 6500-seat arena, a monorail and various other attractions.

Climate

Las Vegas experiences about 320 days of sunshine per year and an average high temperature of 80 degrees Fahrenheit. This high-desert community at an elevation of 2174 feet has an arid climate, low humidity and a yearly rainfall of about 4 inches. Spring and fall generally bring the mildest weather, when daytime highs are in the comfortable 70-degree range. Winter months, by contrast, can be quite cool, with highs in the 50s and lows in the 30s.

At the peak of summer, the temperature regularly climbs above 100 degrees. But the heat is easily escaped via air conditioning, swimming pools or jaunts to water parks. Scenic Mount Charleston in the Spring Mountains National Recreation Area also offers a break from the heat with its cooler upper-elevation temperatures.

Laughlin is located on the northeast edge of the Mojave Desert at an elevation of 510 feet and has a high mean temperature of about 85 degrees. In this hot, dry region, the summer months routinely sizzle well above the 100-degree mark, sometimes climbing above 120 degrees. But relief is always close at hand in the form of air conditioning and the frigid water of the Colorado River. Sometimes higher-than-average humidity triggers summer thunderstorms and flash floods, turning the area's dry washes into turbulent rivers. Winters can be equally severe, with below-freezing temperatures. Rainfall averages about 4 inches a year.

Roaming around Laughlin.

Shopping

Most of the big resort hotels in Las Vegas and Laughlin have shopping venues. These usually feature a dozen or so stores selling designer fashions, furs, jewelry, artwork, toys and international gifts. Shopping at Mandalay Bay provides access to fine wines, original artwork, leather goods and jewelry. The opulent shops at the Bellagio present creations from European designers and fine jewelers. A French shopping district at Paris Las Vegas includes a French wine shop and a pastry store. Next door, the Shops in Desert Passage resemble an open-air bazaar straight out of the movie *Casablanca*. (See the *Las Vegas Valley* chapter for more detailed listings.)

As for outlet shopping, Fashions Outlets of Las Vegas in Primm is tough to beat with its giant mix of high-end stores and discounted brand-name shops. In the heart of the Las Vegas Strip is Belz Factory Outlet World, also with mostly high-end merchandise.

The larger hotels are good places to find shops that carry such necessities as aspirin, toothbrushes, film, postage stamps, magazines and other miscellaneous items. These shops are usually centrally located near the front entrance of the hotel, the registration desk or the casino.

For the real souvenir hound there is also no shortage of trinket shops. Hats, shirts, coffee mugs, salt-and-pepper shakers, leather purses, turquoise jewelry, dice, playing cards and poker chips are widely available. In Las Vegas, these shops are mainly along The Strip area of Las Vegas Boulevard from Charleston Boulevard south to Tropicana Avenue; downtown, they are located one block off Fremont between Main and 4th streets.

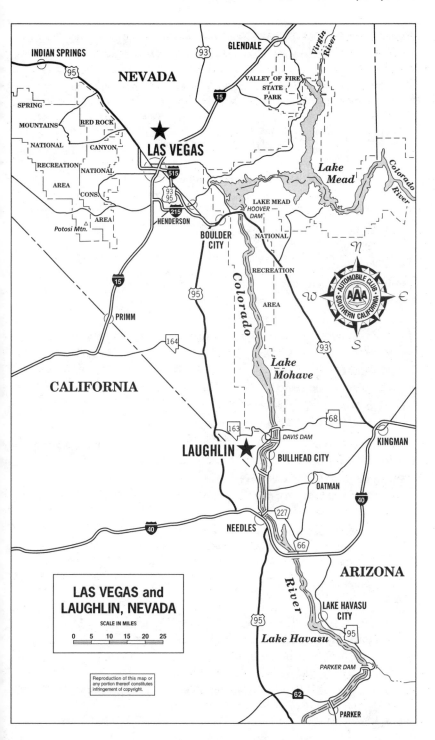

♠ TIPPING

A tip or gratuity for services rendered is not only customary in Las Vegas, it's expected. Although entirely at the customer's discretion, prompt, friendly and quality service merits a tip. There is a staggering array of service personnel in Las Vegas and Laughlin—including card dealers, slot people, showroom maitre d's and pool attendants—who supplement their income with tips. When in doubt about the amount, 15-20% of the total bill is usually appropriate. Following are some helpful guidelines:

Bartenders and Cocktail Servers
For parties of two to four people, a tip of $1-2 per round is standard; more for larger groups.

Bell Captains, Bell Caps and Skycaps
$1-2 per bag or $5 if you have several bags. For concierge or VIP services, a $5 tip is appropriate.

Child-care Attendants
A tip of $2-3 per hour of child-care service is appreciated.

Dealers
It is customary to make a small bet for the dealer or tip a chip when you are winning.

Hotel maids
$2-5 a day is appreciated.

Lounge/Pool Attendants
$1-2 in the attendant's tray is customary for towels, etc.

Masseuse/Masseur
The 15-20% rule is standard.

Showroom Maitre d's/Ushers
$5-20 should assist in getting desired seating in showrooms with unreserved seats.

Slot People/Keno Runners
A $1 tip now and then is appropriate for good service.

Taxi Drivers
15-20% is standard, more if the driver helps with luggage.

Tour Guides
$1-2 per person at the end of the trip is suggested.

Valet Parking Attendants
$2 is standard, more if they assist with luggage.

Waiters/Room Service
The 15-20% rule applies for both. When ordering room service, be sure to ask if the tip is included in the bill.

History

Las Vegas is Spanish for "The Fertile Plain," so named for its numerous springs and once verdant landscape. The surrounding harsh and unforgiving Mojave Desert protected this oasis for centuries from all but the native Paiute Indians. It was not until 1829 when the first known inhabitants of European descent settled. By comparison, Laughlin is a much more recent arrival, beginning in 1966 with Don Laughlin's aerial view of this once barren, formidable landscape. From his private plane, the native Midwesterner saw investment potential along a vacant stretch of the Colorado River, near Davis Dam and the sparsely populated town of Bullhead City, Arizona.

The discovery of abundant spring water at what is now **Las Vegas** shortened the Spanish Trail to Los Angeles, eased the rigors for Spanish traders and hastened the rush west for California gold. Some 14 years later, John C. Frémont, an American soldier and explorer, led an overland expedition west and camped at Las Vegas Springs. Today, Fremont Street and numerous other area landmarks carry his name.

The modern history of Las Vegas began in 1855, when a small group of Mormon settlers arrived. They came to protect the mail route between Los Angeles and Salt Lake City, but for the next three years also cultivated fruits and vegetables and mined lead at Potosi Mountain.

The Mormons abandoned their mining activity when the bullets made from their ore proved to be flaky and brittle due to an extremely high silver content—a problem other miners would liked to have had. American Indian raiding parties also added to their problems. The Mormons' 150-square-foot adobe fort was abandoned in 1858; a portion of it can be seen today near the intersection of Las

Fremont Street in 1929.

Vegas Boulevard North and Washington Avenue (see Old Las Vegas Mormon Fort State Historic Park in the *Las Vegas Valley* chapter).

In 1864, Nevada was admitted to the Union as the 36th state, although the 11,000 square miles surrounding Las Vegas were part of Arizona Territory. It was not until two years later that Congress ceded this region to Nevada, establishing the current state borders.

Farming and ranching were the main economic focus of Las Vegas until the coming of the railroad. On May 15, 1905, the Union Pacific Railroad auctioned off 1200 lots in a single day—lots that soon sprouted gambling houses, saloons and stores. In 1910, Nevada passed an anti-gambling law so strict that it even forbade the Western custom of flipping a coin for the price of a drink. Despite the law, which remained in effect for 20 years, gambling continued to flourish in the form of "underground" games, where patrons uttered a secret password to play.

Legalized gambling returned to the state in 1931, at the height of the Great Depression. It was also the same year construction started on the Boulder Canyon Project. Thousands of jobless citizens—victims of the nation's economic slump—streamed into the Las Vegas-Boulder City area looking for work. At its peak, the project employed 5128 people and had an average monthly payroll of $500,000.

In 1935 President Franklin Roosevelt dedicated the structure, known then as Boulder Dam. In April 1947, by congressional action, the 726-foot-high structure was officially designated Hoover Dam, the name by which it is known today.

The great hydroelectric project on the Colorado River originally brought power to Las Vegas, and this abundant source of electricity helped create the famous neon city. (Today Las Vegas' power primarily comes from coal-burning power stations.) In 1941 a group of Los Angeles investors, speculating on the resort potential of the area, built El Rancho Vegas, the first hotel on what became the Las Vegas Strip. Shortly thereafter, the Last Frontier was completed, followed by the Flamingo, a hotel and casino built by the infamous mobster Benjamin "Bugsy" Siegel. (Six months after the Flamingo's December 1946 opening, Siegel was murdered by an unknown assailant in Beverly Hills, California.)

The momentum established by these early resorts has continued ever since, taking off in the post-World War II years as the town emerged to become a major tourist destination. High-rise hotels with blazing marquees began to rise along a stretch of Las Vegas Boulevard that would soon be known simply as "The Strip." The Desert Inn, Sands, Riviera, Dunes and Stardust were but a few of those to open during the 1950s, and their names soon became familiar far beyond the Nevada state line.

Casino gambling was the main draw at most venues, but entertainment helped seal Las Vegas' reputation as a playground getaway. In 1941, when El Rancho Vegas was the only Strip resort, singers, comedians, strippers and other performers entertained guests in its small, intimate showroom.

The celebrated "Rat Pack" helped establish Las Vegas as a tourist destination.

Other resorts copied that successful format by featuring big-name entertainers of their own. Comedian Jimmy Durante and pianist Liberace were among the first headliners to play Las Vegas. The Stardust blazed a new path in the 1950s when it made a stage-spectacular its main entertainment feature. The hotel imported *Lido de Paris* from France, a critically acclaimed show that enjoyed a 31-year run. The Tropicana followed suit with another French import when it bought the U.S. rights to *Folies Bergere* in 1960. It remains a favorite to this day, complete with its trademark show-stopping cancan number.

Casino lounges emerged during the post-war years, offering dusk-to-dawn entertainment while spawning such crowd-pleasers as Don Rickles and Bob Newhart. For insurance, the hotels began importing the likes of Judy Garland and Red Skelton from Hollywood on a regular basis. Meanwhile, the famed "Rat Pack" of Frank Sinatra, Dean Martin and Sammy Davis Jr. crooned to hundreds of sellout audiences during their heyday in the 1950s and '60s. Sinatra would remain a star attraction decades later, packing the crowds into the early 1990s.

While headliners like Wayne Newton and Siegfried & Roy have become synonymous with Las Vegas in recent decades, no one did more for the town's entertainment image than the "King" himself, Elvis Presley. Between 1969 and 1976, Presley performed to more than 1500 sellout crowds at the Las Vegas Hilton, a one-man windfall for tourism.

Though gambling remained the number one lure, in 1976 the town faced competition for the first time when New Jersey voters approved a ballot measure to open casinos in Atlantic City. Las Vegas confronted the challenge by transforming itself into a family-friendly destination. As early as 1968, Circus Circus opened on The Strip, with carnival games and midway-style rides beneath its circus tent-shaped roof, although the transformation did not take off until the late 1980s.

The $630 million Mirage, the first new resort hotel in 15 years, opened in late 1989 featuring a white tiger habitat, a 20,000-gallon aquarium and a man-made volcano among its many non-casino attractions. A year later came the Excalibur, a 4000-

El Rancho Vegas was the first resort on The Strip when it opened in 1941.

room property designed like a medieval castle, with jousting knights, court jesters and entire floors devoted to non-gambling entertainment. The '90s building frenzy was underway, reaching its peak in late 1993 when three huge properties—the Luxor, Treasure Island and MGM Grand—opened within three months of each other. With more than 5000 rooms, the $1 billion MGM Grand became the world's largest hotel property.

While the 1993, 12,000-room, single-year spurt has not been eclipsed, growth continues, and with it a trend toward opulence. The 1998 opening of the most expensive hotel property in history, the $1.7 billion Bellagio, demonstrated a continued faith in the ability of Las Vegas to attract high rollers. The elegant hotel features an indoor botanical garden and a restaurant with original works of art by Picasso. Mandalay Bay Resort and Casino, which opened in 1999, incorporates a tropical theme throughout its property, featuring an 11-acre wave pool, the Shark Reef aquarium, and a House of Blues—not to mention the five-diamond-rated Four Seasons Hotel on its property.

In a town where bigger has always been better, a new breed of resort has established itself. Modeling and miniaturization are their focus. New York, Venice and Paris have been scaled and relocated in a way that could only be Vegas. The Statue of Liberty, the Empire State Building and the Chrysler Building re-create the Big Apple's skyline at New York-New York. Romantic Venice is found at the Venetian, complete with gondoliers plying canals, the Ca D'Oro (Palace of Gold), the Bridge of Sighs and even the Rialto Bridge. Paris Las Vegas features a 50-story replica of the Eiffel Tower, where 100 feet above The Strip guests may dine in a gourmet restaurant, or ride a glass elevator to the top to an observation deck that provides panoramas of the city.

Adding to the concept of the city as "a Disneyland for adults" is the construction of the ultramodern, $650-million Las Vegas Monorail. The privately-funded project, completed in 2004, connects eight hotel/casinos and the convention center, enabling visitors to travel from one end of the Strip to the other in as little as 14 minutes.

The town's long-held reputation for cheap buffets has given way to a growing recognition for fine dining. Restaurateur Wolfgang Puck has been credited with pioneering the so-called "food revolution" that has swept Las Vegas in recent years, resulting in three AAA five-diamond-rated restaurants on the Strip and a smorgasbord of award-winning chefs being imported to create dining destinations throughout the city.

The Las Vegas population has grown dramatically in recent years. Clark County is now home to 1.6 million people, having more than doubled since 1990. Perhaps befitting that growth, Las Vegas has never paid great homage to its history, choosing instead to focus on tomorrow. As an example, when the Hilton Corporation tore down an older section of the Flamingo Hotel in 1993, it also razed the fortress-like "Bugsy Suite" with its false stairways and bulletproof office that the notorious gangster used before his death. The Flamingo name survives, but each year entire hotels of bygone eras are felled to clear the way for bigger and better ones.

Even when Las Vegas does preserve the past, it reinvents itself in order to adapt to the ever-changing tastes of visitors. Take Fremont Street, the one-time "Glitter Gulch," which lost out years ago to The Strip as the center of gambling and entertainment action. A four-block section of the street was closed to traffic in 1995 and transformed into the Fremont Street Experience, a pedestrian mall crowned by a 90-foot-high canopy with more than 2 million lights. The street now hosts a series of dazzling sound and light shows every night, as well as an open-air Neon Museum.

Fremont Street transformed.

Henderson, a suburb of Las Vegas built during World War II to house defense workers, has emerged as something of an "anti-Strip" resort destination. The fast-growing city, a mix of planned residential communities, parks and shopping malls, offered few enticements to tourists until recently. Lake Las Vegas Resort, a new Tuscan-inspired enclave built around an artificial lake on the former site of a swamp at the edge of town, is the latest challenger to make a pitch for the hearts and wallets of visitors to Southern Nevada.

As the 21st century unfolds, water shortfalls may slow the region's long-term growth. Most of Las Vegas' water comes from the Colorado River, which Nevada must share with seven other states. If present trends continue, the state will use up its allotment, which will curtail growth if new supplies are not developed.

Before 1966, what is now **Laughlin** consisted of one rundown restaurant at the end of a dirt road. The area was known as South Pointe, the name of a construction camp that housed workers for nearby Davis Dam. (South Pointe's population disappeared following completion of the dam in 1953.) Entrepreneur Don Laughlin, fresh from a successful 10-year gaming venture in Las Vegas, purchased the deteriorating restaurant and renovated it as a casino in 1966, appropriately naming it Riverside. In 1977, the growing community was officially named after its entrepreneur-founder.

Initially, Laughlin's customers were residents of Bullhead City, Arizona, enticed by the free ferry service from a parking lot on the Arizona side of the river. As news of the friendly, informal atmosphere of the Riverside Casino got out, people from greater distances showed up. Soon the new business was a great success, which induced Laughlin to expand his operation. Others quickly saw the potential for the gaming business along the shores of the Colorado, so beginning in 1967 with what is now the Golden Nugget (originally called the Bob Cat), additional casino/hotels began to rise. Today nine major casinos occupy the west riverbank of the Colorado at Laughlin; another sits a block back from the water, and still another lies nine miles to the south of town on the Fort Mojave Indian Reservation. Those casinos were the main draw for the 4.6 million people who visited Laughlin in 2000.

Laughlin supplanted Lake Tahoe in 1987 as Nevada's third-largest gaming resort (after Las Vegas and Reno), and plans for further growth are a major topic of local conversation. Laughlin has clearly come a long way from its humble beginnings, when coyotes outnumbered the town's population. The town's 8200 residents are still outnumbered, however—this time by more than 11,000 slot machines.

Across the river in **Bullhead City**, the boomtown atmosphere is equally intense. Rugged mountains provide a scenic backdrop and contain mines and ghost towns of historic importance. Katherine Mine, Chloride and Oatman give travelers an enticing glimpse into the world of the Wild West. More than 37,000 people reside in Bullhead City today.

With wonderfully jagged mountaintops, winding roads and alluring vistas, a drive along Historic Route 66 through **Oatman** and **Kingman**, Arizona, is more than pleasing to the eye. It also serves as a reminder of those who, during the 1930s, migrated from the parched Midwest on this very road, seeking a better life.

Once a dusty rest stop along I-15 known as State Line, **Primm** has become a destination in its own right with its modern hotel-casinos, thrill rides and a golf course. The town changed its name in 1996 to honor Gary Primm, the developer and former owner of the three hotel-casinos that put this California-Nevada border outpost on the map.

Casino Games

From 1931 until the mid-1970s, Nevada was the only state that offered legalized gambling. This fact alone helped make Las Vegas the single most-popular tourist destination in the United States.

Before embarking on one of the many games of chance, it's a good idea to become familiar with a game's rules and strategy. Gambling instruction is offered in most casinos and, in some cases, on the hotel's cable TV channel. Understanding a game's intricacies will not only increase your odds of winning but also make it more enjoyable to play. Do not expect dealers or croupiers to be of much help; they have a job to do and will offer assistance and advice only when they can. A good way to get to know a game is to watch the action for a while before joining in; observation is an inexpensive way of learning some of the more obvious lessons.

Video poker is a favorite of casino patrons.

Many books devoted to the art of casino gambling have complete explanations of the rules, strategy, odds, wagering and systems that claim to give players an advantage. But be skeptical of the systems: statistically they might work in the long run, but few players have the time and the resources to last, or the concentration and mental dexterity that are often required. The serious student will spend time practicing at home before venturing into a casino. And a last piece of advice: Before placing any bets, determine how much you can afford to lose and set that money aside for gambling. Should it cross to the other side of the tables, exercise caution. It is not just a cliché that in Las Vegas, people can lose everything they have.

BACCARAT A game very similar to chemin de fer, baccarat (pronounced Ba-Ca-Rah) is played with eight decks of cards dealt from a box called a "shoe." Two cards are given to each of two players, with one player being designated the bank. The object of the game is to come as close to the number nine as possible. All tens and face cards are counted as zero. Other people at the table bet on either the bank or the player.

BINGO Most bingo games in Las Vegas and Laughlin are played on "boards" with three bingo cards on each board. There is both open-play and party bingo at most casinos. In open-play bingo, each board costs between 10¢ and 40¢ per game. Party bingo is played at set hours; cards cost $1 to $4 each with a $3 to $6 minimum; approximately 10 to 12 games are played during each party session.

BLACKJACK Also called "21," blackjack is one of the most popular card games, mainly because it's fast and easy to learn. The object of the game is to beat the dealer by getting as close to 21 as possible without going over that count.

CARIBBEAN STUD POKER This game, based on Five Card Stud but played on a layout similar to Blackjack, was the first casino table game to offer a separate progressive jackpot in addition to regular wagers.

CRAPS The most complicated casino game, craps offers dozens of different ways to bet on the dice. The action is fast and the amount of money exchanging hands is considerable. Craps is not a good game for the timid, but it's fun to watch.

KENO This is an adaptation of an ancient Chinese game. Players mark a series of favorite numbers between one and 80 that appear on the blank keno ticket. Twenty numbers are then drawn at random. The amount of money won depends on the type of ticket played and how many winning numbers were selected. Many restaurants and lounges have keno runners who take the bets. Keno is also a popular slot game.

LET IT RIDE Players do not play against the dealer or other players in this game, based on five-card stud poker. Each player places three equal bets and receives three cards; two additional cards are placed face down in front of the dealer. After looking at their first three cards, the player may ask for their first bet back or they may "Let It Ride." The objective is to get the best possible hand by using the three cards and the dealer's two face-down cards.

PAI GOW This ancient Chinese game involves 32 dominoes that are shuffled by the dealer and then placed in eight stacks of four each. Up to eight players are dealt one stack each. The object of the game is to set the four dominoes into two pairs for the best ranking combinations.

PAI GOW POKER A combination of poker and Pai Gow, this game is played with an ordinary deck of 52 cards plus one joker. The joker is used as an ace or to complete a straight or flush. Players are dealt seven cards each, which are arranged into two hands. One hand contains five cards and is known as the "high hand," while the other hand has only two cards and is called the "low hand." The object of the game is to win the bet by having both the high and low hands rank higher than the respective hands of the banker. The ranking is determined by traditional poker rules.

POKER The rules for casino poker are similar to home games, except that the house provides a dealer who manages the game without playing a hand. The house makes money by taking a small percentage of each pot. Five Card Stud is a well-known form of poker; the object of the game is to create the highest hand possible with the various cards dealt. Let It Ride is one of many variations. Check the rules carefully before sitting down at a game.

RACE AND SPORTS BOOKS Bets can be made on practically any horse race, boxing match, or professional or collegiate game (most Nevada events, except boxing matches, are excluded) from the comfort of race and sports books. Live events are shown on giant, satellite-fed screens. Most of the major hotels have race and sports books.

ROULETTE The roulette wheel has 36 numbers plus a green zero and a green double zero. Bets can be made on one number, a group, a color or a column of numbers. Odds on roulette range from 35-to-1 to even money. For example, if the player wins by betting on a single number, he or she is paid $35 for every $1 wagered. This is strictly a game of luck and intuition, so there's no reason to worry about skill level. Low stakes games are common, so a few dollars can keep a player going for quite some time.

SLOT MACHINES One-armed bandits and video poker comprise the majority of slots, but video blackjack, video keno and a variety of other games are offered. Quarter and dollar machines are the most prevalent, and most slots don't even require coins or tokens—they accept U.S. bills of many denominations. There are a variety of ways to win, including multiple pay lines, fixed jackpots and progressives (slots linked to statewide networks). To win the big jackpots and progressives requires more than the minimum bet; some machines accept up to 10 bets (or coins) at once.

Family Activities

After more than a decade of promoting itself as a family-friendly destination, Las Vegas appears to be reverting back to its former image as a an adult-oriented city. However, both Las Vegas and Laughlin still offer a number of diversions for the younger set

Despite the focus on casinos and entertainment for mature audiences, there is an abundance of attractions suitable for both children and adults. The Stratosphere Tower, the tallest structure west of the Mississippi, is crowned with three thrill rides, including the highest roller coaster in the world. New York-New York Hotel & Casino entices visitors with a popular "twist and shout" coaster of its own, the Manhattan Express.

Year-round fun can be found at Circus Circus Hotel & Casino's Adventuredome, a five-acre, climate-controlled, indoor amusement park whose attractions include the nation's only double-loop, double-corkscrew, indoor roller coaster. The hotel also boasts a carnival-style arcade and circus acts.

Mandalay Bay's Shark Reef puts some teeth in the aquarium experience, with over 2000 animals from 100 different species; exhibits are appropriate for all ages, with touch tanks geared to kids. Luring crowds with its pyramid structure and enormous outdoor sphinx, Luxor Las Vegas has an eclectic mix of Egyptian replicas, including a full-size reproduction of King Tut's tomb. Other attractions on The Strip appealing to children include the Excalibur Hotel & Casino's medieval cas-

Kids at GameWorks' Surge Rock attraction.

tle-themed exterior and Renaissance village interior. Carnival-style arcade games and nightly jousting tournaments can all be found here, as well as Merlin's Magic Motion Machine, a motion-simulator ride. At the Mirage, children will enjoy Siegfried & Roy's Secret Garden and Dolphin Habitat as well as the white tiger display.

Visitors to Primm will find the Desperado roller coaster and other thrill rides at Buffalo Bill's Resort & Casino, while Henderson touts the Ethel M Chocolates Factory and Ron Lee's World of Clowns, all appealing to the young ones. In Laughlin, the Ramada Express has a narrow-gauge railroad with a steam locomotive that takes passengers for a ride around the property. The unofficial welcoming committee of Oatman, Arizona, an Old West mining town near Laughlin, is a group of friendly but wild burros that roam the streets, often greeting visitors in hopes of a carrot snack. Entertaining gunfights are staged daily on town streets.

♠ Kidding Around

Following is a quick reference list of family activities in this book:

Marriage Information

Two words spoken as often in Las Vegas as "hit me" and "double down" are without a doubt, "I do." Where else but in this unique community are marriage licenses issued so frequently (one every 5½ minutes), and would Elvis impersonators preside over the ceremonies? Seven days a week, 24 hours a day on weekends (correct change required), wedding vows are taken at drive-up windows, on bungee jumping platforms and boats, in helicopters, hotel suites and churches, and at dozens of wedding chapels. Ninety miles to the south, Laughlin now has its own branch of the Clark County Clerk's Office, and couples there can get hitched on the Colorado River aboard Mississippi-style riverboats or in any number of wedding chapels.

Marriages in Las Vegas have doubled in the past two decades—now averaging 120,000 per year—due in part to the ease of getting a marriage license. Historically, the most popular wedding day here is Valentine's Day, with New Year's Eve running a close second. Among the famous who have married in Las Vegas are Paul Newman and Joanne Woodward, Elvis and Priscilla Presley, Frank Sinatra and Mia Farrow, Richard Gere and Cindy Crawford, and Bruce Willis and Demi Moore.

LAS VEGAS Marriage Bureau, *Clark County Courthouse, 200 S 3rd St. (702) 455-4415. Open Mon-Thu 8 am-midnight, and continuously (24 hours) from Fri 8 am-Sun midnight; holidays, 24 hours. License fee, $55 in cash.*

LAUGHLIN Justice Court Office, *Regional Government Center, 101 Civic Wy. (702) 298-4622. Open Tue-Thu 8 am-4:30 pm, Fri to 8 pm, Sat-Sun 8 am-noon and 1-4 pm. Closed Mon and legal holidays. License fee, $55 in cash.*

To purchase a marriage license, the couple must simply appear at the Marriage Bureau in Las Vegas or the Justice Court in Laughlin. No legal residency is

A formal affair at Bellagio.

required. Blood tests are not needed and there is no waiting period. Persons cannot be nearer of kin than second cousins or cousins of half-blood. Applicants must be 18 or older; minor age 16 or 17 must have the consent of parents or legal guardians. Persons giving consent must have proof of identity and guardianship; proof of age may be required as well. If the bride or groom was previously married, divorce must be final in the state in which it was granted; no papers are required.

Marriage ceremonies can be performed in Las Vegas at the Office of Civil Marriages, 309 South 3rd Street, or in one of the many wedding chapels in town (more than 50 at last count). One witness to the ceremony is required by law. The commissioner's office charges $50, and exact change is required. Hours are 8 a.m. to 10 p.m. daily, including weekdays and holidays; no appointment is necessary. Wedding

A wedding gondola ride at the Venetian.

chapel fees depend on the elaborateness of the ceremony. Many large hotels and casino complexes have wedding chapels on the grounds. For a list of wedding chapels, see the Las Vegas telephone directory yellow pages under "Wedding."

The Laughlin-Bullhead City area offers wedding services at several chapels and aboard riverboats. Ceremonies can also be performed in the Justice Court Office (appointments are required); there is an additional recording fee for the service. For more information, call the Justice Court Office. Wedding chapels can be found in the Laughlin-Bullhead City telephone directory yellow pages under "Wedding Chapels and Ceremonies."

Las Vegas Valley

How many guestrooms a gambling resort has or how "loose" the casino slots may be is largely irrelevant. Fantasy and surrealism reign on The Strip, where traffic crawls as drivers shamelessly gawk at the huge pyramid and sphinx of the Egyptian-themed Luxor, the soaring Manhattan skyline of New York-New York and the imposing Eiffel Tower in front of Paris Las Vegas. Without a doubt, audacious creativity, unabashed flamboyance and a dash of irreverence have proved a winning formula in wooing visitors to modern-day Las Vegas.

POINTS OF INTEREST

Attractions are listed alphabetically by city or area—**Henderson, Downtown Las Vegas Area, Las Vegas Strip and Vicinity** and **North Las Vegas Area.** Listings connected to hotel properties do not imply AAA endorsement for the lodging establishment.

Henderson

CLARK COUNTY MUSEUM *13 miles SE of Las Vegas at 1830 S Boulder Hwy (US 93/95). (702) 455-7955. Open daily 9 am-4:30 pm. Closed Jan 1, Thanksgiving and Dec 25. Adults $1.50; ages 55 and older and 3-16, $1.* This 25-acre museum houses regional memorabilia, artifacts, and historic buildings, many fully restored to reflect their respective eras. Outdoor exhibits include authentic rolling stock, mining

Candy-making at Ethel M.

equipment and a "ghost town" comprised of several structures dating to the 1880s. The indoor Exhibit Center features themed displays, an outdoor classroom with plants native to the Mojave Desert, and a permanent Southern Nevada timeline exhibit that dates from prehistoric times to the present.

ETHEL M CHOCOLATES FACTORY *8 miles SE of The Strip, off Sunset Rd at Mountain Vista; 2 Cactus Garden Dr. (702) 433-2500 (recorded information). Open daily 8:30 am-7 pm. Closed Thanksgiving and Dec 25. Free.* Ethel M's self-guided tour offers a behind-the-scenes look at the ingredients and machinery used in the candy-making process. At the end of the tour, participants may sample their favorite Ethel M chocolate and shop for other tempting treats in the gift store. Adjacent to the factory is a 2½-acre cactus garden featuring rare and exotic plants.

HENDERSON BIRD VIEWING PRESERVE *2400 Moser Dr. (702) 566-2940. Open daily 6 am-3 pm. Closed during National Security Alerts, level Orange or higher. Free; guided tours by appointment.* This preserve, adjacent to a water reclamation facility, includes a visitor center, numerous trails and observation stations with benches.

LAKE LAS VEGAS RESORT *1600 Lake Las Vegas Pkwy, off Lake Mead Pkwy (SR 564). (702) 564-1600, (800) 564-1603, marina (702) 568-6024.* A literal oasis in the desert, this new Mediterranean-style resort destination is centered around a 320-acre private man-made lake, 17 miles from The Strip, just west of Lake Mead. Resort hotels, spas, championship golf courses, shopping, dining, and a full-service marina with boat rentals and yacht cruises are all part of the mix.

Gondola Adventures *(877) 446-6365. Times and prices vary; reservations required.* Champagne, lunch and dinner cruises on Lake Las Vegas are available, complete with singing gondolier.

MonteLago Village Resort *(866) 752-9558.* Lake Las Vegas Resort is anchored by this $500 million waterfront complex with cobblestone streets, gourmet restaurants, upscale boutiques and art galleries, luxury condos, and, of course, a casino. MonteLago's centerpiece, the AAA five diamond-rated Ritz-Carlton, Lake Las Vegas, is distinguished by a mini re-creation of Florence's famed Ponte Vecchio bridge.

RON LEE'S WORLD OF CLOWNS *Off Gibson and Warm Springs rds, at 330 Carousel Pkwy. (702) 434-1700. Open Mon-Fri 8:30 am-4:30 pm. Closed major holidays. Free tour.* The mold-making and painting processes of clown figurines are shown during this self-guided tour. Through windows, visitors may watch the artisans at work; a video at each station explains the process being done. A large gift shop retails the final products.

Downtown Las Vegas Area

FREMONT STREET EXPERIENCE *Fremont St from 4th to Main sts in downtown Las Vegas. (702) 678-5600. Free nightly shows on the hour, dusk-midnight.* The four blocks of downtown once known as "Glitter Gulch" are now a pedestrian-only zone covered by a 90-foot-high latticed canopy embedded with 2.1 million lights. The high-tech, computer-controlled light and music show debuted in 1995.

GOLDEN GATE HOTEL & CASINO *1 Fremont St. (702) 385-1906.* The oldest hotel in town, this historic 106-room downtown haunt (opened in 1906 as Hotel Nevada with $1-day rooms) preserves much of the flavor of a long-gone Las Vegas. The casino walls are virtually papered with century-old photos of San Francisco; the 24-hour deli is renowned for its bargain-priced shrimp cocktail, a local tradition it reputedly began.

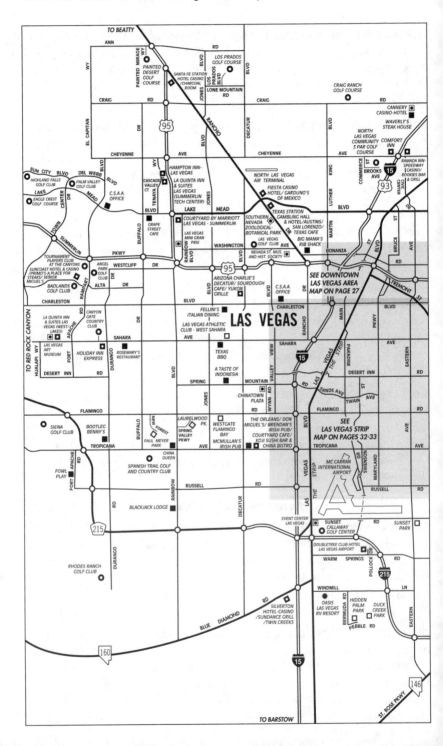

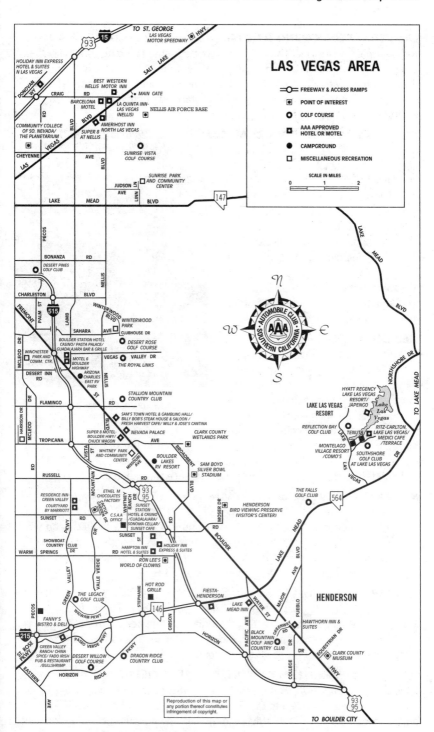

LAS VEGAS CLUB CASINO & HOTEL *18 E Fremont St. (702) 385-1664. Hall of Fame open 24 hours. Free.* The city's only sports-themed lodging (originally the Overland Hotel), this 410-room facility is home to the Sports Hall of Fame, a hallway crammed with a huge and varied collection of memorabilia ranging from baseball bats to football uniforms, and autographed photos of players. The exhibit extends into the hotel's restaurants and casino.

LAS VEGAS NATURAL HISTORY MUSEUM *900 Las Vegas Blvd N. (702) 384-3466. Open daily 9 am-4 pm. Adults, $6; ages 55 and older, students and military, $5; ages 3-11, $3; ages 2 and younger, free.*
The museum features an animated dinosaur exhibit, which includes a 35-foot *Tyrannosaurus rex;* an international wildlife room with mounted animals; a 3000-gallon tank filled with live sharks; a whale and dolphin exhibit; and a display of plants and wildlife native to Southern Nevada and the Southwest desert. Children may illuminate various animals in an African Savanna exhibit.

LIED DISCOVERY CHILDREN'S MUSEUM *833 Las Vegas Blvd N. (702) 382-3445. Open Tue-Sun 10 am-5 pm. Closed Mon, except most school holiday Mon. Adults, $6; military, ages 1-17 and 55 and older, $5; infants and museum members, free.* Kids will enjoy this unusual

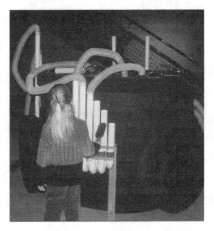

Lied Discovery Children's Museum

museum, which includes over 100 hands-on exhibits in the arts, humanities and sciences—if they like, children can pick a job, earn a paycheck, deposit it in a bank and shop for groceries. There's also a science tower and a weather station.

NEON MUSEUM *At E end of Fremont Street Experience, in front of Neonopolis; 3rd St cul-de-sac between Fremont and Ogden sts. (702) 387-6366. Open 24 hrs. Free. Tours of the Boneyard, $5 per person; by appointment only.* Refurbished neon signs, salvaged from defunct Las Vegas hotels and businesses, are exhibited in two open-air museum "galleries." Tours are also available of the museum's **Neon Boneyard**, a collection of non-restored signs on a site near downtown.

NEONOPOLIS *At E end of Fremont Street Experience, 450 Fremont St at Las Vegas Blvd. (702) 477-0470. Open Sun-Thu 11 am-9 pm, Fri-Sat to 10 pm. Free.* Restaurants, shops, a movie theater and a giant arcade pepper this 250,000-square-foot entertainment complex, modeled after San Diego's Horton Plaza. Dozens of vintage neon signs add to the experience.

NEVADA STATE MUSEUM AND HISTORICAL SOCIETY *2 miles W of downtown in Lorenzi Park, 700 Twin Lakes Dr. (702) 486-5205. Open daily 9 am-5 pm. Closed Jan 1, Thanksgiving and Dec 25. Adults, $4; ages 65 and older, $3; ages 17 and younger, free.* Two of the galleries in this lakeside museum present permanent

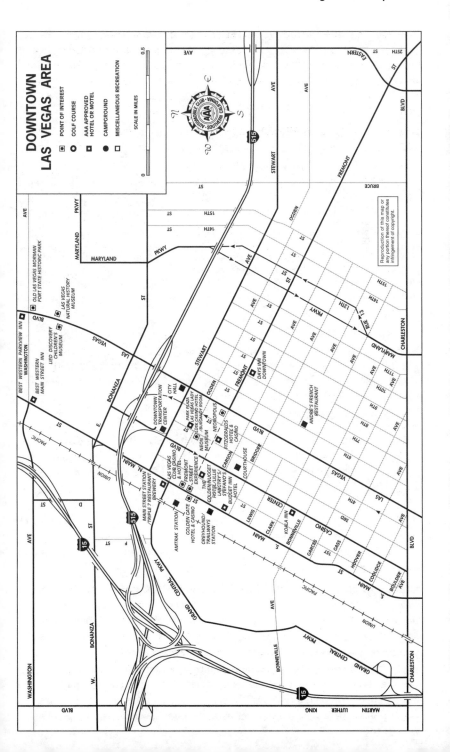

♠ A Quick Guide to Las Vegas & Vicinity

Police (non-emergency)

Boulder City (702) 293-9224

Henderson (702) 565-8933

Metropolitan Las Vegas, Mount Charleston and
North Las Vegas (702) 649-9111

Time (775) 844-1212

Weather Conditions (702) 248-4800

Information Guides

A variety of weekly and biweekly publications, distributed in lodgings and other tourist venues, provide information on attractions, dining and entertainment.

Radio Stations

These stations broadcast news, weather and traffic.

Highway News: KHWY (99.5 FM), KIXW (101.5 FM); News/Sports/Talk: KBAD (920 AM), KDWN (720 AM), KENO (1460 AM), KLAV (1230 AM), KXNT (840 AM), KNUU (970 AM); Public Radio/Classical: KNPR (89.5 FM); Spanish: KDOL (870 AM/1280 AM).

Television Stations

The area's major television stations include channels 3 (NBC), 5 (FOX), 8 (CBS), 10 (PBS), 13 (ABC), 21 (WB) and 25 (UPN). For a complete list of radio and television programs, consult *Las Vegas Review-Journal* or *Las Vegas Sun*.

displays on natural history. Exhibits on the history of the Southern Nevada region occupying a third gallery change annually. A research library is also located here. American Indian jewelry, and books and videos about Nevada's history can be purchased in the museum store.

OLD LAS VEGAS MORMON FORT STATE HISTORIC PARK *1 mile N of downtown, 500 E Washington. (702) 486-3511. Open daily 8 am-4:30 pm. Closed holidays. Adults, $3; ages 6-12, $2; ages 5 and younger, free.* This fort, built by Mormon settlers in 1855, is the oldest building of its kind in Nevada. It provided shelter for gold-seekers, emigrants and other travelers along the Spanish Trail/Mormon Road. Sections of the park have been renovated. In order to maintain the character of the fort, its walls have been reconstructed with parts reflecting a state of disrepair; a re-created stream flows along the same route as the park's original stream; and a pioneer demonstration garden has been planted.

Historic photographs, interpretive panels and antiques from the mid-1800s are on display.

SOUTHERN NEVADA ZOOLOGICAL-BOTANICAL PARK *3 miles NW of downtown; 1775 N Rancho Dr. (702) 647-4685. Open daily 9 am-5 pm. Closed Jan 1, Thanksgiving and Dec 25. Adults, $7; ages 2-12 and 62 and older, $5.* This limited zoological-botanical park exhibits a collection of mostly small animals and exotic birds. Featured are the last family of Barbary apes in the U.S., animals ranging from alligators to tigers, and all species of venomous reptiles found in Southern Nevada. Birds on display range from ravens and talking parrots to golden eagles and ostriches. A snack bar and gift shop are located on the grounds. Off-road tours of the surrounding desert area that include the perimeter of "Area-51" are also available.

Las Vegas Strip and Vicinity

ADVENTUREDOME—*See Circus Circus Hotel, Casino & Themepark.*

A.J. HACKETT BUNGY *810 Circus Circus Dr, adjacent to Circus Circus Hotel, Casino & Themepark. (702) 385-4321. Open daily 11 am-8:30 pm; bungee jumpers must have registered to jump at least ½ hour before closing time. $59 per person; same-day additional jumps, $20; additional jumps at other times, $29.* This New Zealand-based company has several locations around the world and a record of 1.5 million incident-free jumps. Participants plunge 171 feet from North America's highest double platform over a 12-foot pool.

ATOMIC TESTING MUSEUM *1 mile E of The Strip in Frank H Rogers Science & Technology Bldg, 755 E Flamingo Rd. (702) 794-5150. Open Mon-Fri 9 am-5 pm. Free.* The history of the Nevada Test Site is depicted through interactive multimedia exhibits, photographs, memorabilia and other Cold War artifacts, including pieces of equipment donated by nuclear laboratories. This new museum is an affiliate of the Smithsonian Institute.

BALLY'S LAS VEGAS *3645 Las Vegas Blvd S, at Flamingo Rd. (702) 739-4111.* Home of the long-running showgirl cabaret *Jubilee!*, this colorful hotel/casino served as a location for the film *Honeymoon in Vegas*.

Jubilee! **All Access Backstage Walking Tour** *(702) 946-4567. Mon, Wed and Sat at 2 pm. Tour, $15; with purchase of* Jubilee! *show ticket, $10. Children must be 13 years or older.* This one-hour tour takes visitors behind the scenes of the technically complex production, dressing rooms and all. A close-up look at the show's spectacular Bob Mackie costumes is included.

BELLAGIO *3600 Las Vegas Blvd S. (702) 693-7111, (888) 987-6667. Via Bellagio open daily 10 am-midnight.* This Tuscan-style resort, which opened in 1998, is known for its elegant and distinctive Old World look. The grand front lobby has an 18-foot ceiling with a colorful chandelier designed by glass sculptor Dale Chihully; the Conservatory and Botanical Garden features seasonal trees and flowers with theatrical lighting. Via Bellagio, a glass-enclosed shopping promenade, offers 100,000 square feet of upscale boutiques such as Giorgio Armani,

♠ Public Transportation

Downtown Transportation Center *300 N Casino Center Blvd and Stewart Ave. (702) 228-7433. DTC serves as a transportation hub for Citizens Area Transit (CAT) buses and the downtown trolley. Most bus lines connect to the center, as does the trolley system. The center is open daily 6 am-10 pm, with customer service available until 6:45 p.m. Holiday service varies.*

Strip Bus *(702) 228-7433. Online at www.rtcsouthernnevada.com. 1-way fares for routes 301, 302 and 303: adults, $2; ages 62 and older, 6-17 and persons with disabilities (with reduced-fare photo ID card), $1. 1-way fares for all other routes: adults, $1.25; ages 62 and older, 5-17 and persons with disabilities (with reduced-fare ID), 60¢. All-day pass, $5. Exact change is required. Tokens (called CAT Coins) or a monthly pass can be purchased at the Downtown Transportation Center.* Twenty-four hours a day, the CAT bus (Route 301) runs at 10-minute intervals along The Strip between the southernmost point, Vacation Village, and the northernmost point, the Downtown Transportation Center. The Strip Express (Route 302) runs this same route daily at 15- to 20-minute intervals from 10 a.m. to midnight.

Local residential bus service to several areas, including Henderson and Boulder City, is also available. Call for more information.

Downtown Trolley *(702) 229-6024. Fares: adults, 50¢; ages 62 and older, ages 17 and younger and disabled, 25¢.* Shuttle buses designed to look like trolleys depart the Downtown Transportation Center daily every 20 minutes from 7 a.m. to 11 p.m. The route traveled is along Ogden Ave. (eastbound) to the Charleston Plaza Shopping Center and Fremont St. (westbound). The entire route takes 30 minutes to travel. (Do not confuse this trolley with the Strip Trolley.) See *Downtown Las Vegas* map.

Strip Trolley *(702) 382-1404. Fare: $1.75. All-day pass, $5. Exact change is required.* Like the Downtown Trolley, the Strip Trolley also uses shuttle buses designed to look like trolleys. The trolley line operates daily 9:30 a.m. to 2 a.m. along Las Vegas Boulevard South, from Mandalay Bay on the south end to the Stratosphere Tower on the north end. An additional loop includes the

Gucci, Chanel and Tiffany & Co. The hotel is also home to Cirque du Solieil's long-running aquatic circus, "O," and two AAA five-diamond restaurants, Le Cirque and Picasso; the latter displays original paintings and ceramic pieces by its famous namesake.

Bellagio Gallery of Fine Art *Open daily 9 am-9 pm; last admission sold at 8:30 pm. Admission (audio tour included) $15; ages 65 and older, 12 and younger and Nev residents, $12. Wheelchair accessible.* This gallery features rotating exhibits from major museums and private collections throughout the world, favoring the Impressionist Movement of the 1870s as well as contemporary artists.

♠ Public Transportation

Las Vegas Hilton and a portion of Paradise Rd. The trolleys pass by each stop about every 15 minutes. (Do not confuse this trolley with the Downtown Trolley.) See *Las Vegas Strip* map.

Taxi *$3 base fare plus $1.80 per mile; 40¢ per minute for standing still. Pickups at McCarran International Airport pay $1.20 tax per load.* Taxis are plentiful, particularly at the entrances of the major resort hotels. A typical trip half the length of The Strip will cost $10-17; from the airport to the middle of The Strip, $10-12; and from the airport to downtown, $18-24. The airport taxi queue is located on the east side of baggage claim. The following companies provide service in Las Vegas: ABC Union/NLV, (702) 736-8444; Ace (702) 736-8383; Checker/Star/Yellow, (702) 873-2227; Desert, (702) 873-2000; Henderson, (702) 384-2322; Nellis, (702) 248-1111; Western, (702) 736-8000. Upon request, ABC Union, Ace, Nellis and Western provide vans with wheelchair lifts at regular taxi rates.

Airport Shuttle A variety of companies offer shuttle bus service between McCarran Airport and downtown, Strip and Off-Strip hotels. Typical costs are $4-5 for Strip hotels, $5-7 for downtown lodgings and $7 and up for Off-Strip destinations. Round-trip fares are available at a discount. Shuttles are located on the west side of baggage claim.

Free Shuttles and Trams Courtesy shuttle buses offer transportation between Harrah's Las Vegas Casino & Hotel and Rio Suite Hotel & Casino; Hard Rock Hotel and Casino, the Forum Shops at Caesar's Palace, Fashion Show Mall, and Stardust Resort and Casino; Barbary Coast Hotel, Gold Coast Hotel and The Orleans; Fashion Show Mall and various locations; Sam's Town Hotel & Gambling Hall and various locations; The Palms Casino Resort, Fashion Show Mall, Forum Shops, and The Shops at Desert Passage. Shuttles typically run every 20-30 minutes but times vary; check with the venue for more information. Free trams run 24/7 between Bellagio and Monte Carlo Resort & Casino; and between Mandalay Bay Resort & Casino, Luxor Las Vegas and Excalibur Hotel & Casino.

Fountains of Bellagio *Shows daily; 7 pm-midnight every 15 minutes; Mon-Fri 3-7 pm and Sat-Sun noon-7 pm on the half-hour. Free.* A fountain show takes place on the eight-acre lake entrance to Bellagio, with water soaring up to 240 feet in the air, choreographed to music ranging from Sinatra to Pavarotti.

BONANZA GIFT & SOUVENIR SHOPS *2460 Las Vegas Blvd S. (702) 385-7359. Open daily 8 am-midnight.* This store offers what is likely the largest assortment of Las Vegas souvenirs in town—rooms full of T-shirts, key chains, gag gifts and other ephemera not found in the city's upscale shopping malls.

LAS VEGAS STRIP

- ■ POINT OF INTEREST
- ○ GOLF COURSE
- ▫ AAA APPROVED HOTEL OR MOTEL
- ● CAMPGROUND
- □ MISCELLANEOUS RECREATION

SCALE IN MILES
0   0.5

CALIFORNIA STATE AUTOMOBILE ASSOCIATION OFFICE

CHARLESTON BLVD

FREMONT ST

CHARLESTON BLVD

ECONO LODGE

HOWARD JOHNSON LAS VEGAS STRIP

RONDY'S DINER

STRATOSPHERE CASINO HOTEL & TOWER/ ROXY'S DINER

BONANZA GIFT & SOUVENIR SHOPS

GOLDEN STEER

SAHARA HOTEL & CASINO

WET 'N WILD

TRAVELODGE LAS VEGAS STRIP

HILTON GRAND VACATION CLUB ON THE LAS VEGAS STRIP

GUINESS WORLD OF RECORDS MUSEUM

CIRCUSLAND

CIRCUS RV PARK

CIRCUS CIRCUS HOTEL CASINO & THEMEPARK/ BLUE IGUANA A.J. HACKETT BUNGY

STARDUST RESORT AND CASINO

LAS VEGAS SPORTING HOUSE

PALACE STATION HOTEL & CASINO/ THE BROILER/ PALACE CAFE

COFFEE PUB

SCANDIA FAMILY FUN CENTER

ELVIS-A-RAMA MUSEUM

FASHION SHOW

TREASURE ISLAND

THE MIRAGE/ RENOIR/ SAMBA BRAZILLIAN STEAKHOUSE/ KOKOMOS

THE VENETIAN RESORT HOTEL CASINO/ LUTECE/ VALENTINO LAS VEGAS/ RANCHO / THE VENETIAN CASINO ROYALE AND HOTEL

THE WYNN COLLECTION OF FINE ART

VILLA ROMA INN

RIVIERA HOTEL & CASINO/RISTORANTE ITALIANO

SOMERSET HOUSE MOTEL

FLYAWAY INDOOR SKYDIVING

MARRIOTT SUITES LAS VEGAS

PIERO'S

COURTYARD BY MARRIOTT CONVENTION CENTER

RESIDENCE INN LAS VEGAS CONVENTION CENTER

LAS VEGAS CONVENTION CENTER

LAS VEGAS HILTON/ ANDIAMO/ HILTON STEAKHOUSE/ PARADISE CAFE

HILTON GRAND VACATIONS CLUB AT THE LAS VEGAS HILTON

HOMESTEAD STUDIO SUITES HOTEL - LAS VEGAS /MIDTOWN

LA SCALA

LAS VEGAS COUNTRY CLUB

BEST WESTERN MARDI GRAS INN & CASINO

EMBASSY SUITES CONVENTION CENTER

LAS VEGAS ATHLETIC CLUB-MARYLAND PARKWAY

LAS VEGAS NATIONAL GOLF CLUB

SAHARA AVE

DESERT INN RD

SPRING MOUNTAIN RD

MARYLAND PKWY

EASTERN AVE

PARADISE RD

LAS VEGAS BLVD

S. MAIN ST

INDUSTRIAL RD

RANCHO DR

KING RD

MARTIN L. KING BLVD

GRAND CENTRAL PKWY

JOE W. BROWN DR

KAREN AVE

TWAIN AVE

SANDS AVE

DESERT INN RD

TEODY DR

HIGHLAND DR

THE STRIP

MONORAIL

TROLLEY ROUTE

LAS VEGAS TROLLEY ROUTE

15

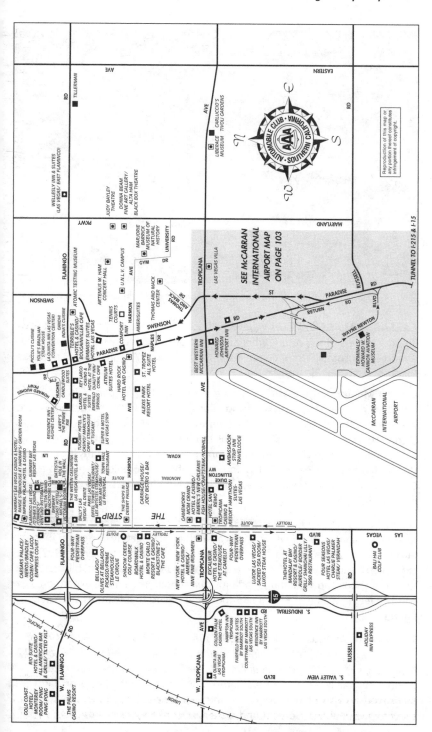

Bellagio's fountain show combines water, music and light to great effect.

CAESARS PALACE *3750 Las Vegas Blvd S. (702) 731-7333.* The glory that was Rome is revived at this resort, where even the gift shop teddy bears wear togas. Amidst the "classical" architecture is the 50,000-gallon Atlantis Aquarium, featuring over 500 exotic tropical fish.

Caesars Magical Empire Shows *Tue-Sat 4:30-10 pm. $75. Tours, Tue-Sat 11:30 am-3:30 pm. Free.* Magic, mystery and dining converge in this attraction, where visitors are entertained before and during their meals. Greeters dressed as Roman centurions lead guests to one of 10 dining chambers or two séance rooms, where a magician takes charge and performs an array of mystical feats during dinner. Tours of the dining and entertainment complex, including a Lumineria show with dancing, fire, smoke and lighting effects, are available during pre-dining hours.

Forum Shops *(702) 733-9000, (888) 910-7223. Open daily at 10 am; Sun-Thu to 11 pm, Fri-Sat to midnight.* This upscale indoor mall features a Roman motif, talking statues and a domed "sky" that changes from night to day. A 1997 expansion doubled the mall's size to 533,000 square feet, and established more than 110 shops and restaurants. Atlantis, the centerpiece for the expansion, is a hall 160 feet in diameter with an 85-foot-high ceiling that features animated figures.

The Race for Atlantis *(702) 733-9000, (888) 910-7223. Open daily at 10 am; Sun-Thu to 11 pm, Fri-Sat to midnight. Adults $10; ages 55 and older, $9; ages 12 and younger, $7 (42" height requirement).* The Race for Atlantis is one of the world's few 3-D IMAX motion simulators. Super-sized three-dimensional images and sound systems immerse guests in the experience through the use of a headset with a visor and personal sound system.

CENTAUR ART GALLERIES *In Fashion Show Mall, 3200 Las Vegas Blvd S at Spring Mountain Rd. (702) 737-1234. Open Mon-Fri 10 am-9 pm, Sat to 8 pm, Sun 11 am-6 pm. Free.* Major shows of museum-quality works—including mammoth exhibits devoted to such artists as Dali, Picasso and Chagall—are the mainstay of this shop.

CHINATOWN PLAZA *2 miles W of The Strip; 4255 Spring Mountain Rd. (702) 221-8448. Open 10 am-10 pm daily.* This shopping plaza has more than 30 specialty stores that carry jewelry, handcrafted furniture, clothing and other merchandise from the Orient. In addition to several restaurants, one of the largest Asian supermarkets in Nevada is located here.

CIRCUS CIRCUS HOTEL, CASINO & THEMEPARK *2880 Las Vegas Blvd S. (702) 734-0410.* This resort, one of the town's original casino-theme parks, offers what is perhaps the quintessential Las Vegas experience.

Adventuredome *Recorded information (702) 794-3939. Hours vary; call for information. Free admission; all-day ride pass, $21.95 for 48" and taller; $13.95 for 33-47"; individual ride tickets, $3-5. Military and Nev residents, $2 off adult pass. Some rides have height requirements.* The Adventuredome is a climate-controlled amusement park spanning five acres. It is the largest fully enclosed themepark in the United States. Featured rides include the nation's only indoor double-loop, double-corkscrew roller coaster; a water flume ride with a 60-foot free fall; Hot Shots Laser Tag, a high-tech version of the old game of tag; Chaos, a thrill ride; and a number of tamer attractions suitable for younger children. Themed gift shops, a restaurant and snack bar are also on premises.

Circus Acts *Under the big top. Open daily 11 am-midnight. Performances every half hour. Free.* Acts include acrobatic antics on both the high and low wires, juggling, trapeze artists, animal acts and unicycle-balancing acts. The stage is surrounded by the old-fashioned Midway, which offers a plethora of carnival games.

CLARK COUNTY WETLANDS PARK *8 miles E of The Strip, at the terminus of Tropicana Ave. Visitor center open daily 10 am-4 pm; trails open dawn-dusk. Free. Guided tours available. Summer visitors should be aware of extreme heat.* The standout feature of this 2900-acre park on the eastern edge of Las Vegas Valley is the Nature Preserve, a desert wildlife and plant habitat with five miles of trails.

ELVIS-A-RAMA MUSEUM *Behind the Fashion Show Mall at 3401 Industrial Rd. (702) 309-7200. Open daily 10 am-7 pm. Adults $9.95; ages 13 and younger and seniors, $7.95. Tribute shows at 11 am, noon and 1 pm; free. Concerts, call for schedule; $14.95 and up.* From gold records to blue suede shoes, this museum displays the world's second-largest collection of Elvis memorabilia—$5.5 worth of costumes, cars, movie posters, concert footage, contracts and other artifacts. Impersonators offer 15-minute tribute shows and hour-long concerts.

Elvis Presley's car and '50s attire may be found at the Elvis-A-Rama Museum.

EVENT CENTER LAS VEGAS *Located near McCarran International Airport; 121 E Sunset Blvd. (702) 317-7777. Call for hours. Individually priced attractions.* At this indoor/outdoor facility (formerly Sports Center Las Vegas), visitors may hit home runs in batting cages designed like real baseball stadiums, race on NASCAR tracks designed by Jeff Gordon, or play miniature golf. The complex is home to the American Basketball Association's Las Vegas Rattlers.

EXCALIBUR HOTEL & CASINO *3850 Las Vegas Blvd S. (877) 750-5464. Court Jester's Stage, 11 am-7:30 pm. Free.* This huge, castle-shaped hotel is themed throughout after the medieval days of King Arthur. Puppets, jugglers and musicians perform on the Court Jester's Stage.

Fantasy Faire Midway *Lower level. Motion-simulator theaters open Sun-Thu 10 am-midnight, Fri-Sat 10 am-1 am; hours may vary. $3 per person.* Among the attractions here are two motion-simulator theaters, including **Merlin's Magic Motion Machine**, medieval-themed midway games, and strolling entertainers.

Tournament of Kings *(702) 597-7600. Open daily; seatings at 6 and 8:30 pm. Tickets, $43.95 plus tax.* A Camelot-themed dinner show is performed while guests dine on a four-course meal consisting of soup, game hen, potato and a dessert. King Arthur, his sons Mordred and Chris, wizards, knights and fire-breathing dragons battle during the meal.

FLAMINGO LAS VEGAS *3555 Las Vegas Blvd S. (702) 733-3111.* One of the first resorts on the Strip, opened by Benjamin "Bugsy" Siegel in 1946, the hotel is now home to Gladys Knight and The Second City improv group. Renowned for its pink neon facade, the Flamingo has been completely rebuilt since its early days.

Wildlife Habitat & Arboretum *Lobby level. Open 24 hours. Penguin feeding times 8:30 am, 3 pm. Free.* This 15-acre oasis is a mini tropical paradise, featuring exotic plants, waterfalls, penguins, birds, fish, turtles and, of course, the hotel's trademark pink flamingos.

FLYAWAY INDOOR SKYDIVING *200 Convention Center Dr, just E of Las Vegas Blvd S. (877) 545-8093. Open daily 10 am-7 pm. Classes scheduled on the hour and half hour. First flight, $50. Two flights, $75. Participants must be in good physical condition; minors must be accompanied by parent or guardian.* Participants "fly" in a vertical wind tunnel, simulating the freefall experience of skydiving.

GAMEWORKS LAS VEGAS *In Showcase Mall, 3785 Las Vegas Blvd S. (702) 432-4263. Open Sun-Thu 10 am-midnight, Fri-Sat 10 am-2 am. Hours may vary in summer. Game prices vary.* This virtual-reality arcade, created by Steven Spielberg, Sega Enterprises and Universal Studios, touts more than 200 video games of every description. Among the many attractions players can try their luck on are ski slopes, battlefields and raceways. The centerpiece is Surge Rock, a 75-foot-tall rock-climbing structure. The facility also maintains a full-service bar and food services.

GUINNESS WORLD OF RECORDS MUSEUM *2780 Las Vegas Blvd S. (702) 792-3766. Open daily 9 am-5 pm. Adults, $6.50; ages 55 and older, students and military, $5.50; ages 5-11, $4.50.* Rare videos and artifacts commemorate record-breaking feats from the worlds of entertainment, art, sports and science. Literally thousands of records can be accessed from the "Guinness World of Records" and "World of Sports" data banks. A special display highlights Las Vegas' history, casinos and entertainers.

HARD ROCK HOTEL AND CASINO *1 mile E of the Strip; 4455 Paradise Rd. (888) 473-7625. Exhibit open 24 hrs daily. Free.* Distinguished by its landmark 90-foot neon guitar, the hotel offers a colorful outdoor light show but is best known for a mammoth assemblage of rock 'n' roll memorabilia. The $3 million collection includes concert outfits and costumes, guitars, gold records, posters and photographs; Jimi Hendrix, Elvis Presley, Madonna, Eric Clapton and many other rock stars are represented.

HOWARD W. CANNON AVIATION MUSEUM *At McCarran International Airport, 5757 Wayne Newton Blvd. Main exhibit, 2nd floor mezzanine above baggage claim, near glass elevators. (702) 455-7968. Open 24 hours. Free.* Through photographs and memorabilia, this small museum-without-walls recalls pioneer airlines and aviators of Southern Nevada, including Howard Hughes.

IMPERIAL PALACE HOTEL & CASINO *3535 Las Vegas Blvd S. (800) 634-6441. Dealertainers parade, daily 6 pm. Free. Luau, Apr-Oct on Tue-Thu eves. Admission.* Gaming and entertainment have been combined here, with celebrity impersonator dealers or "Dealertainers" parading through the casino, entertaining and dealing blackjack. The hotel is home to a long-running Polynesian revue and poolside luau.

The Auto Collections *(702) 794-3174. Open daily 9:30 am-9:30 pm. Adults, $6.95; ages 65 and older and 4-12, $3; ages 3 and younger, free.* This museum, located on the fifth level of the hotel's parking structure, features more than 300 antique, classic and special-interest autos, antique trucks, motorcycles, and cars once owned by gangsters and world-famous celebrities. It also houses one of the world's largest collections of Model J Duesenbergs. Vehicles are available for purchase.

The Auto Collections at Imperial Palace.

LAS VEGAS ART MUSEUM *8 miles W of The Strip; 9600 W Sahara Ave. (702) 360-8000. Open Tue-Sat 10 am-5 pm, Sun 1-5 pm. Adults $5; ages 55 and older, $3; students with ID, $2.* This 30,000-square-foot institution, which has a permanent collection of more than 200 works, is an affiliate of the Smithsonian Institute and features exhibits drawn from the latter's vast holdings.

Architecture as art at Las Vegas Art Museum.

LAS VEGAS CONVENTION CENTER *1 mile E of The Strip; 3150 Paradise Rd. (702) 892-0711.* With more than 3.2 million square feet of meeting and exhibit space, the convention center is able to host some of the largest tradeshows anywhere. This $150 million facility offers 144 meeting rooms with seating capacities up to 7500, as well as two on-site restaurants with more than 600 seats each.

LAS VEGAS HILTON *E of The Strip, 3000 Paradise Rd. (702) 732-5111.* This longtime Vegas flagship, once host to Elvis Presley's crowd-pleasing act, now draws fans of one of television's legendary shows.

Star Trek: The Experience *Open daily 11 am-11 pm. (702) 697-8750. Adults, $29.99; ages 12 and younger and 65 and older, $26.99. Includes 1 admission to each ride and unlimited time in museum area. Museum-only pass, $19.99. Deep Space Nine, free. Minimum height for rides, 42." Wheelchair patrons must be able to sit in theater seats.* This multi-faceted attraction includes two 22-minute simulated-motion thrill rides, a museum-quality exhibit, shops and a restaurant. Participants are attacked by humanoids in the new **Borg Invasion 4D** adventure, which employs the first 3-D motion picture to be photographed and projected digitally, and state-of-the-art audio-visual effects. The movie combines

♠ Las Vegas Monorail

(702) 699-8200. Daily 8 am to midnight. Fare: 1-Ride Pass, $3. 10-Ride Pass, $25. 1-Day Pass, $15. 3-Day Pass, $40.

The Robert N. Broadbent Las Vegas Monorail is the first fully automated urban monorail rapid transit system in the U.S. The four-mile route parallels the east side of Las Vegas Boulevard, conveniently connecting eight major resorts.

Beginning at MGM Grand Hotel and Casino, the monorail travels north, with stations at Paris Las Vegas/Bally's Las Vegas, Flamingo Las Vegas, Imperial Palace Hotel & Casino/Harrah's Las Vegas Casino & Hotel, Las Vegas Convention Center, Las Vegas Hilton and Sahara Hotel & Casino.

The $650 million privately funded system, which opened in 2004, originated in an earlier venture that connected MGM Grand and Bally's. The driverless electric trains are designed to handle 4000 passengers each way per hour. There are plans to extend the system to McCarran Airport and downtown Las Vegas; a reduced-fare bus (Route 551) transports monorail users from the Sahara Avenue station to downtown in the meantime.

live action and animation, and features actors familiar from the *Star Trek* feature films and TV shows. Real actors are also involved in the **Klingon Encounter** (formerly called The Voyage Through Space), an excursion to the 24th century that consists of a simulated space battle and a flight to safety. Fantasy is presented as fact in **History of the Future**, a self-guided museum exhibit of more than 200 *Star Trek* costumes and props. *Star Trek* characters mingle with visitors at the **Deep Space Nine Promenade**, a free-of-admission shopping and dining experience which offers the largest collection of officially licensed *Star Trek* merchandise in the world. At Quark's Bar and Restaurant, the menu includes Romulan Ale (German pilsner), Glop on a Stick (corn dog) and The Wrap of Khan (chicken fajita wrap).

LAS VEGAS MINI GRAN PRIX *6 miles W of The Strip, 1401 N Rainbow Blvd. (702) 259-7000. Open daily at 10 am; Sun-Thu to 10 pm, Fri-Sat to 11 pm. Hours may vary. Closed Dec 25. $5.50 per ticket or $25 for 5. Must be 36" tall to ride Dragon roller coaster, 54" for go-karts. Grand prix drivers must be 16 years old and possess a valid driver's license.* This motor-amusement center features racetracks where children and adults alike can test their driving skills. Vehicles range from "Kiddie Karts" and go-karts to sprint karts and Grand Prix vehicles.

LAS VEGAS VILLA *E of The Strip, 4982 Shirley St. (702) 795-8119. Tours, $15; ages 12 and younger, free. Reservations required. Dining options.* Liberace's luxurious former home, a 20,000-square-foot mansion with crystal chandeliers, mirrored walls, hand-carved doors and imported marble floors, may be toured by appointment.

LIBERACE MUSEUM *2 miles E of The Strip at 1775 E Tropicana Ave. (702) 798-5595, shuttle service (702) 335-3530. Open Mon-Sat 10 am-5 pm, Sun noon-4 pm. Closed Jan 1, Thanksgiving and Dec 25. Adults, $12; ages 65 and older and students, $8; ages 6 and younger, free. Children must be accompanied by an adult. Tribute concerts Tue-Thu and Sat at 1 pm; $10.* The museum's collection of memorabilia, antiques and classic cars includes Liberace's million-dollar wardrobe and extensive fur collection, his gold and diamond stage jewelry and a piano once played by Chopin. The recently expanded and renovated museum also displays the entertainer's miniature piano collection, a photographic history of his life, and a re-creation of his former office and bedroom. Hour-long tribute concerts are offered as well.

LUXOR LAS VEGAS *3900 Las Vegas Blvd S. (702) 262-4555 (recorded information), (888) 777-0188.* From the massive sphinx outside to the elegant atrium lobby, this pyramid-shaped resort endeavors to make a visit to Egypt unnecessary.

Pharaoh's Pavilion *Open daily 9 am-11 pm. IMAX shows screen daily; call for show times. Museum admission, $5. Show admission, $9.95. All-attractions pass, $24.95; tickets should be purchased 15 minutes in advance.* The Luxor's entertainment complex transports guests back in time to a replica of King Tut's Tomb and Museum, reconstructed to exacting detail; an audiotape-guide assists in this self-paced tour. The seven-story high IMAX theater offers various 2D and 3D movies. Motion simulator rides, a virtual reality roller coaster and high-tech arcade games are also available.

MANDALAY BAY RESORT & CASINO *3950 Las Vegas Blvd S. (702) 632-7777.* With its 11-acre sand beach and its lush indoor foliage, this resort is designed to resemble an exotic tropical paradise. Colorful birds take flight in the high-ceilinged lobby; the gift shops and boutiques offer everything from imported rum to Balinese carvings.

House of Blues *(702) 632-7600. Restaurant open Sun-Thu 8 am-midnight; Fri-Sat to 1 am. Nightclub open daily 11 pm-2 am. Hours may vary. Club cover charge,*

$10. This restaurant/live-music venue has a huge collection of publicly displayed folk art. The restaurant features Southern-inspired cuisine and a traditional Sunday gospel brunch; the club offers live rock, and rhythm and blues music.

Shark Reef *Open daily 10 am-11 pm. Adults $15.95; ages 5-12, $9.95; ages 4 and younger, free.* This mini aquarium features over 100 species of fish and reptiles from the world's tropical waters, including a dozen varieties of sharks. The main tank holds nearly 1.3 million gallons of water.

Shark Reef at Mandalay Bay.

MGM GRAND HOTEL AND CASINO
3799 Las Vegas Blvd S. (702) 891-1111. A 45-foot tall, 100,000-pound bronze lion, perched atop a 25-foot pedestal, greets visitors and guests of the country's biggest resort. The hotel, which opened late in 1993, features Art Deco decor, and a re-creation of New York's celebrated Studio 54 nightclub.

CBS Television City *Studio Walk. Open daily 10 am-10 pm. Closing time may vary. Allow 1 hour. Children must be 10 years old and accompanied by an adult. Free.* Screenings of new shows from CBS, MTV, Nickelodeon and other networks are offered at this facility, followed by audience surveys.

Lion Habitat *Open daily 11 am-10 pm. Free.* This indoor enclosure provides a showcase for public appreciation of the animals, and permits lions to encircle guests via a see-through walkway tunnel that runs through the habitat.

THE MIRAGE *3400 Las Vegas Blvd S. (702) 791-7111, (800) 627-6667. White Tiger Habitat open daily 24 hours. Free.* The former home of Siegfried & Roy's stage show features a Polynesian design, an indoor tropical rain forest and, at the front desk, a 20,000-gallon tropical fish aquarium. The Royal White Tigers of Nevada featured in the magic show are still on view in the White Tiger Habitat, located on the hotel's southwestern side just off the casino. Street of Shops is a winding boulevard of designer boutiques; Renoir, a AAA five-diamond restaurant, is a chic dining room decorated with paintings by its namesake and other Impressionists.

Siegfried & Roy's Secret Garden and Dolphin Habitat *Memorial Day-Labor Day open Mon-Fri 11 am-7 pm, Sat-Sun and major holidays from 10 am; remainder of year open at 11 am, closing hours vary. Adults, $12; ages 10 and younger accompanied by an adult, free. Dolphin Habitat only after 3:30 pm, $6.* The Secret Garden features eight zoological environments with animals from the Siegfried & Roy show, which can be observed through a floor-to-ceiling wall of glass, while they sleep, eat and play. A close look at nine Atlantic bottle-nose dolphins is the main draw of the Dolphin Habitat, which offers continuous 15-minute tours focused primarily on the facility's underwater viewing room.

The Volcano *Shows daily 7 pm-midnight. Free.* Located at the hotel's front entrance, the volcano's fiery eruptions occur every 15 minutes and never fail to momentarily stop traffic. This was one of the first of the modern-day "attractions" on the Strip.

NEW YORK-NEW YORK HOTEL & CASINO *3790 Las Vegas Blvd S. (702) 740-6969.* Las Vegas' stunning replication of Manhattan's skyline includes several scaled landmarks, notably the Empire State Building, the Chrysler Building, the Century Building, the Statue of Liberty, and a 300-foot long Brooklyn Bridge. Adding to the New York-style ambiance of the hotel, which opened in 1997, are an elegant Art Deco lobby, Greenwich Village and Little Italy—where visitors can purchase soft pretzels, Manhattan clam chowder, Italian-sausage sandwiches and, of course, New York-style pizza.

New York-New York

Coney Island Emporium *Second level. Open daily at 8 am, Mon-Thu to midnight, Fri-Sun to 2 am.* This arcade re-creates an early 1900s atmosphere complete with old-fashioned midway carnival games and attractions, as well as modern video games that feature the latest in high-tech gadgetry.

ESPN Zone *Open Sat 11 am-1:30 am; Sun to 12:30 am; Mon-Thu 11:30 am-12:30 am; Fri to 1:30 am.* This sports-themed dining and entertainment complex is comprised of the Sports Arena, which offers 10,000 square feet of interactive and competitive attractions; the Screening Room, which features multi-game viewing of televised games; and the Studio Grill, a restaurant with sports-themed artwork.

Manhattan Express *Open daily 10 am, Sun-Thu to 11:30 pm, Fri-Sat to midnight. Tickets $12.50, additional rides $6.* Next to the emporium, this roller coaster travels upside down and through part of the casino, reaching a height of 203 feet. Riders experience a unique "heartline" twist and dive maneuver, which causes a momentary sensation of weightlessness.

THE PALMS CASINO RESORT *Near the Rio Suite Hotel & Casino, 4321 W Flamingo Rd. (702) 942-7777, (866) 942-7777.* This vacation getaway-themed hotel features an eclectic mix of restaurants and bars—including the 55th floor glass-walled "ghostbar" with a spectacular view of the city. The Palms and the nearby Rio Suite Hotel & Casino are proof the glitz and glamour of Las Vegas have spread beyond The Strip.

PARIS LAS VEGAS *3645 Las Vegas Blvd S. (702) 946-7000.* Famous architectural landmarks from Europe's City of Light create a Parisian environment, replete with a two-third scale Arc de Triomphe, facades of the Paris Opera House and the Louvre, as well as a replica of the Hotel de Ville.

Eiffel Tower Experience *Open daily 10 am-1 am, weather permitting. Mon-Thu: Adults $9; ages 6-12 and 65 and older, $7; ages 5 and younger, free; Fri-Sun: Adults $12; ages 6-12 and 65 and older, $10; ages 5 and younger, free.* Hotel guests of Paris Las Vegas, Bally's Las Vegas, Caesar's Palace, Flamingo Las Vegas and the Las Vegas Hilton may purchase 2 tickets for the price of 1. The real Eiffel Tower, built in France for the 1889 World's Fair, has been duplicated at one-half scale on the Las Vegas Strip, using Gustav Eiffel's original blueprints. A restaurant inside the superstructure is 100 feet above the Strip. Guests may also take a glass elevator to an observation deck on the 50th story.

Le Boulevard *Most shops open daily 9 am-10 pm.* The authentic-looking French shopping venue modeled after the Rue de la Paix—complete with cobblestone streets and winding alleys—offers over 31,500 square feet of elegant boutiques and shops, including a bakery and a wine cellar, and eight restaurants.

RIO SUITE HOTEL & CASINO *3700 Flamingo Rd. (702) 252-7777.* This off-Strip, Brazilian-themed resort has carved out a wild and colorful reputation for itself; the hotel's Club Rio and the 51st-floor VooDoo Lounge, accessible via glass elevator, are two of the most popular nightspots in town. The hotel's Ipanema Beach is a real sand beach at the edge of a tropical lagoon.

Masquerade Show in the Sky *Masquerade Village. Daily, times change frequently; call for information. Viewing free; participation $9.95.* Floats suspended from the ceiling parade through the casino, bearing costumed performers who throw beaded necklaces to the crowd below. Guests can participate in the carnival-like activity.

SAHARA HOTEL & CASINO *2523 Las Vegas Blvd S. (800) 851-1703.* This Moroccan-themed resort is one of the last Las Vegas hotel-casinos remaining from the famed Rat Pack days.

NASCAR Cafe *(702) 737-2750. Open Mon-Thu 11 am-10 pm, Fri to 11 pm; Sat 10 am-midnight; Sun 9 am-10 pm. Speed operates Mon-Thu noon-9 pm, Fri noon-midnight; Sat 11 am-midnight. Cyber and Coaster Ride Passes, $10 each; All Day Attractions Pass, $17.95.* This themed entertainment complex offers NASCAR memorabilia and racing shown on giant TV screens with surround sound. The complex's Las Vegas Cyber Speedway puts visitors behind the wheel of an Indy racecar with amazing realism. Speed: The Ride, a roller coaster launched from the cafe, blasts riders through a 72-foot loop; it then accelerates to its top speed of 70 mph as it zips through the resort's marquee and up an incline 224 feet above ground, before repeating the process in reverse.

SAM'S TOWN HOTEL & GAMBLING HALL *6 miles E of The Strip, 5111 Boulder Hwy. (702) 456-7777. Free Strip shuttle.* This off-Strip, Western-themed hotel on the eastern perimeter of the city features a Western store, a 56-lane bowling center and two RV parks.

Sam's Town Mystic Falls Park *Water show daily at 2, 6, 8 and 10 pm. Free.* A nine-story atrium encloses this 25,000-square-foot indoor park, which houses lifelike animals, lush tropical foliage, waterfalls and meandering footpaths. Restaurants with patio seating, shops and the hotel itself surround the park. Featured is the Sunset Stampede, a 10-minute choreographed water show with laser lights.

SCANDIA FAMILY FUN CEN-TER *On the W side of I-15, S of Sahara Ave; 2900 Sirius Ave. (702) 364-0070. Open daily from 10 am; Oct-May, Sun-Thu to 10 pm, Fri-Sat to midnight; Jun-Sep, open to 1 am. Unlimited all-day wristband, $17.50; Supersaver all-attraction pass, $12.95; individual ride admissions, $4.50. Unlimited golf: adults $7.50; children over 36", $5.95.* The amusement center features three elaborate 18-hole miniature golf courses, go-karts, bumper boats, baseball batting cages and a large video game arcade. Snack bar on site.

Scandia Family Fun Center

SIEGFRIED & ROY'S SECRET GARDEN AND DOLPHIN HABITAT—*See The Mirage.*

THE SHOPS IN DESERT PASSAGE *3667 Las Vegas Blvd S, across from Bellagio. (702) 866-0710. Open daily at 10 am; Mon-Fri to 11 pm, Sat-Sun to midnight.* This 500,000-square-foot shopping mall is designed to look and feel like an open-air bazaar. Inspired by traditional trading areas in Bombay, Tangiers and Marrakech, the shopping environment includes a 10-story terraced mountain and a North African harbor complete with indoor thunderstorms. The complex includes 140 retail shops, eight restaurants and two nightclubs.

SIRENS OF TI—*See Treasure Island.*

STRATOSPHERE CASINO HOTEL & TOWER *2000 Las Vegas Blvd S. (702) 380-7777, (800) 998-6937.* The focus of this landmark hotel is the tallest free-standing observation tower in the United States, rising 1149 feet above the Strip.

Stratosphere Tower *Open daily from 10 am; Sun-Thu to 1 am, Fri-Sat and holidays to 2 am. Admission, $9; Nev residents, hotel guests, ages 4-12 and 65 and over, $6. X Scream, $8. Big Shot, $8. High Roller, $4. Call for additional pricing. Must be 48" tall to ride Big Shot and High Roller, 54" for X Scream.* An eye-catching sight with its futuristic, Space Needle-like appearance and soaring height, the tower features two observation platforms, a revolving restaurant with 360-degree views, and three thrill rides: **High Roller**, the world's highest roller coaster; **Big Shot**, an acceleration ride; and **X Scream**, a new high-tech teeter-totter that dangles riders high over The Strip. The Tower Shops promenade combines over 30 boutiques with themed street scenes of Paris, New York and Hong Kong.

TREASURE ISLAND *3300 Las Vegas Blvd S. (702) 894-7111.* This elegant resort, home of Cirque du Soleil's *Mystère*, is distinguished by its colorful 18th-century village exterior, as carefully detailed as a movie set; inside, the hotel is designed to resemble a Caribbean hideaway.

Mystère challenged the concept of Las Vegas entertainment.

Sirens of TI *Siren's Cove, at the hotel's main entrance on The Strip. Shows daily at 7, 8:30 10 and 11:30 pm. No performances during inclement weather or high winds; subject to last-minute cancellation. Free.* Temptresses of the sea clash with a band of renegade pirates in this new extravaganza (replacing the long-running "Battle of Buccaneer Bay") that features music, dance and fiery explosions.

TROPICANA RESORT & CASINO *3801 Las Vegas Blvd S. (702) 739-2411, (800) 468-9494.* This glitzy mainstay of The Strip is the home of the long-running *Folies Bergere.*

Air Play *Shows daily at 11 am and 1, 3, 5, 7 and 9 pm. Free.* Acrobats, jugglers, aerialists and dancers perform half-hour shows in the casino, under the Tiffany glass ceiling.

Casino Legends Hall of Fame *(702) 739-5444. Open daily 9 am-9 pm. Adults, $6.95; ages 55 and older, $5.95; ages 17 and younger, free, must be accompanied by an adult.* This 6000-square-foot exhibit space features more than 15,000 items of memorabilia, including Liberace and Elvis costumes, old slot machines and historic photographs of Vegas.

UNIVERSITY OF NEVADA, LAS VEGAS *E of the Strip, 4505 S Maryland Pkwy. (702) 895-3011. For campus tours, call (702) 895-3443 or visit the admissions office, Maude Frazier Hall, Rm 114. A brochure for the self-guided arboretum tour of the campus is available from the UNLV News and Public Information Ofc, the*

Museum of Natural History and the grounds department. More than 23,000 students attend classes on the 335-acre campus. The school, which opened in 1957, is home to a $55 million high-tech research library.

Donna Beam Fine Art Gallery *In the Alta Ham Fine Arts Bldg, Rm 145-A. (702) 895-3893. Open Mon-Fri 9 am-5 pm. Closed Sat-Sun and major holidays. Free.* The gallery hosts changing exhibitions by students, faculty and invited artists.

Marjorie Barrick Museum of Natural History *On campus; E of Swenson St at end of Harmon Ave. Metered parking adj to museum. (702) 895-3381. Open Mon-Fri 8 am-4:45 pm, Sat 10 am-2 pm. Closed Sun and holidays. Free.* The museum encompasses permanent exhibits on the archaeology, geology and biology of the desert Southwest, an outdoor botanical garden, and taxidermy displays of indigenous animals.

Performing Arts Center *Adj to Maryland Pkwy; N end of Academic Mall. Schedule and ticket information (702) 895-2787. Tickets range from free to $75.* The center, comprised of the Artemus W. Ham Concert Hall, Judy Bayley Theatre and Alta Ham Black Box Theatre, regularly presents major international performing artists in classical and popular music, dance, theater and opera. It is also home to the Nevada Symphony Orchestra, Nevada Opera-Theatre and the Community Concert Association, whose seasons run from September through May and include professional performances in ballet, symphonic and chamber music, and opera.

Sam Boyd Silver Bowl Stadium *Off campus; via US 93/95 (use Russell Rd exit) in Silver Bowl Regional Park. Ticket information (702) 895-3905.* The stadium is home to the university's NCAA football team, the Rebels, from September through November. It also hosts motocross competitions and concerts in the summer.

Thomas and Mack Center *Off Tropicana Ave at Swenson St. Events schedule and ticket information (702) 895-3905.* This 18,500-seat indoor arena hosts sporting events, concerts and shows. From November through February it is the home court for the school's NCAA Runnin' Rebels basketball team.

THE VENETIAN RESORT HOTEL CASINO *3355 Las Vegas Blvd S. (702) 414-1000.* Full-scale replicas of Venice's most famous landmarks have been spectacularly re-created at this elegant 4049-room resort, including the Ca D'Oro (Palace of Gold); St. Mark's Square, including its 315-foot Campanile Tower; the Bridge of Sighs; Doge's Palace, with Lady Justice who sits atop the palace; and the Rialto Bridge.

Gondola Rides *(702) 414-4500. Offered Sun-Thu 10 am-11 pm, Fri-Sat to midnight; last gondola leaves 15 min prior to closing. Same-day reservation (beginning at 9 am) required in person at the loading dock in St Mark's Square. Adults, $15; ages 12 and younger, $6. Private gondola for two, $60. Cash only.* Gondoliers serenade visitors in Italian as they propel their guests up and down the canals traversing the Grand Canal Shoppes.

Grand Canal Shoppes *(702) 414-4500. Open daily at 10 am; Sun-Thu to 11 pm, Fri-Sat to midnight.* A collection of international boutiques and specialty stores is featured in a Venetian streetscape, complete with strolling carnival characters and street performers who entertain throughout the day.

Guggenheim Hermitage Museum *(702) 414-2440. Open daily 9:30 am-8:30 pm. Adults, $15; Nev residents and ages 65 and older, $12; students, $11; ages 6-12, $7; ages 5 and younger, free.* Rotating exhibits of masterpieces from the collections of the Solomon R. Guggenheim Museum in Manhattan and the prestigious State Hermitage Museum in St. Petersburg, Russia, are shown in this 7660-square-foot facility off the hotel's front lobby.

Grand Canal Shoppes

Madame Tussaud's Interactive Wax Museum *Open daily at 10 am; Mar-Oct to 10 pm, rest of year closing hours vary. Adults, $19.95; ages 60 and older, Nev residents and students with ID, $14; ages 6-12, $9.95; ages 5 and younger, free.* Wax likenesses of more than 100 celebrities are exhibited in themed-display areas, including Las Vegas legends Frank Sinatra and Sammy Davis Jr., sports greats Babe Ruth and Muhammad Ali, Hollywood stars Marilyn Monroe and Harrison Ford, and music personalities Louis Armstrong and Gloria Estefan.

THE VOLCANO—*See The Mirage.*

THE WYNN COLLECTION OF FINE ART *3145 Las Vegas Blvd S. (702) 733-4100.* Temporarily closed, the personal collection of hotelier Steve Wynn will reopen with the completion his new resort Wynn Las Vegas (on the former site of the Desert Inn), slated for 2005.

XPLEX LAS VEGAS *8 miles S of McCarran Airport, 15000 Las Vegas Blvd S. (702) 260-6355. Open Tue-Sun; Sept-May, 9 am-5 pm; Jun-Aug, 3-11 pm. Kart rentals, $30 and up per half-hour session. Reservations required. Drivers must be 12 years old and 50" tall for kart rental; training sessions available for children ages 5-12.* Motorsports enthusiasts and fans may satisfy their "need for speed" at this professional kart racing facility, modeled after the famed Le Mans track in France.

North Las Vegas Area

CANNERY CASINO-HOTEL *2121 E Craig Rd. (702) 507-5700.* Part of a North Las Vegas revitalization plan, this 28-acre complex includes a 201-room hotel-casino. Although it opened in 2003, its industrial theme resembles a post-WWII factory, complete with a 120-foot smokestack out in front.

FLOYD LAMB STATE PARK *15 miles NW of Las Vegas off US 95, E at Durango; 9200 Tule Springs Rd. (702) 486-5413. Open daily 8 am-dusk. Closed Jan 1 and Dec 25. Entrance fee $6 per vehicle.* The 2040-acre park, a former stagecoach rest stop and "dude" ranch, includes Tule Springs Ranch, four small lakes and the surrounding natural desert area. Fishing is permitted in all four lakes, which are stocked with rainbow trout in winter and catfish in summer; largemouth bass live in the lakes, but the catch is low. Swimming, wading and boating are not allowed. Picnic tables and grills are located throughout the park and are available on a first-come, first-served basis. Self-guided hiking trails traverse tree-shaded groves and pass by the lakes. Visitors may roam the grounds of the old Tule Springs Ranch, one of the best Pleistocene fossil sites in western North America, and take a self-guided tour of 22 historic structures. The buildings, closed to the public, are identified in a park brochure, available at the entrance station.

Floyd Lamb State Park

LAS VEGAS MOTOR SPEEDWAY *7000 Las Vegas Blvd N. (702) 644-4444. Call for ticket prices and program information.* This racing complex hosts a wide range of events throughout the year on its 1.5-mile oval, the most prominent of which is the Las Vegas 400 NASCAR Winston Cup race each March. Several smaller tracks accommodate everything from drag racing to road-course events.

NELLIS AIR FORCE BASE *Main gate at Las Vegas Blvd and Craig Rd. (702) 652-1110.* Nellis, a weapons testing and tactical fighter training center, is also the home of the Thunderbirds, the Air Force's precision flying team. The Thunderbirds are often away performing at air shows throughout the country, but they do perform at the Nellis AFB Open House, which is held once a year; call for schedule.

THE PLANETARIUM *1 mile E of I-15 at Community College of Southern Nevada, 3200 E Cheyenne Ave. (702) 651-4759. Programs Fri at 6 and 7:30 pm, Sat at 3:30 and 7:30 pm; no late seating. Adults $5; ages 11 and younger and 55-over, $3.* Multi-media shows on astronomy are presented at Southern Nevada's only public planetarium and observatory, with telescope viewing available after the second showing.

GUIDED TOURS

The tours listed in this section generally last a day or half-day, though some of the trips to more distant places involve an overnight stay. Be sure to contact the companies in advance for complete information and reservations;

many tours offer hotel pickup and discounted children's rates. Also, check refund policies to avoid losing your deposit in the event of a late cancellation. Scheduled tours are subject to cancellation if there is an insufficient number of passengers.

Tours listed are provided as a convenience for our readers; inclusion in this publication does not imply endorsement by the Automobile Club of Southern California.

Las Vegas

ADVENTURE BALLOONS *(702) 241-6889, (800) 346-6444.* Las Vegas Valley.

ADVENTURE PHOTO TOURS *3111 S Valley View Blvd, Ste X-106. (702) 889-8687, (888) 363-8687.* Grand Canyon, Hoover Dam, Red Rock Canyon, Valley of Fire State Park, Death Valley, Zion, Bryce Canyon and "Area-51" land tours.

ANNIE BANANIE'S WILD WEST TOURS *1824 Wincanton Dr. (702) 804-9755.* Valley of Fire, Lake Mead, Red Rock Canyon.

DESERT ECO-TOURS *Southern Nevada Zoological-Botanical Park, 1775 N Rancho Dr. (702) 647-4685, 648-5955. Reservations required; age restrictions on some tours.* "Area-51," Colorado River, Rainbow Canyon, Cathedral Gorge land tours.

DESERT STAR HOT AIR BALLOON ADVENTURES *9672 Marble Peak Ct. (702) 240-9007.* Las Vegas Valley.

GRAY LINE TOURS *Coach USA, 795 E Tropicana. (702) 644-2233.* Grand Canyon, Colorado River, Hoover Dam/Lake Mead, Red Rock Canyon/Mount Charleston, Las Vegas land tours and air/land tours.

KEY TOURS *3305 W Spring Mountain Rd, Ste 18. (702) 362-9355, (800) 777-4697.* Hoover Dam, Laughlin and Primm land tours.

ROCKY TRAILS *1930 Village Center Circle, (702) 869-9991, (888) 867-6259.* Grand Canyon, Death Valley, Valley of Fire, Red Rock Canyon, Colorado River land tours.

SHOWTIME TOURS OF LAS VEGAS *1550 S Industrial Rd. (702) 895-9976.* Grand Canyon, Hoover Dam, Las Vegas, Laughlin, Oatman air and air/land tours, and river rafting.

SIGHTSEEING TOURS UNLIMITED (STU) *6380 S Valley View. (702) 471-7155, (800) 377-2003.* Grand Canyon, Hoover Dam, Lake Mead, Las Vegas, Red Rock Canyon, Primm, Laughlin, Colorado River, off-road Hummer tours, air and land tours.

SUNDANCE HELICOPTERS, INC. *5596 Haven St. (702) 736-0606, (800) 653-1881.* Grand Canyon, Hoover Dam/Lake Mead and Las Vegas helicopter tours.

♠ Grand Canyon Flights

In 1987, the U.S. Congress passed a law prohibiting flights below the canyon rim, and directed the National Park Service (NPS) and the Federal Aviation Administration (FAA) to designate safe routes for flights over the national park area. Congress also mandated that the NPS work to re-establish the "natural quiet" of the canyon. The NPS then proposed to the FAA that flight-free zones be established over 45 percent of the Grand Canyon, that air-tour operators be restricted to flying in specific routes over the least-used parts of the park, and that pilots be required to stay above the canyon rim. The law took effect in September 1988. A report, which evaluated both safety and noise pollution generated by park over-flights, was submitted to Congress in 1994. The NPS and FAA are working together to develop a final use plan for the canyon that may restrict the number of flights and/or the noise level that the flights may generate. According to a government spokesperson, those flying over the canyon can still view much of the grandeur of the park. The main concerns are passenger safety and the noise level.

North Las Vegas

AIR VEGAS AIRLINES *2642 Airport Dr. (702) 736-3599, (800) 255-7474.* Grand Canyon helicopter tours.

LOOK TOURS *2634 Airport Dr #103. (702) 233-1627, (800) 609-5665.* Grand Canyon, Hoover Dam, Lake Mead, Las Vegas, Red Rock Canyon, Laughlin, Oatman, Colorado River, air and land tours.

SCENIC AIRLINES *2705 Airport Dr. (702) 638-3300, (800) 634-6801.* Grand Canyon, Colorado River, Las Vegas, Hoover Dam, Bryce Canyon, Monument Valley, air/land tours.

SHOWROOM ENTERTAINMENT

Headline entertainment is second only to gambling in the number of visitors it attracts to Las Vegas. The big showrooms typically feature a well-known singer or comedian backed by an opening act, or a glitzy revue with elaborate sets and costumes. While magicians, impressionists and Elvis impersonators abound, the latest trend is the importation of Broadway shows. Facilities listed here seat 500 or more.

Show tickets can be purchased by phoning or visiting the hotel's showroom box office or by contacting a local ticket agency. A number of ticket agencies in Las Vegas specialize in booking entertainment. Refer to the telephone directory yellow pages under "Ticket Sales/Events" or "Tourist Information."

Many showrooms offer advance ticket sales and reserved seating. Be sure to ask at the time of purchase if the seats are reserved. If you have assigned seats, you should arrive approximately 30 minutes prior to show time. If seats are not assigned, it is advisable to arrive at least an hour prior to curtain. Dinner shows may require even earlier arrival, although such options—once common—are disappearing.

Prices change frequently and without notice. While some hotels offer free afternoon lounge shows, admission costs for long-running revues and big-name headline acts have increased dramatically in recent years. At press time, prices ranged from $15 to $200, with an average of $50-60 per person, not including taxes and gratuities; these amounts will often be raised for especially popular entertainers, as well as for opening and closing nights and New Year's Eve.

Large production shows often run indefinitely, many of them for several years. As of press time, shows scheduled to run indefinitely appear in the listings, but *shows are subject to change without notice. Verify shows, times and prices in advance.*

Although the early and late shows are basically the same in terms of content, children are generally not admitted to the late shows. The hour alone prevents most children from enjoying themselves, and entertainers feel freer to use language and discuss subjects that might not be appropriate for a general audience. For this reason, not only children but sensitive adults should attend the early shows. Production shows with nudity usually do not admit children; call the theater's box office in advance for any applicable age restrictions.

Nightclubs and dance clubs have become an increasingly popular aspect of Vegas' nightlife in recent years. Among the most popular venues are the MGM Grand's trendy Studio 54, named for the renowned 1970s New York City club; Mandalay Bay's exotic rumjungle; the glass-walled ghostbar at Palms Casino Resort; Venus, the "retro" lounge at the Venetian; and Gilley's, the country-western honky-tonk at the New Frontier. Many of the clubs have dress codes.

Showroom listing does not imply AAA endorsement for the lodging establishment. For the most current information, refer to the Auto Club's "Nevada Show Sheet"—available to AAA members at all Southern California district offices and on the Internet at http://www.aaa-calif.com—or consult the various entertainment guides available at the Las Vegas Convention and Visitors Authority and elsewhere.

Las Vegas

BALLY'S LAS VEGAS *3645 Las Vegas Blvd S. (702) 946-4567. Donn Arden's Jubilee!* (indefinitely; minimum age 18).

BELLAGIO *3600 Las Vegas Blvd S. (702) 693-7722, (888) 488-7111. "O"* featuring Cirque du Soleil (indefinitely; tickets can be purchased 90 days in advance).

CAESARS PALACE *3570 Las Vegas Blvd S. (702) 474-4000. A New Day* featuring Celine Dion (indefinitely).

FLAMINGO LAS VEGAS *3555 Las Vegas Blvd S. (800) 221-7299. Gladys Knight* (indefinitely). *The Second City* (indefinitely).

THE GOLDEN NUGGET *129 Fremont St. (866) 946-5336. The Amazing Jonathan* (indefinitely).

HARD ROCK HOTEL AND CASINO *4455 Paradise Rd. (888) 473-7625.*

HARRAH'S LAS VEGAS CASINO & HOTEL *3475 Las Vegas Blvd S. (702) 369-5222. Clint Holmes* (indefinitely). *Mac King Comedy Magic Show* (indefinitely).

HOTEL SAN REMO *115 E Tropicana Ave. (702) 597-6028. Showgirls of Magic* (indefinitely; minimum age 21).

IMPERIAL PALACE HOTEL & CASINO *3535 Las Vegas Blvd S. (702) 794-3261, (800) 634-6441. Legends in Concert* (indefinitely; age 1 and younger, free; dinner options available; smoke-free theater).

LAS VEGAS HILTON *3000 Paradise Rd. (702) 732-5755.*

LUXOR LAS VEGAS *3900 Las Vegas Blvd S. (888) 777-0188. Blue Man Group: Live at Luxor* (indefinitely).

MANDALAY BAY RESORT & CASINO *3950 Las Vegas Blvd S. (877) 632-7400, House of Blues (702) 632-7600.*

MGM GRAND HOTEL AND CASINO *3799 Las Vegas Blvd S. (702) 891-7777, (800) 929-1111.*

THE MIRAGE *3400 Las Vegas Blvd S. (702) 791-7111. Danny Gans* (indefinitely).

MONTE CARLO RESORT & CASINO *3770 Las Vegas Blvd S. (702) 730-7160, (877) 386-8224. Lance Burton, Master Magician* (indefinitely).

NEW YORK-NEW YORK HOTEL & CASINO *3790 Las Vegas Blvd S. (702) 740-6815. Rita Rudner* (indefinitely). *Zumanity* (indefinitely).

THE ORLEANS *4500 W Tropicana Ave. (702) 365-7075.*

O'SHEA'S CASINO *3555 Las Vegas Blvd S. (702), (866) 737-1343. Hip-Nosis* (indefinitely).

THE PALMS CASINO RESORT *4321 W Flamingo Rd. (702) 942-7777.*

PARIS LAS VEGAS *3645 Las Vegas Blvd S. (702) 946-4567.*

RIO SUITE HOTEL & CASINO *3700 Flamingo Rd. (702) 777-7776. Scintas* (indefinitely). *Penn & Teller* (indefinitely).

RIVIERA HOTEL & CASINO *2901 Las Vegas Blvd S. (702) 794-9433, (800) 634-3420. An Evening at La Cage* (indefinitely; minimum age 18; dinner options available). *Splash* (indefinitely; minimum age 18).

STARDUST RESORT AND CASINO *3000 Las Vegas Blvd S. (702) 617-5577. Wayne Newton* (indefinitely).

STRATOSPHERE CASINO HOTEL & TOWER *2000 Las Vegas Blvd S. (702) 380-7711, (800) 998-6937. Viva Las Vegas!* (indefinitely). *American Superstars* (indefinitely).

SUNCOAST HOTEL & CASINO *9090 Alta Dr. (702) 636-7075.*

TREASURE ISLAND *3300 Las Vegas Blvd S. (702) 894-7111, (800) 392-1999. Mystère* featuring Cirque du Soleil (indefinitely; tickets can be purchased 90 days in advance).

TROPICANA RESORT & CASINO *3801 Las Vegas Blvd S. (702) 739-2411. Folies Bergere* (indefinitely; minimum age 16; early show, all ages). *The Magic of Rick Thomas* (indefinitely). *The Comedy Stop* (minimum age 21).

THE VENETIAN RESORT HOTEL CASINO *3355 Las Vegas Blvd S. (702) 933-4230. Michael Flatley's Lord of the Dance* (indefinitely).

ANNUAL EVENTS

Parades, rodeos, art fairs, fireworks displays and golf tournaments are just a few of the many annual community events that Las Vegas and environs have to offer. For detailed information about each event, please call the telephone numbers shown, or consult with the local chamber of commerce or visitor information bureau. In addition, casino tournaments take place throughout the year. In Las Vegas, spectator sports include boxing, baseball, soccer, football, basketball and hockey.

Spectator sports are popular throughout the year. The Las Vegas 51s baseball club (702-386-7200), affiliated with the Los Angeles Dodgers, plays its home games at Cashman Field April through September. The Thomas and Mack Center is the home of UNLV's NCAA basketball team, the Runnin' Rebels (702-895-3905), who play November through February. Sam Boyd Stadium is the home venue for Rebels university football; the season runs September through November.

Auto racing is a fast-growing sport at the Las Vegas Motor Speedway, which hosts the Las Vegas 400 NASCAR race in March and many other events throughout the year. For more information, call (702) 644-4444. Other exciting sporting events include top-flight **boxing matches** at the Las Vegas Hilton, Caesars Palace, Mandalay Bay and MGM Grand hotels.

Casino tournaments in bridge, blackjack, slot play, craps, poker, gin rummy and bowling take place in many casinos. Anyone interested in these tournaments should contact the hotel or venue directly for dates and play information; room reservations should be made well in advance, as room space is often at a premium during a tournament.

January

LAS VEGAS INTERNATIONAL MARATHON *(702) 240-2722.* The full marathon has been run every year since 1967, and the half-marathon since 1993. Each event attracts more than 4000 participants from all 50 states and more than 35 countries.

April

CITY OF LIGHTS JAZZ FESTIVAL *Desert Breeze Park, Las Vegas. (702) 228-3780.* Many of the top names in jazz have appeared at this one-day festival.

HENDERSON HERITAGE DAYS *Various locations, Henderson. (702) 565-8951.* This 10-day event celebrates Henderson's heritage with a beauty pageant, live music, chili cookoff, talent show, car show, softball tournament, parade, 5-K run and charity basketball tournament.

NATIVE AMERICAN ARTS FESTIVAL *Clark County Museum, Henderson. (702) 455-7955.* American Indian food and art, dancing, craft demonstrations and storytelling are featured during this three-day festival.

May

ARTFEST *Convention Center, Henderson. (702) 267-4055.* This two-day outdoor event features over 200 artists displaying their work and more than two dozen entertainment acts on three stages, plus a children's art workshop.

June

CINEVEGAS FILM FESTIVAL *Brenden Theaters, The Palms Casino Resort, Las Vegas. (702) 368-2890.* This nine-day film festival features American and international works, including independent and cult movies.

September

LAS VEGAS MARIACHI FESTIVAL *Various locations, Las Vegas. (800) 637-1006.* This day-long mariachi festival

Native American Arts Festival

features top-name entertainers and bands, and is one of the most prestigious of its kind in the U.S.

SUPER RUN *Water St, Henderson. (702) 267-2171.* This three-day event features a classic car show and concerts.

October

LAS VEGAS INVITATIONAL *Tournament Players Club in Summerlin; TPC at the Canyons; and Bear's Best Las Vegas. (702) 242-3000.* This PGA Tour event (formerly the Invensys Classic at Las Vegas) lasts five days.

Mariachi Festival

RENAISSANCE FAIRE *Sunset Park, Las Vegas. (702) 455-8200.* Historical reenactments, jousting, theatrical performances, food and strolling minstrels highlight this four-day event.

December

CHILDREN'S CHRISTMAS PARADE *Water St, Henderson. (702) 799-3500.* Held on a Saturday, this parade features floats, horses and a visit from Santa Claus.

LAS VEGAS BOWL *At Sam Boyd Silver Bowl Stadium, off Russell Rd exit and US 93/95. (702) 895-3905.* This annual college football bowl game pits a Mountain West Conference team against a Pac-10 Conference squad.

NATIONAL FINALS RODEO *UNLV's Thomas and Mack Center, Las Vegas. (702) 895-3905.* This professional rodeo event takes place over 10 days and features saddle bronc, bareback and bull riding; calf roping; steer wrestling; and barrel racing.

NEW YEAR'S EVE CELEBRATIONS *Various locations. (702) 892-7575.*

OUTSIDE LAS VEGAS

From the grandeur of Hoover Dam to the pine forests of Mount Charleston, a world of opportunity beckons those who venture beyond the lures of Las Vegas. Most of the surrounding region remains undeveloped, with a host of opportunities awaiting the adventurous traveler. **Boulder City,** *southeast of Las Vegas, is a tidy town that has maintained its down-home, historic atmosphere and serves as gateway to Hoover Dam and the many diversions of* **Lake Mead National Recreation Area.** *For breathtaking desert views, visitors may head west to* **Red Rock National Conservation Area** *or northeast to* **Valley of Fire State Park,** *both within an hour's drive of the Strip. Close as well is* **Spring Mountains National Recreation Area,** *home of Mount Charleston, the third-highest peak in Nevada; it's less than an hour's drive to the northwest. And at the California-Nevada border, the tiny town of* **Primm** *has emerged as a family entertainment center and tourist destination in its own right, thanks to the Desperado roller coaster and other thrill rides at its resort hotels.*

POINTS OF INTEREST

Attractions are listed alphabetically by city or area—**Boulder City, Lake Mead National Recreation Area, Overton, Primm, Red Rock Canyon National Conservation Area, Spring Mountains National Recreation Area** and **Valley of Fire State Park**. Listings of attractions located on hotel properties do not necessarily imply AAA approval of the lodging facilities.

Boulder City

BOOTLEG CANYON TRAIL SYSTEMS *1011 Yucca St off US 93. (702) 293-3472. Open 24 hours. Free. No motorcycles allowed.* An extensive network of downhill and cross-country mountain biking and hiking trails awaits adventurers who follow the signs to the top of the mountain with the letters "BC" painted in white.

BOULDER CITY HISTORIC DISTRICT *23 miles SE of Las Vegas via US 93/95 on US 93/Nevada Hwy. Chamber of Commerce located at 465 Nevada Wy. (702) 293-2034.* Created in 1931 to house the thousands of workers who built nearby Hoover Dam, Boulder City was the country's first fully developed, master-planned community. It is also only city in Nevada where gaming has always been, and still is, illegal. While the rest of the country strug-

The past is preserved at Historic Boulder Dam Hotel.

gled during the Great Depression, this sparkling new community thrived—the population swelled to more than 8000 while the dam was being built. Through the 1940s, Boulder City flourished as a regional government center and tourism point for the dam and Lake Mead. The community remained under the jurisdiction of the federal government until an act of Congress permitted the burgeoning city to become an incorporated municipality in 1960. A self-guided tour of the Boulder City Historic District is outlined in a brochure available at the local chamber of commerce.

The city's best-known structure and focal point is **Historic Boulder Dam Hotel**, a pine-shingled, Dutch Colonial-style building on Arizona Street. Built in 1933 to accommodate a growing tourist industry, the 33-room hotel was Southern Nevada's finest inn, boasting private baths and showers in each room—a rarity for the times—and an elegant lobby paneled in rare southern gumwood. The hotel hosted a steady stream of Hollywood celebrities, American politicians, European aristocrats and Far Eastern royalty. Today the hotel is the home of the Boulder City/Hoover Dam Museum and the Boulder City Arts Council and Art Gallery.

Boulder City/Hoover Dam Museum

BOULDER CITY/HOOVER DAM MUSEUM

1305 Arizona St (in Historic Boulder Dam Hotel). (702) 294-1988. Open daily to 5 pm; Mon-Sat at 10 am, Sun at noon. Closed most major holidays; open July 4. Admission, $2; ages 8-16 and ages 55 and older, $1; ages 7 and younger, free. This small museum exhibits Hoover Dam-related artifacts, including a display of a dam workers' tent-house and a variety of historical photographs.

HOOVER DAM *30 miles SE of Las Vegas via US 93/95 on US 93. (800) 634-6787, (886) 291-8687. Guided tours daily 9 am-4:30 pm. Closed Thanksgiving and Dec 25. Admission, $10; ages 62 and older, $8; ages 7-16, $5; ages 6 and younger, free. Parking on Nev/Ariz side, $5 per vehicle. Note: Due to security concerns, access to and tours of Hoover Dam may be restricted. Call for current status.* This 726-foot-high dam is a National Historic Landmark and considered one of the engineering wonders of the world. Built during the Great Depression with the skill, long hours and dedication of thousands of construction workers, it was completed in 1935—two years ahead of schedule. Not only did the dam help control the sometimes violent Colorado River, but it provided a cheap source of electricity, which aided the development of Las Vegas and Southern California. As an additional bonus, the dam created Lake Mead, America's largest manmade reservoir and a popular recreation spot.

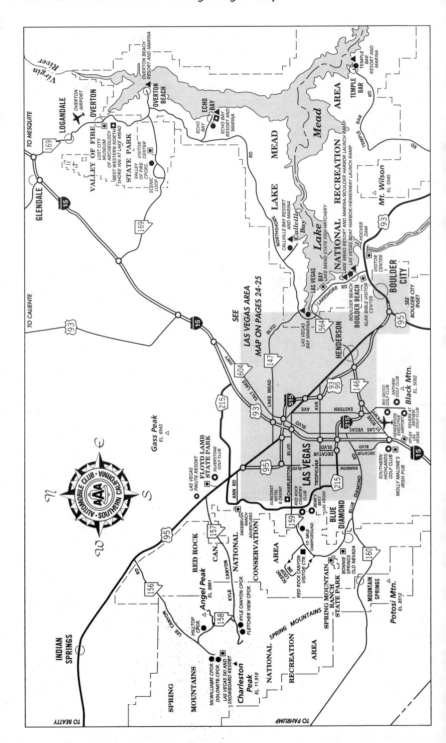

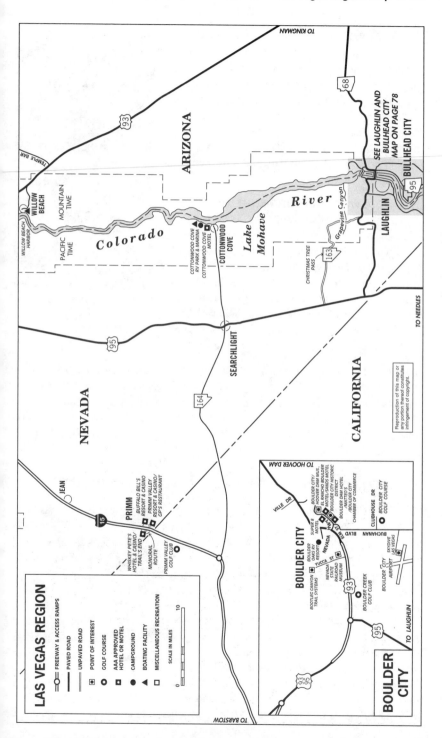

In 1995, a $123-million visitor center and five-story parking structure opened to the public. The three-level visitor center features an exhibit gallery, revolving theater and observation platform. Two high-speed elevators operate daily to lower visitors 520 feet into the walls of Black Canyon for the Discovery Tour of the dam's power plant. The view from the bottom of Hoover Dam is awe-inspiring, leaving no doubt that this structure is truly an engineering spectacle.

NEVADA STATE RAILROAD MUSEUM *600 Yucca St at Boulder Hwy. (702) 486-5933. Train rides 2nd Sat of month at 9 and 10:30 am, noon and 1:30 pm. Fare $5; ages 65 and older, $4; ages 5-11, $3; ages 4 and younger, free.* This new museum offers excursion rides on the historic Boulder Branch Line, built in 1931 to haul equipment and material for the construction of Hoover Dam. The

Just below Hoover Dam.

seven-mile round-trip ride aboard vintage Pullman coaches lasts 45 minutes and provides river, mountain and desert views.

SKYDIVE LAS VEGAS *At Boulder City Airport, 1401 Airport Rd #4. (702) 759-3483. Open daily 8 am-3 pm. Closed Dec 25 and Jan 1. Reservations recommended. Prices for jumps begin at $155. Jumpers must be over 18 with photo ID, under 245 lbs and height/weight proportionate. Video packages available.* This full-time skydiving school offers the ultimate thrill ride, a tandem free-fall/parachute jump from 7000 feet above sea level.

Lake Mead National Recreation Area

LAKE MEAD *25 miles SE of Las Vegas. Alan Bible Visitor Center located 4 miles NE of Boulder City on US 93. (702) 293-8990 (visitor center), 293-8906 (park information). The visitor center is open daily 8:30 am-4:30 pm. Closed Jan 1, Thanksgiving and Dec 25. The 6 major recreation areas on Lake Mead are **Boulder Beach**, 28 miles SE via US 93 and SR 166; **Las Vegas Bay**, 17 miles E via SR 147/Lake Mead Blvd; **Callville Bay**, 29 miles E via SR 147, Northshore and Callville*

This way to Lake Mead.

*Bay rds; **Echo Bay**, 54 miles NE via SR 147, Northshore Rd and access road to Echo Bay; **Overton Beach**, 60 miles NE via I-15 and SR 169; and **Temple Bar**, in Ariz, 75 miles SE via US 93 and Temple Bar Rd. For emergency assistance in the Lake Mead*

NRA call (800) 680-5851 or (702) 293-8932 (911 is not fully implemented in the Lake Mead NRA). For Lake Mead weather conditions, call (702) 736-3854.

Lake Mead NRA assesses entrance and lake-use fees. Fees may be paid at greeter locations in the recreation area. Entrance fees: 1-5 days—$3 per person by foot or bicycle, $5 per vehicle; annual pass—$20 per vehicle. Lake-use fees (charged in addition to the entrance fee): 1-5 days—$10 for first vessel, $5 each additional vessel; annual pass—$20 for first vessel, $10 each additional vessel.

Lake Mead is the largest manmade reservoir in the United States. It is administered by the National Park Service as part of the Lake Mead National Recreation Area, which also includes Lake Mohave, downstream from Hoover Dam. Lake Mead is 110 miles long and has a shoreline five times that length. Created by Hoover Dam, the lake area offers year-round fishing, swimming, water skiing, camping, hiking, picnicking, scuba diving, sailing, power boating and houseboating. Information about the recreation area can be obtained at the Alan Bible Visitor Center on US 93, which also has a botanical garden, bookstore and exhibits on natural history.

Lake Mead at Hemenway.

Much of Lake Mead's surrounding landscape is rugged desert interspersed with stark grayish-purple mountains, colorful red rock canyons and a variety of desert shrubberies. Mild weather throughout most of the year is punctuated by hot, dry summers, when temperatures often reach over 100 degrees. The desert environment is home to more than 1000 bighorn sheep that roam the rocky ridges, while the manmade lake attracts ducks, cormorants, geese, egrets, herons, ospreys and bald eagles.

The lake offers some of the best sportfishing in the country and an open season on all fish year round (see Water Recreation in the *Recreation* chapter). There are many scenic drives through this dramatic region. A popular one follows Northshore Road, running north from Lake Mead Boulevard (SR 147) to Echo Bay and Overton Beach. An often spectacular view of the surrounding mountains and hills can be seen from this route, where the browns, burnt reds and black rocks of the landscape are contrasted with stark off-whites and tans. Each hill is seemingly formed from a different material, but all are the product of an active geologic past.

The red and black rocks that dominate the scenery speak of the high iron and magnesium content of the volcanic debris. Local sedimentary rocks, such as the sandstone layers evidenced in the nearby hills, were laid down by water and then uplifted at a later time. A high iron content is also evidenced there, often by an entire range of stark red hills. The vividness of the rocks' colors on this drive can often vary not only with the time of day, but also with the direction of travel. What may appear dull and drab through the windshield may look entirely different in the rearview mirror. Drive carefully—one of the greatest hazards here is looking at the landscape instead of the road.

Caution: Care should be taken when traveling in this area.

- Desert thunderstorms in summer and fall can produce both lightning and flash floods. Never camp in a wash or low-lying area. Never drive across flooded roads; many roads have been posted flash-flood areas.

- Summer's extreme temperatures can cause heat exhaustion and heat stroke, as well as cripple a car that does not have adequate coolant in the cooling system. (Refer to the Desert Driving Hints in the *Transportation* chapter.)

- Poisonous snakes and scorpions are indigenous to this area. They usually will not strike unless cornered, but caution should be taken to avoid them.

- Drive only on paved roads or on unpaved roads marked with yellow arrows. Check with rangers about road conditions before traveling unpaved roads.

LAKE MEAD STATE FISH HATCHERY *9½ miles N of Boulder City on SR 166/Lakeshore Rd. (702) 486-6738. Open daily 8 am-4 pm. Free.* This facility is a cold-water hatchery used for trout. Its visitor center features displays on production methods. Currently closed for renovation, the hatchery is slated to reopen to the public in summer 2005.

LAKE MOHAVE *Extends 67 miles N from Davis Dam along the Colorado River. General information (702) 293-8906; Lake Mohave weather (702) 297-1265. Ranger stations can be found at the 3 major recreation areas on the lake:* **Katherine Landing**, *6 miles N of Bullhead City via SR 95, SR 68 and N on an access road; (928) 754-3272.* **Cottonwood Cove**, *55 miles N of Laughlin via Laughlin Cutoff Rd, SR 163, US 95 and an access road E from Searchlight; (702) 297-1265.* **Willow Beach**, *81 miles N of Bullhead City via SR 95, SR 68 to Kingman, US 93 N and an access road W; (928) 767-4000.*

Lake Mohave's teal waters provide a sharp contrast to the desert landscape surrounding it. Its northern section is almost as narrow as the Colorado River itself, with Indian petroglyphs etched on the steep walls of Black Canyon. The midsection widens to almost four miles before narrowing again to the south, where the shore is lined with hundreds of small coves and inlets.

The contrast of the water to the desert is also reflected in the colorful flora and fauna. The lake is an abundant source of water for traditional desert dwellers, as well as a winter home for many migratory bird species. Homes for Gila monsters, scorpions, tarantulas, burros and coyotes, as well as small beavers, muskrats and bighorn sheep can be found in the area. Birds run the gamut from hawks and large crows to roadrunners and blue heron. Spring often brings a display of wildflowers among the desert plants—most notably brittlebush and sand verbena.

Lake Mohave is ideal for boating year round, but those pursuing land adventures will find the best months to visit are October through April. Winters are mild, with daytime temperatures generally ranging from 65 to 85 degrees. Brutally hot summer days are routinely above the 100-degree mark and sometimes reach 120 degrees.

The lake's main appeal is in the variety of recreation it offers. Houseboating and fishing are popular, as are swimming, scuba diving, water skiing, windsurfing and sunbathing. Houseboats can be rented at Katherine Landing and Cottonwood Cove marinas, but reservations must be made well in advance. A fish hatchery at Willow Beach supplies the rainbow trout that are planted in the lake. Lake Mohave has a reputation as one of the best trout and largemouth bass fishing areas in the Southwest.

Overton

LOST CITY MUSEUM OF ARCHEOLOGY *60 miles NE of Las Vegas via I-15 and SR 169; 721 S Moapa Valley Blvd. (702) 397-2193. Open daily 8:30 am-4:30 pm. Closed Jan 1, Thanksgiving and Dec 25. Adults, $3; ages 65 and older, $2; ages 18*

and younger, free. This museum offers visitors a chance to see both original American Indian relics and faithful reconstructions of Pueblo dwellings, as well as a new exhibit on the history of archaeology. The last 10,000 years have seen several cultures in residence, including the Gypsum Cave People, ancient Basket Makers, early Pueblos and, most recently, the Paiute Indians, who came to the area about 900 years ago. Many ruins

Indian Pueblo at Lost City Museum.

near the museum have not yet been excavated, and as the delicate process of unearthing the remains continues, more and more is revealed about the area's past inhabitants.

Primm

PRIMM VALLEY RESORTS *40 miles S of Las Vegas at the Calif/Nev state line on I-15. (702), (800) 386-7867.* Primm, popularly known as State Line for several years, was once a drive-through hamlet for folks on the way to bigger and better things. Today, it is itself a high-wattage destination, offering entertainment, lodging, dining and gaming at three large, resort-style hotels with more than 2600 rooms between them. A sleek, futuristic-looking monorail links Primm Valley Resort & Casino to Buffalo Bill's next door, while another connects it with Whiskey Pete's across the Interstate.

Buffalo Bill's Resort & Casino *On E side of I-15, 31700 S Las Vegas Blvd. Rides per person: Desperado roller coaster, $7; Turbo Drop, $5; log ride, $5; 3-D motion rides, $5 each; virtual reality roller coaster, $4; all-day and half-day wrist bands are also available. Rides subject to periodic closure due to weather.* The Wild West-styled Buffalo Bill's features one of tallest and fastest roller coasters in the U.S. **Desperado** plunges 225 feet and reaches speeds of 80 mph while riders glimpse spectacular views of the surrounding desert. Additional thrills can be had on the **Turbo Drop**, which lifts riders 170 feet above the desert and then drops them, reaching speeds up to 45 mph before bouncing gently on air brakes. A little tamer, but just as fun, are the **Frog Hopper**—a gentle version of the Turbo Drop for small fry—and the

Above, Buffalo Bill Resort and roller coaster; below, Outlet mall.

Adventure Canyon Log Flume Ride, which crisscrosses the path of the roller coaster and finishes with a gentle ride through the casino. Bill's is also home to **The Vault A 3-D Experience**, a motion simulator with a variety of ride scenarios.

Primm Valley Resort & Casino *On E side of I-15, 31900 S Las Vegas Blvd. Fashion Outlets open daily 10 am-8 pm. Closed Dec 25 and Thanksgiving. Bonnie and Clyde exhibit open 24 hours. Free.* Upscale relaxation is the focus of this country club-like retreat, home to the **Primm Valley Golf Club**, which offers two 18-hole championship courses (see Golfing in the *Recreation* chapter), and **Fashion Outlets of Las Vegas**. The most unusual attraction is in the rotunda that connects the resort to the factory outlet mall: a **Bonnie and Clyde display** featuring their bullet-riddled Ford "Getaway Car," wanted posters and other memorabilia, as well as the restored **Dutch Shultz-Al Capone Gangster Car**.

Whiskey Pete's Hotel & Casino *On W side of I-15, 100 W Primm Blvd.* Named for the legendary proprietor of an old rest stop at the state line, the mining town-themed Whiskey Pete's was opened in 1977 by the Primm family. The majestic "castle in the desert" with its soaring towers became a landmark and led to the further development of the area.

Red Rock Canyon
National Conservation Area

18 miles W of Las Vegas via SR 159/W Charleston Blvd or 20 miles W of Las Vegas via SR 160/Blue Diamond Rd. Visitor center located to the left of the scenic loop drive

Above, Spring Mountain; below, hiking in Red Rock Canyon.

entrance. (702) 515-5350 (Bureau of Land Management, Red Rock Canyon NCA). Open daily 6 am; Apr-Sep park to 8 pm, visitors center to 5 pm; Oct-Mar closing hours vary. Closed Jan 1, Thanksgiving and Dec 25. Entrance fee: $5 per vehicle; bicyclists and pedestrians, free.

Just a short drive from the manmade wonders of Las Vegas, Red Rock Canyon features nature at its best. The 13-mile scenic loop drive, plus more than 20 miles of hiking trails, are perfect for sightseeing. Activities like horseback riding mixed with numerous panoramic overlooks, a variety of flora and fauna, American Indian rock art, plus a well-stocked visitor center with exhibit rooms and a bookstore, round out the experience. Picnicking sites are located at Red Spring and Willow Spring.

Because Red Rock Canyon is up to 5000 feet higher in elevation than Las Vegas and has double the annual rainfall—about 8 to 12 inches—a wider variety of plant and animal life is able to flourish here. Cacti, annuals, yucca (such as the Joshua tree) and trees (ponderosa and piñon pines, juniper and willow) are prevalent, as are many types of birds, such as hawks, eagles, falcons, roadrunners, owls, ravens and wrens. Many other birds migrate through during the spring and fall; the visitor center staff can provide a complete list.

Much of the wildlife in Red Rock is visible only during the early morning and late evening hours, when cooler temperatures prevail. Night-dwellers include mule deer, coyotes, mountain lions, badgers, bobcats, jackrabbits and bats. Easier-to-spot diurnal inhabitants are bighorn sheep, wild burros, wild horses and antelope ground squirrels (identified by their white tails).

Reptiles are no strangers to the area, and include tree frogs, geckos, lizards and snakes. There are also three types of poisonous rattlesnakes here—the sidewinder, Mojave green and Mojave speckled. Hot days (above 70 degrees) bring out snakes; use caution when hiking. And remember, all animals, including snakes, are protected at Red Rock Canyon.

The Scenic Loop Drive is a convenient way to view the beauty of Red Rock Canyon; the road is located just off SR 159 and open daily from 6 a.m. to dusk. This one-way, 13-mile route begins near the visitor center, then returns to SR 159 about two miles farther south. The drive offers a close look at the area's Aztec sandstone, plant life and the **Keystone Thrust Fault**. The fault occurred some 65 million years ago and is considered the most significant geologic feature of Red Rock Canyon. It is believed that two of the Earth's crustal plates collided with such force that part of one plate was shoved up and over the younger sandstone. The thrust contact is evidenced by the sharp contrast between the gray limestone and the red sandstone.

Enjoying scenic Red Rock Canyon.

The first two pullouts on the scenic loop have short trails to the base of the **Calico Hills**, where seasonal rain pools can be found. These pools often become temporary homes to small insects, insect larvae and fairy shrimp. Easier hiking can be found a little farther along the drive at the **Sandstone Quarry**, accessed via a short, graded dirt road. From the historic quarry, many small canyons can be explored. A side road leads to the Willow Spring Picnic Area and a ³⁄₁₀-mile hike from the road takes visitors to **Lost Creek Canyon**, the site of a year-round spring and occasional seasonal waterfall.

Farther along the gently curving drive is **Ice Box Canyon Overlook**. From this location, visitors can take a ⁸⁄₁₀-mile hike to a box canyon surrounded by steep walls; the walls keep this canyon cooler than others in the area—hence the name. The end of the hike is reached by "boulder hopping" an additional ½ mile across the canyon bottom. Seasonal pools and an occasional waterfall can also be found here. The last stop along the road is the **Pine Creek Canyon Overlook**, one of the area's most popular hiking trails. The two-mile round trip features a running creek, ponderosa pines and the remains of a historic homestead.

The Scenic Loop Drive is also an excellent way for experienced **bicyclists** to see the area. The one-way paved road assures riders of no oncoming traffic, and since the road's width is two lanes, there is plenty of room for cars to pass. Bicyclists will, however, find the road a bit of a challenge. Its steep, undulating grades gain 1000 feet in altitude over the first five miles, followed by switchbacks at the top of the grade, then by a 1000-foot drop in elevation over the last eight miles. Round-trip mileage is about 15 miles. Bicyclists should beware of weekend and holiday traffic, which can be heavy, and keep a lookout for falling rocks in the switchbacks, and loose pebbles and debris where the road crosses a wash. Since there is no repair facility or air for tires available in the park or in nearby Blue Diamond, cyclists should come prepared to make their own repairs. The visitor center has a brochure detailing the route.

Safety Guidelines:

- Thunderstorms, especially in summer and early fall, can produce both lightning and flash floods. Never drive across flooded roads or cross low-lying areas when water is running.

- Charcoal fires are allowed at designated sites where grills are provided. Ground fires are prohibited.

- Camping is permitted only in designated locations.

- Climbing on sandstone requires equipment and experience. Sandstone is soft and crumbly and can be dangerous to climbers.

- Heat, cold and dehydration can take their toll on hikers. Carry one gallon of water for each person per day. Summer days can bring extreme heat, and temperatures drop rapidly at night.

- All natural and historic features are protected by federal law. This includes animals, plants, rocks and American Indian artifacts. Do not damage, disturb or remove them.

- Do not feed the burros at Red Rock Canyon. Feeding burros encourages them to congregate on the roads, where many have been killed or injured by vehicles. Burros have also been known to bite, kick and step out in front of cars unexpectedly. Use caution and observe them from a distance.

BONNIE SPRINGS OLD NEVADA *Off SR 159/W Charleston Blvd, 5½ miles S of Red Rock Canyon Visitor Center; 1 Gun Fighter Ln. (702) 875-4191. Open daily at 10:30 am; during daylight-saving time to 6 pm, standard time to 5 pm. Petting zoo open daily at 10 am. Train operates Sat, Sun and holidays only. Park admission Mon-Fri, $7 per vehicle (up to 6 people); Sat-Sun $10 per vehicle.* In the 1800s, Bonnie Springs Ranch was a stopover for wagon trains traveling the Old Spanish Trail. In 1952, Al and Bonnie Levinson built a replica of an old Western town. Attractions include staged gunfights and hangings, a melodrama, wax museum, blacksmith display, stagecoach and miniature train rides, horseback rides, and a petting zoo. The zoo houses donkeys, pigs, llamas, deer, a variety of other farm animals and a duck pond; food to feed them can be purchased from on-site vending machines. A Western-themed motel, gift shop, restaurant and saloon are also on the premises.

SPRING MOUNTAIN RANCH STATE PARK *S of Scenic Loop Dr off SR 159, 15 miles W of Las Vegas via Charleston Blvd. (702) 875-4141; summer theater information (702) 594-7529. Day-use area open 8 am-dusk. Visitor center/ranch house and gift shop open daily 10 am-4 pm. Closed Thanksgiving and Dec 25; call for holiday hours. 45-min guided tours of the historic area offered daily; call for schedule. Entrance fee: $6 per vehicle.* This 520-acre park at the base of the majestic Wilson Cliffs overflows with tranquil beauty. During the 1830s, the area was a welcome oasis for weary travelers on the alternate route of the Old Spanish Trail. Through most of the 20th century the site was used as a cattle ranch, changing owners several times (including Howard Hughes), before coming under park protection in 1974. Now listed on the National Register of Historic Places, tours of the historic site and its circa-1860s structures are given throughout the year. A large, grassy day-use area, shaded by scrub oak and mesquite trees, is available for picnickers; tables and barbecue grills are provided. The park hosts many activities, including art shows, plays and musicals, at its outdoor theater June through August, and living history programs in the spring and fall.

Spring Mountains National Recreation Area

35 miles NW of Las Vegas via US 95, turnoff at SR 157/Kyle Canyon Rd or SR 156/Lee Canyon Rd. Open daily. **Field office/visitor center** *(Las Vegas) W of The Strip at 4701 N Torrey Pines Dr. (702) 515-5400. Visitor center only, open Mon-Fri 7:30 am-4:30 pm. Closed Sat, Sun and holidays.* **Main visitor center** *(Kyle Canyon) at Mile Marker 3 on SR 157. (702) 872-5486. Open Mon-Fri 10 am-3 pm, Sat-Sun 9 am-4 pm. Hours may vary. Mount Charleston weather conditions, (702) 736-3854.* Barely a 45-minute drive from the glitz of Las Vegas is Spring Mountains National Recreation Area. Part of the Humboldt-Toiyabe National Forest, Spring Mountains NRA provides a lush reprieve from high temperatures and stark landscapes of the desert. By taking the Spring Mountains Scenic Loop, visitors are exposed to a number of appealing sights as the road climbs to its maximum elevation of 8500 feet. At this elevation, the temperature in the forest is usually 30 degrees cooler than in Las Vegas. Weekend crowds attest to the forest's popularity; weekdays are usually quieter.

Caution: Portions of the national forest may close for the winter as early as October (depending on weather conditions), and tire chains may be required at any time during winter months. Gasoline is not available on the mountain.

Cathedral Rock, Old Mill, Foxtail and **Deer Creek** are enjoyable picnic spots. Another feature to look for is **Mummy Mountain**, so named because it looks like a huge mummy lying on its back. Restaurant dining with outdoor seating is available near Cathedral Rock. Hikers should bring comfortable walking shoes in order to experience the area's beauty up close; numerous hiking trails offer broad vistas and interesting flora and fauna.

Charleston Peak is the third-highest peak in Nevada. A trail to the 11,918-foot summit is usually open between June and October, though weather conditions can lengthen or shorten the hiking season considerably. Hikers should be in good condition before attempting the climb; the gain in elevation from start to finish is almost 4000 feet, and the total round trip is more than 18 miles.

Spring Mountains ski lift.

Mount Charleston taxi service.

LAS VEGAS SKI AND SNOWBOARD RESORT *47 miles NW of Las Vegas via US 95 and SR 156/Lee Canyon Rd. (702) 645-2754. Open Thanksgiving-Easter, daily 9 am-4 pm, weather permitting. All-day tickets, $33; ages 12 and younger, $25; ages 65 and older, $23.* Winter temperatures average 30 to 40 degrees at this resort, which offers 10 different trails. The summit is at 9510 feet; the vertical drop is 1000 feet. Rentals (alpine skis, boots and poles, snowboards), snowmaking, night skiing (depending on snow conditions), ski school, snack bar and day lodge are available. Three double chairs service the area; prices vary, call for information. The nearest AAA-approved accommodations are in Las Vegas. Tire chains may be required when driving in this area.

Valley of Fire State Park

50 miles NE of Las Vegas via I-15 and SR 169 (Valley of Fire Rd) near Overton. (702) 397-2088. Open daily sunrise-sunset. Entrance fee: $5 per vehicle. Camping fee: $14 per vehicle (includes entrance fee). Visitor center located just off Valley of Fire Rd, midway into the park. Open daily 8:30 am-4:30 pm. Closed Dec 25. So named because of the effect of bright sunlight reflecting off red sandstone, Nevada's oldest state park is a visually stunning area that contains dozens of unique geological formations and remnants of an ancient American Indian civilization.

During the dinosaur age 150 million years ago, these great sandstone formations were created from shifting sand dunes and years of uplifting, faulting and erosion. Prehistoric inhabitants of the area included the Basket Maker people, and later, Ancestral Puebloan farmers from the nearby Moapa Valley.

Nevada's oldest state park offers countless natural formations, brilliantly red in color, and all different shapes and sizes. Located near the east entrance station is **Elephant Rock**, one of the most photographed formations in the park; it resembles an elephant's profile when viewed from the hill behind, looking toward Valley of Fire Road. **Seven Sisters**, another striking formation, is also easily visible from Valley of Fire Road; it is just east of the visitor center. **The Beehives**, weathered by wind and water, are near the west entrance station. The remnants of petrified logs are also within in the park, although thoughtless visitors have taken so many samples that the amount of petrified wood is considerably depleted. For examples of **petroglyphs**—pictures carved into rock—**Atlatl Rock** is one of the best. Situated near the center of the park along Scenic Loop Road, the petroglyphs of the towering

rock are easily viewed by walking up a steep, metal staircase. Visitors who brave the 83 mesh-covered steps to the top will be rewarded with the sight of ancient, well-preserved figures carved into the rock.

Another site known for its petroglyphs is Mouse's Tank, a natural basin named after an early renegade who used the area as a hideout. Water collects in the rock after a rainfall, occasionally remaining in the tank for months.

Clockwise, Elephant Rock, The Beehives; and petroglyphs

Because of its rare beauty, Valley of Fire has been used many times as the background for motion pictures. There are numerous hiking trails, as well as camping and picnicking facilities. The visitor center has an outdoor botanical garden, displays of local fauna, and information about the park and its hiking trails.

Caution: Care should be taken when traveling in this area.

- Thunderstorms, especially in summer and early fall, can produce both lightning and flash floods. Camp only in designated areas and never drive across flooded roads.

- All natural and historic features are protected. This includes animals, plants, rocks and American Indian artifacts. Do not damage, disturb or remove them.

- Care should be taken when hiking in canyon areas. Taking shortcuts may be dangerous. Never hike alone. Register at the visitor center before hiking backcountry areas. No overnight backpacking.

GUIDED TOURS

The tours listed in this section generally last less than a day, though some of the trips to more distant places involve an overnight stay. Contact the companies in advance for complete information and reservations; many tours offer hotel pickup and discounted children's rates. Also, check refund policies to avoid losing your deposit in the event of a late cancellation. Scheduled tours are subject to cancellation if there is an insufficient number of passengers.

Tours listed are provided as a convenience for our readers; inclusion in this publication does not imply endorsement by the Automobile Club of Southern California.

Boulder City

BLACK CANYON RIVER ADVENTURES *4 mi NE of Boulder City on US 93, in Hacienda Hotel and Casino. (800) 455-3490. Reservations advised.* Motorized raft trips down the Colorado River, from Hoover Dam to Willow Beach.

COLORADO RIVER TOURS *205 Rainier Ct. (702) 291-0026.* El Dorado Canyon land tours (oldest gold mine in Nevada); Colorado River kayak and canoe trips, and rentals.

DOWN RIVER OUTFITTERS *1631 Industrial Rd. (702) 293-1190, (800) 748-3702.* Colorado River kayak and canoe trips from Hoover Dam to Willow Beach.

LAKE MEAD CRUISES *(702) 293-6180. Reservations recommended.* Lake Mead stern-wheeler cruises depart from Lake Mead Cruises Landing. Sightseeing, dinner/dance and breakfast cruises.

SHOWROOM ENTERTAINMENT

Primm's showrooms, while not as pervasive or as elaborate as those in Las Vegas, still add a noteworthy dimension to this growing tourist destination.

Tickets for shows may be purchased by phoning or visiting the hotel's showroom box office or by contacting a local ticket agency. Refer to the telephone directory yellow pages under "Ticket Sales/Events" or "Tourist Information."

Listing does not imply AAA endorsement for the lodging establishments. For the most current information, refer to the Auto Club's "Nevada Show Sheet," available to AAA members at all Southern California district offices.

Primm

Located along I-15 at the California-Nevada state line, this emerging destination offers production shows, headliners, special events and lounge entertainment. Times and prices vary with entertainers.

PRIMM VALLEY RESORTS *(702), (800) 386-7867.*

Buffalo Bill's Resort & Casino *On E side of I-15.*

Primm Valley Resort & Casino *On E side of I-15.*

Whiskey Pete's Hotel & Casino *On W side of I-15.*

ANNUAL EVENTS

The Boulder City area plays host to a number of annual events, while Logandale, more than 50 miles northeast of Las Vegas, hosts the Clark County Fair each year. For detailed information about each event, please call the telephone number shown, or consult with the local chamber of commerce or visitor information bureau.

April

CLARK COUNTY FAIR *Clark County Fairgrounds, Logandale. (702) 398-3247.* This four-day event features livestock shows, pony rides, arts and crafts booths, a PRCA rodeo and carnival rides.

May

SPRING JAMBOREE & CRAFT FAIR *Bicentennial Park, Boulder City. (702) 293-2034.* An arts and crafts fair, classic car show, food booths and music are all part of this two-day springtime festival.

July

DAMBOREE *Central Park, Boulder City. (702) 293-2034.* This old-fashioned Fourth of July celebration includes a parade, games, children's activities, live music, a carnival and fireworks.

October

ART IN THE PARK *Bicentennial Park, Boulder City. (702) 293-4111, ext 725.* With arts and crafts on display in more than 300 booths, this two-day show is the largest of its kind in the western United States.

December

CHRISTMAS PARADE *Boulder City. (702) 293-2034.* A Saturday night parade down the Nevada Highway, ending at Bicentennial Park, helps celebrate the holiday season.

PARADE OF LIGHTS *Lake Mead. (702) 293-2034 (Boulder City).* Boats ranging in length from 16 to 34-plus feet gather on the nation's largest manmade lake to ring in the Christmas season with an evening's blaze of festive, twinkling lights.

Laughlin-Bullhead City

*Ninety miles south of Las Vegas are the booming towns of **Laughlin, Nevada**, and **Bullhead City, Arizona**. Perched on opposite banks of the Colorado River, they lack the vibrant atmosphere of Las Vegas, although Laughlin alone draws some 5 million tourists annually. The town's relaxed pace, bargain-priced lodging and entertainment attracts visitors. Popular music of the '60s through the '90s draws both baby-boomers and seniors to lounges and showrooms. And some 10,000 to 15,000 "snowbirds" migrate from colder climates each year to make the area their winter home. Moreover, the region boasts many worthwhile attractions, ranging from hiking trails to historic mining towns, such as Oatman, Arizona. And of course, there's abundant recreation on the Colorado River.*

POINTS OF INTEREST

Attractions are listed alphabetically. ***Note:*** The State of Arizona does not observe daylight-saving time; Mountain Standard Time is in effect year round.

COLORADO BELLE HOTEL & CASINO *In Laughlin at 2100 S Casino Dr. (702) 298-4000.* This resort-casino is a striking 608-foot replica of a Mississippi paddle-wheel riverboat. It features nautically themed hotel rooms and restaurants, a microbrewery/sports bar, a 100-game video arcade, and a strolling Dixieland band on Friday and Saturday nights.

COLORADO RIVER MUSEUM *In Bullhead City, AZ, at 2201 SR 68, ¼ mile N of the Laughlin Bridge. (928) 754-3399. Open Sep-Jun, Tue-Sun 10 am-4 pm (Ariz time). Closed major holidays and Jul-Aug. Donation.* Housed in a former Catholic church built in 1947

Watersports are popular in Laughlin.

during the Davis Dam construction, this small museum features a model of Fort Mojave in the late 1800s and an exhibit on the Rose Massacre that took place nearby, geologic maps of the area, historical photographs, and a hands-on children's gallery where kids can grind corn and create rock art. Items donated to the museum include a steamboat anchor, mining tools, antique barbed wire, American Indian artifacts, a dinosaur footprint, and an 1884 piano that was shipped around Cape Horn.

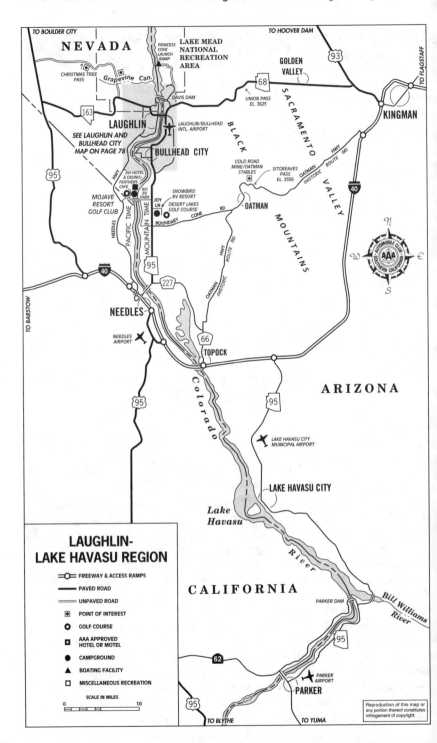

DAVIS CAMP COUNTY PARK *In Bullhead City, AZ, on SR 95, ½ mile N of the Laughlin Bridge. (928) 754-7250, reservations (877) 757-0915. Open Mar 15-Oct 15, 6 am-dusk; rest of year from 7 am. $5 per vehicle entrance fee, $5 per person holiday weekends; $7 launching fee Mar 15-Oct 15. Fees may vary for special events.* The park offers a stretch of sandy beach for swimming and fishing, or launching personal watercraft, inner tubes, rafts or rubber boats. The area from the park north to Davis Dam is noted for its excellent striped bass and rainbow trout fishing. Visitors have found that a hike into the park's south section can provide views of a variety of birds and small wildlife. RV camping only is permitted along the river (see *Campgrounds & Trailer Parks*); fishing requires a license (see Water Recreation under *Recreation*).

Davis Dam, on the Colorado River.

DAVIS DAM *2 miles N of Laughlin via Casino Dr and SR 163. (928) 754-3628.* Designed to help regulate the delivery of water to the lower Colorado River region and Mexico, this rock-fill and earthen structure is augmented by concrete intakes and spillways. In addition to its importance for flood control, the dam provides hydroelectric power for regional industry and irrigation for farming. The powerhouse is no longer open for tours, but the dam can still be viewed up close.

DON LAUGHLIN'S RIVERSIDE RESORT HOTEL & CASINO *In Laughlin at 1650 S Casino Dr.* The high-rise resort that spurred the town's development houses a Western dance hall, a cineplex with first-run movies, and an RV park.

Don Laughlin's Classic Car Collection *(702) 298-2535, ext 5678 or 5103. Open daily 9 am-10 pm, Fri to 11 pm. Free.* The collection features antique, classic and futuristic "concept" automobiles from the Imperial Palace in Las Vegas and Don Laughlin's private collection. The cars are exhibited in two rooms: a glass-walled room facing Casino Drive, and the Exhibition Hall on the third floor of the hotel's 26-story tower.

Don's Kid Kastle *(702) 298-2535, ext 5191; (800) 227-3849. Open daily at 10 am; Sun-Thu to 11 pm; Fri-Sat to midnight. Hourly fee per child: Mon-Thu $6, Fri-Sun $6.50. For ages 3 months-12 years.* Activities include group play, nonviolent video games, and a giant castle where children may climb, slide and explore.

♠ A Quick Guide to Laughlin-Bullhead City

Emergency 911

Highway Conditions   Arizona (888) 411-7623 • Nevada (702) 486-3116

Time/Weather

Arizona   (520) 763-3000

Nevada time (775) 844-1212

Weather   (702) 248-4800

Emergency Road Service for AAA Members

(800) AAA-HELP (in the USA and Canada)

(800) 955-4TDD (for the hearing impaired)

Radio Stations

For a complete list of radio programs, consult the daily newspapers.

Classic Rock: KLUK (97.9 FM), KRRK (101.1 FM); **Contemporary Rock:** KZUL (104.5 FM); **Country:** KFLG (94.7 FM and 1000 AM), KGMN (104.7 FM), KWAZ (97.9 FM); **News/Talk:** KATO (1230 AM), KZZZ (1490 AM); **Oldies:** KRCY (105.9 FM).

Television Stations

In Laughlin, the major television stations include channels 3 (NBC), 5 (FOX), 8 (ABC) and 13 (CBS). In Bullhead City, Ariz., the major network programs appear on channels 5 (CBS), 10 (FOX), 12 (NBC) and 13 (ABC). For a complete list of television programs, consult the daily newspaper or hotel listings.

Riverside Lanes *(702) 298-2535, ext 5160; (888) 590-2695. Open Sun-Thu 8 am-midnight, Fri-Sat to 2 am. Call for lane availability and prices. Cosmic Bowling, Wed 8 pm-midnight, Fri-Sat 9 pm-1 am. First come, first served.* The bowling center, which features 34 lanes with automatic scoring, offers Cosmic Bowling three nights a week. The facility is illuminated with black lights and equipped with glow-in-the-dark pins and balls on these evenings; running lights, along the sides of the lanes, help bowlers aim at the incandescent pins.

GRAPEVINE CANYON/CHRISTMAS TREE PASS *7 miles W of Davis Dam on SR 163 (about 6 miles W of Casino Dr), N on dirt access road (a small sign indicates the turn). (928) 754-3272. No restrooms or drinking water available.* This canyon offers excellent viewing of American Indian rock carvings of animals, fertility symbols and spiritual signs. Varying in age from 150 to more than 600 years, they are reached by a half-mile path from the parking area. Hikers will travel along the edge of a wash to a small incline in the canyon.

♠ A Quick Guide to Laughlin-Bullhead City

Public Transportation

Shuttles and Ferries All of the hotels in Laughlin have large on-site parking lots. A water taxi runs between the casino docks at the Riverside, Edgewater, Pioneer, Golden Nugget and Harrah's; the fare is $1 one way and $2 round trip. On those occasions when the water level of the river (controlled by Davis Dam) is too low for the taxis to travel safely, parking lot pickups are made by shuttle buses.

In addition, Citizen Area Transit (CAT) operates a 24-hour bus route in Laughlin, covering the business district and residential area. The fare for those 18 and over is $1.50, and 75¢ for ages 65 and older and 5 to 17.

Taxi Laughlin and Bullhead City both have taxi service, but the Arizona-based taxi companies are not allowed to operate in Nevada unless called to take a passenger from Laughlin into the state of Arizona. They are also not allowed to take passengers from one casino to another or from one location in Nevada to another.

The Laughlin taxi companies charge a base fare of $2.80 plus $1.80 for each mile; 40¢ per minute waiting time. In Bullhead City, the base fare is $1.50 plus $1.50 for each mile.

The following companies provide service in Laughlin: Desert, (702) 298-7575; Lucky, (702) 298-2299. In Bullhead City: Bullhead City Taxi/Mojave, (928) 754-7433; Lucky, (928) 754-1100; Rebel, (928) 754-2000; AA Taxi Cab, (928) 754-7845.

Heading north from the Grapevine Canyon parking lot (toward US 95) leads to Christmas Tree Pass, which gets its name from the piñon and juniper trees that locals have decorated with ribbons, plastic lids, paper and other bits of "trash" for many years. About four miles out of Grapevine Canyon the wide, graded dirt road narrows considerably to allow access for only one car in each direction; this section is not recommended for RVs. As the road leaves Christmas Tree Pass, it widens out again for another five miles to US 95. *Note:* This road is subject to heavy washout during periods of rain.

Four-wheel-drive enthusiasts will find several backcountry roads that the National Park Service has approved for public access. They lead to secluded coves on the lake or into the desert mountain backcountry. It is advisable to check with the ranger for information about road conditions. *Caution:* Flash flooding can occur during inclement weather and sudden summer thunderstorms. Watch for unfenced mine shafts and pits. Stay out of abandoned mines; deep shafts, rotten timbers and flammable or poisonous gases can be concealed inside the tunnels.

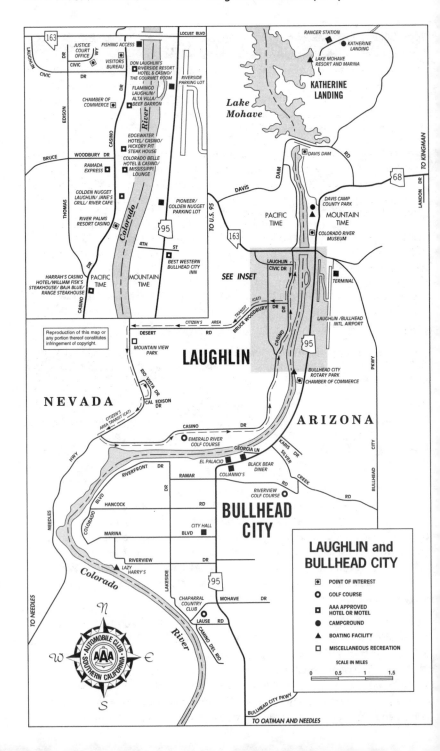

OATMAN *23 miles SE of Bullhead City, Ariz via SR 95 and Boundary Cone Rd, on Historic Route 66 (Oatman Hwy). (928) 768-6222.* Located in the rugged Black Mountains between Kingman and Bullhead City on Historic Route 66, Oatman is an old mining town that has been seen in many movies and TV shows and is still brimming with the fervor of the Old West. Many of the original buildings are still in use, housing tourist-oriented enterprises, as well as a post office and several Western-style restaurants and saloons.

This once-prosperous gold-mining community flourished from 1905 to 1942, its local mines yielding nearly $36 million in gold at the peak of production. The onset of World War II led to the town's demise, when Congress halted all mining not essential to the war effort; mining activity resumed in recent years but ceased again in 1998 when the price of gold fell below a cost-productive level.

Today Oatman has about 150 residents, down from a whopping 10,000 during its heyday in the 1930s. Oatman's fortuitous position along the original Route 66 (US 66) from Chicago to Los Angeles has undoubtedly helped preserve it; this town was an important last stop for travelers before entering the Mojave Desert into California.

Get your kicks on Historic Route 66, in Oatman.

A number of Wild West-style attractions can be seen here, including the afternoon **gunfights** staged three times daily by "Outlaw Willie," the Ghostrider Gunfighters and their female counterparts, the Oatman Gold Diggers. Other spots to see include the Oatman Jail (now a museum); a variety of old mining equipment displayed along the street and in shops; the historic **Oatman Hotel**, where movie legends Clark Gable and Carole Lombard spent their wedding night in 1939; and the town's unofficial welcoming committee of wild **burros**. These cute but stubborn animals are descendants of the burros miners turned loose years ago. They freely roam the streets in search of carrot handouts, a snack that can be purchased in local stores, but visitors are strongly discouraged from feeding them anything else.

The spectacular scenery offered up on the road through the Black Mountains, from Topock (on I-40) north to Oatman along **Historic Route 66** (Oatman Highway), may be the biggest attraction of all. For another scenic drive, take Route 66 northeast out of Oatman to Kingman. The road goes past the historic mining camp of **Gold Road**, climbs to the summit of the Black Mountains, then crosses the wide Sacramento Valley to **Kingman**.

At times, the road becomes a series of narrow hairpin curves as it winds its way up to the pass. But those with an adventurous spirit will be rewarded with panoramic views of Arizona and Nevada (maybe even California on a clear day) from the tri-state lookout point just before the summit of Sitgreaves Pass. From here, descend the eastern slope of the Black Mountains into the Sacramento Valley, an area populated with creosote bushes, yucca plants and, in season, a sprinkling of wildflowers. For the return to the Laughlin Bridge, take SR 68 west from Kingman across the flat Sacramento Valley, through a pass at the north end of the Black Mountains and down into the Colorado River Valley back to the bridge. Total mileage (from Oatman) is 60 miles. **Note:** This trip is not recommended for large RVs or trailers.

Caution: When exploring near these areas, a four-wheel-drive vehicle is recommended for travel on unpaved roads. Flash flooding can occur during summer thunderstorms, and heavy rains are possible in any season. When exploring old gold camps, watch out for unfenced mine shafts and pits. Never enter abandoned mines; deep shafts, rotted timbers and flammable or poisonous gases can be concealed in the tunnels.

Gold Road Mine *On Historic Route 66, 2½ miles NE of Oatman, Ariz. (928) 768-1600. Open daily 10 am-5 pm. Basic tour (1 hr): adults $12; ages 4-11, $6; ages 3 and younger, free. Extended tour (2½ hrs): $24. Extreme tour (4 hrs): $50 (by reservation only; minimum age 13). Surface tour (1 hr): $10.* This mine, begun by a Mexican prospector who tripped over a chunk of quartz while searching for his lost burro, has been in production off and on for more than 100 years. The tours start with a bumpy ride up a steep hill on a vehicle called a "getman," so named because it gets men up to and down from work. The basic tour takes visitors about 300 feet underground in a historic mine; a signpost marks a point where visitors are directly under Route 66. The extended and extreme tours explore other areas of the mine, while the surface tour focuses on gold ore processing.

RAMADA EXPRESS HOTEL & CASINO *In Laughlin at 2121 S Casino Dr. (800) 243-6846.* This 1501-room resort is distinguished by its Victorian decor and a collection of authentic train memorabilia displayed throughout the hotel and casino.

American Heroes Foundation Museum *(702) 298-6246. Open daily 8 am-5 pm. Free.* Thousands of personal mementos have been donated to this museum. Exhibits include diaries, medals, uniforms, military equipment, flags and models. There are also home-front items such as rationing stamps and propaganda pamphlets. The museum focuses on the WW II era, although there are small exhibits from the Korean and Vietnam wars.

Gambling Train of Laughlin *Open Mon-Thu 11 am-7 pm, Fri-Sun 10 am-10 pm. Free.* This narrow-gauge train offers rides (but no gambling) around a railroad-themed hotel. The locomotive is a replica of the Genoa, an 1890s-era steam engine that hauled freight and passengers on the Virginia and Truckee line in western Nevada.

RIVER WALK *Don Laughlin's Riverside Resort to River Palms Resort Casino. Open 24 hours. Free.* A stroll on this footpath along the river (accessed by walking through or between the hotels) provides a respite from the casinos and a pleasant way to experience the Colorado River.

GUIDED TOURS

The tours listed in this section generally last less than a day. (More extensive touring information is available in the *Las Vegas Valley* chapter.) Be sure to contact the companies in advance for complete information. Scheduled tours are subject to cancellation if there is an insufficient number of passengers.

Tours listed are provided as a convenience for our readers; inclusion in this publication does not imply endorsement by the Automobile Club of Southern California.

LAUGHLIN RIVER TOURS, INC. *Laughlin. (702) 298-1047, (800) 228-9825. Depending on cruise, departures at Edgewater, Flamingo Laughlin or River Palms boat docks. Tickets available at docks of all three hotels. Inquire ahead for current prices.* Laughlin-Bullhead City area tours take place aboard a paddle-wheeler and offer unique perspectives of the towns.

U.S.S. RIVERSIDE *At Don Laughlin's Riverside Resort Hotel & Casino, 1650 S Casino Dr, Laughlin. (702) 298-2535, ext 5770; (800) 227-3849, ext 5770. Departures from Don Laughlin's Riverside boat dock. Ticket booth located on the ground level of the hotel, next to boat dock.* Boat tours of the Laughlin-Bullhead City area and Davis Dam. Weddings held aboard.

A riverboat taxi cruises the Colorado.

SHOWROOM ENTERTAINMENT

Laughlin does not offer the elaborate, long-running stage shows or top-flight entertainers for which Las Vegas is famous. But its showrooms, cabarets and lounges do offer a variety of entertainment, ranging from headline performers to lounge acts. While the hotels listed here have facilities that seat 500 or more, many smaller venues are popular as well.

Lounge entertainment is available at all of the casinos, although some do not offer shows Monday.

The Riverside's Western Ballroom on the second floor of the hotel's south tower features a tea dance every Sunday from 2 to 6 p.m.; reservations are not required. In the evenings, the ballroom features live country music and dancing on its 1400-square-foot dance floor. Popular nightspots may also be found at Don Laughlin's Riverside Resort Hotel & Casino and The Golden Nugget Laughlin. Also, the Ramada Express offers dance contests Tuesday through Saturday at 4 p.m. in the Caboose Lounge. Times and prices vary with entertainers.

Showroom listing does not imply AAA endorsement for the lodging establishment. For the most current information, refer to the Auto Club's "Nevada Show Sheet," available to AAA members at all Southern California district offices.

DON LAUGHLIN'S RIVERSIDE RESORT HOTEL & CASINO *1650 S Casino Dr. (702) 298-2535.*

FLAMINGO LAUGHLIN *1900 S Casino Dr. (702) 298-5111, (800) 352-6464.*

HARRAH'S CASINO HOTEL *2900 W Casino Dr. (702) 298-4600.*

RAMADA EXPRESS HOTEL & CASINO *2121 S Casino Dr. (702) 298-4200, (800) 243-6846. On the Wings of Eagles* (Indefinitely; free).

The Flamingo Laughlin marquee.

RIVER PALMS RESORT CASINO *2700 S Casino Dr. (702) 298-2242.*

ANNUAL EVENTS

Car and motorcycle rallies, rodeos, fireworks displays and even a sidewalk egg fry are among the many community events that Laughlin and environs offer annually. For information about each event, please call the telephone numbers shown, or consult with the local chamber of commerce or visitor information bureau.

In addition, casino tournaments take place in many Laughlin casinos. Anyone interested in these tournaments should contact the hotel or venue directly for dates and play information; room reservations should be made well in advance, as room space is often at a premium during a tournament.

January

BED RACES AND CHAMBER POT PARADE *Oatman, Ariz. (928) 768-6222.* Five-person teams push old iron beds to the finish line on a zigzag racecourse. Costumed contestants parade down the street, competing for best-costume prizes.

LAUGHLIN DESERT CHALLENGE *Starts and finishes at corner of Big Bend Dr and Edison Wy, Laughlin. (800) 227-5245.* More than 200 of the world's top drivers compete over two days in an off-road race through the rough terrain outside of Laughlin.

March

CLARK GABLE-CAROLE LOMBARD LOOK-ALIKE CONTEST *Oatman Hotel, Oatman, Ariz. (928) 768-4274.* Individuals are given the opportunity to exchange vows, and even spend the night, in the same bridal suite where Clark Gable and Carole Lombard spent their honeymoon.

LAUGHLIN RODEO DAYS *Casino Dr, Laughlin. (702) 298-2214, (800) 227-5245.* This five-day PRCA Rodeo featuring the Laughlin River Stampede draws more than 500 partici-pants, who compete for prize money in eight traditional rodeo events. Entertainment, vendor booths, coun-try-western dances and festivities are part of the fun, and take place at area resorts and hotels.

Bucking the odds at Laughlin Rodeo Days.

April

DESERT TWIRLERS DO IT ON THE RIVER JAMBOREE *Mohave Valley Elementary School, 13 mi S of Bullhead City, Ariz. (928) 763-3424.* This two-day event features square and round dancing, plus daytime workshops.

LAUGHLIN RIVER RUN *Casino Dr, Laughlin. (800) 357-8223.* This four-day motorcycle rally features Harley-Davidsons and is billed as the West Coast's largest motorcycle event. Activities include a Miss River Run contest, a stunt com-petition and a custom bike show. Live entertainment and food are also featured.

June

RIVER DAYS *Colorado Riverfront, Laughlin. (702) 298-2214, (800) 227-5245.* Amateur and professional riders compete over two or three days in Formula One races on the Colorado River along the Laughlin shoreline. An exposition showcases the latest in personal watercraft equipment and accessories.

July

FOURTH OF JULY FESTIVITIES *Various locations. (702) 298-2214 (Laughlin); (928) 565-2204 (Bullhead City, Ariz.), (928) 768-6222 (Oatman, Ariz).* Independence Day is celebrated in a wide range of community events.

OATMAN SIDEWALK EGG FRY *Oatman, Ariz. (928) 768-6222.* This annual Fourth of July event features an egg-and-spoon race, traditional sidewalk egg fry, egg-toss and chicken-leg contest, and usually a gun-fighter reunion.

September

OATMAN GOLD CAMP DAYS *Oatman, Ariz. (928) 768-6222.* The Burro Biscuit Throwing Contest is the highlight of this Labor Day weekend event. Other activities include a crazy hat contest, chili cookoff and barbecue.

November

CHRISTMAS BUSH CONTEST *Oatman, Ariz. (928) 768-6222.* Shopkeepers and residents decorate bushes for the holidays, beginning in late November, along Historic Route 66 leading into Oatman from the west.

December

PARADE OF LIGHTS *Katherine's Landing, Ariz. (928) 754-3245.* Boats gather on Lake Mohave to celebrate the Christmas season with an evening's blaze of festive, twinkling lights.

NEW YEAR'S EVE CELEBRATIONS *(702) 298-2214 (Laughlin).* Traditional New Year's Eve festivities take place on both sides of the Colorado River.

Recreation

With an average of nearly 300 sunny days a year, Las Vegas and the Laughlin-Bullhead City areas are ideal spots for outdoor sports. Not only are there acres of lush green golf courses, tennis courts and seemingly endless swimming pools, but the canyons and mountains offer horseback riding amid dramatic backdrops, and Lake Mead National Recreation Area provides year-round boating, fishing, water-skiing and more.

GOLFING

Golf is one of the principal outdoor attractions in Las Vegas, as well as a popular sport in Laughlin-Bullhead City. That it is an $890 million-a-year business in Southern Nevada is no surprise. Las Vegas features several championship courses, some of which host PGA and LPGA tournaments, plus several less demanding courses where the weekend golfer can enjoy a quick round.

The desert climate offers nearly ideal playing conditions all year, with the exception of very high midday temperatures in July and August, which prompt an early tee time.

Golfing in Boulder City.

Public, semi-private and private courses are listed alphabetically by city. Information given for each course includes its name, location, street address, phone number, the earliest tee time available, yardage, par, slope, USGA ratings (from the preferred tee of the course), greens fees and facilities. Greens fees are given for weekday and weekend play during peak season. Some courses may not allow walking so the greens fee includes the mandatory golf cart fee. Some courses have senior citizen rates; call for information. Unless otherwise stated, each course is open daily.

Nine-hole courses may show par, slope and USGA rating that reflect nine holes played twice. It follows that a 9-hole course may list an 18-hole fee because they require 18 holes of play.

All semi-private and private courses have restrictions on public play ranging from members and guests only to liberal reciprocal agreements with members of other courses. Information on private courses is not listed. As it is impossible to list all of the restrictions for each course, telephoning the course is highly recommended in lieu of knowing a member. As fees vary, rate ranges are listed. Reservations are advised at most courses; some country clubs require reservations months in advance.

Information in this section is published as it is received from the individual courses. The listings have been made as complete as possible.

Boulder City

BOULDER CITY GOLF COURSE Public
1 mile S of US 93 via Buchanan Blvd; 1 Clubhouse Dr. (702) 293-9236. Rate range: $45-50. Beginning tee time: 6 a.m. The course is 18 holes; 6110 yards; par 72; 110 slope; 68.3 rating. Clubhouse, driving range, golf shop, golf pro, clubs, power and hand golf carts; restaurant, snack bar, cocktails, coffee shop, beer, wine.

BOULDER CREEK GOLF CLUB Public
S of SR 93; 1501 Veterans Memorial Dr. (702) 294-6534. Rate range including mandatory golf cart: $120-130. Beginning tee time: 7 a.m. The Coyote Run course is 9 holes; 3052 yards; par 36; 121 slope; 33.8 rating. The Desert Hawk course is 9 holes; 3028 yards; par 36; 113 slope; 34.2 rating. The Eldorado Valley course is 9 holes; 3130 yards; par 36; 118 slope; 33.8 rating. Golf shop, clubhouse, golf pro, driving range, clubs, power and hand golf carts; restaurant, snack bar, cocktails.

Henderson

ANTHEM COUNTRY CLUB Private

BLACK MOUNTAIN GOLF AND COUNTRY CLUB Semi-Private
2 miles E of I-515 via E Horizon Dr; 500 Greenway Rd. (702) 565-7933. Rate range including mandatory golf cart: $75-100. Beginning tee time: 6 a.m. The **Desert/Founders** course is 18 holes; 6529 yards; par 72; 129 slope; 71.1 rating. The **Founders/Horizon** course is 18 holes; 6541 yards; par 72; 123 slope; 70.7 rating. The **Horizon/Desert** course is 18 holes; 6480 yards; par 72; 129 slope; 70.5 rating. Clubhouse, driving range, golf shop, golf pro, locker room, night lighting on driving range, clubs, power and hand golf carts; restaurant, cocktails, beer, wine.

DESERT WILLOW GOLF COURSE Public
1½ miles S of I-215 via Green Valley Pkwy; 2020 Horizon Ridge. (702) 263-4653. Rate range including mandatory golf cart: $35-45. Beginning tee time: 7:30 a.m. The course is 18 holes; 3820 yards; par 60; 91 slope; 59.1 rating. Clubhouse, driving range, golf shop, golf pro, clubs, power golf carts; restaurant, snack bar, cocktails.

DRAGON RIDGE COUNTRY CLUB Semi-Private
2 miles N of I-215 via Stephanie St; 552 Stephanie St. (877) 855-1505. Rate range including mandatory golf cart: $150-225. The course is 18 holes; 5888 yards; par 72; 122 slope; 67.8 rating. Clubhouse, driving range, golf shop, golf pro, night lighting on driving range and golf course, clubs, power golf carts; snack bar, cocktails, beer, wine, restaurant.

THE FALLS GOLF CLUB Public

3 miles N of SR 146; 1605 Lake Las Vegas Pkwy. (702) 740-5258. Rate range including mandatory golf cart: $190-260. Beginning tee time: 6:30 a.m. The course is 18 holes; 7250 yards; par 72; 136 slope; 74.7 rating. Clubhouse, driving range, golf shop, golf pro, locker room, night lighting on driving range and golf course, clubs, power golf carts; restaurant, snack bar, cocktails, beer, wine.

THE LEGACY GOLF CLUB Public

1 mile N of I-215/SR 146 via Green Valley Pkwy; 130 Par Excellence Dr. (702) 897-2187. Rate range including mandatory golf cart: $130-150. Beginning tee time: sunrise. The course is 18 holes; 6211 yards; par 72; 119 slope; 69.3 rating. Clubhouse, driving range, golf shop, golf pro, clubs, power golf carts; restaurant, snack bar, cocktails, beer, wine.

REFLECTION BAY GOLF CLUB Public

8 miles E of I-515 via SR 146 and Lake Las Vegas Pkwy; 75 MonteLago Blvd. (702) 470-4653. Rate range including mandatory golf cart: $235-260. Beginning tee time: 6:30 a.m. The course is 18 holes; 6391 yards; par 72; 128 slope; 70.3 rating. Clubhouse, driving range, golf shop, golf pro, locker room, night lighting on driving range and golf course, clubs, power golf carts; restaurant, snack bar, cocktails, beer, wine.

REVERE AT ANTHEM GOLF CLUB Public

10 miles S of I-215 via Eastern Ave, Anthem Pkwy and Hampton Rd; 2600 Hampton Rd. (702) 259-4653. Rate range including mandatory golf cart: $165-225. The **Concord** course is 18 holes; 7034 yards; par 72; 126 slope; 72.8 rating. The **Lexington** course is 18 holes; 7143 yards; par 72; 139 slope; 73.6 rating. Clubhouse, driving range, golf shop, golf pro, clubs, power golf carts; snack bar, cocktails, coffee shop, restaurant.

RIO SECCO GOLF CLUB Public

5 miles E of I-15 via SR 146 and Seven Hills Dr; 2851 Grand Hills Dr. (702) 889-2400. Rate range including mandatory golf cart: $175-250. Beginning tee time: 7:30 a.m. The course is 18 holes; 6375 yards; par 72; 125 slope; 71 rating. Clubhouse, driving range, golf shop, golf pro, locker room, clubs, power golf carts; restaurant, snack bar, cocktails, beer, wine.

SOUTHSHORE GOLF CLUB AT LAKE LAS VEGAS Private

Las Vegas

ANGEL PARK GOLF CLUB Public

3 miles W of US 95 via Summerlin Pkwy; 100 S Rampart Blvd. (702) 254-4653. Rate range including mandatory golf cart: $125-145. The **Mountain** course is 18 holes; 5718 yards; par 71; 116 slope; 67.8 rating. The **Palm** course is 18 holes; 5438 yards; par 70; 113 slope; 67.8 rating. Clubhouse, driving range, golf shop, golf pro, locker room, night lighting on driving range and golf course, clubs, power golf carts; restaurant, snack bar, cocktails, beer, wine.

BADLANDS GOLF CLUB Semi-Private
3½ miles W of US 95 via Summerlin Pkwy and Rampart Blvd; 9119 Alta Dr. (702) 363-0754. Rate range including mandatory golf cart: $135-190. Beginning tee time: sunrise. The **Desperado/Diablo** course is 18 holes; 6430 yards; par 72; 122 slope; 70.6 rating. The **Desperado/Outlaw** course is 18 holes; 6175 yards; par 72; 120 slope; 69.7 rating. The **Diablo/Outlaw** course is 18 holes; 6331 yards; par 72; 121 slope; 70.7 rating. Clubhouse, driving range, golf shop, golf pro, locker room, clubs, power golf carts; restaurant, snack bar, cocktails.

BALI HAI GOLF CLUB Public
½ mile S of Russell Rd; 5160 Las Vegas Blvd S. (702) 450-8000. Rate range including mandatory golf cart: $245-295. Beginning tee time: 6 a.m. The course is 18 holes; 6601 yards; par 71; 125 slope; 70.2 rating. Clubhouse, driving range, golf shop, golf pro, locker room, clubs, power golf carts; restaurant, snack bar, cocktails, beer, wine.

BEAR'S BEST LAS VEGAS Public
10 miles W of I-15; 11111 W Flamingo Rd. (702) 804-8500. Rate range including mandatory golf cart: $195-245. Beginning tee time: 6:30 a.m. The course is 18 holes; 6043 yards; par 72; 122 slope; 68.3 rating. Clubhouse, driving range, golf shop, golf pro, locker room, clubs, power golf carts; restaurant, snack bar, cocktails.

CALLAWAY GOLF CENTER Public
1½ miles NE of I-15; 6730 S Las Vegas Blvd. (702) 896-4100. Rate range: $25-30. Beginning tee time: 7 a.m. The course is 9 holes; 1185 yards; par 27; 0 slope; 0 rating. Driving Range, golf shop, golf pro, night lighting on driving range and golf course, power and hand golf carts; restaurant, cocktails, beer, wine.

CANYON GATE COUNTRY CLUB Private

CRAIG RANCH GOLF COURSE Public
3 miles W of I-15/US 93; 628 W Craig Rd. (702) 642-9700. Rate: $19. The course is 18 holes; 6001 yards; par 70; 105 slope; 66.8 rating. Clubhouse, driving range, golf shop, golf pro, clubs, power and hand golf carts; snack bar, beer.

DESERT PINES GOLF CLUB Public
1½ miles NE of I-515 via Eastern Ave; 3415 E Bonanza Rd. (702) 388-4400. Rate range including mandatory golf cart: $135-175. Beginning tee time: sunrise. The course is 18 holes; 6464 yards; par 71; 112 slope; 66.8 rating. Clubhouse, driving range, golf shop, golf pro, locker room, night lighting on driving range and golf course, clubs, power golf carts; restaurant, snack bar, cocktails.

DESERT ROSE GOLF CLUB Public
2 miles E of SR 582 via Sahara Ave and Winterwood Blvd; 5483 Clubhouse Dr. (702) 431-4653. Rate range including mandatory golf cart: $59-79. Beginning tee time: 6:30 a.m. The course is 18 holes; 6135 yards; par 71; 114 slope; 69 rating.

Driving Range, golf shop, golf pro, clubs, power and hand golf carts; restaurant, snack bar, cocktails, beer, wine.

EAGLE CREST GOLF COURSE Semi-Private

4½ miles W of US 95 via Summerlin Pkwy and Anasazi Dr; 2203 Thomas Ryan Blvd. (702) 240-1320. Rate including mandatory golf cart: $60. Beginning tee time: 6:30 a.m. The course is 18 holes; 1765 yards; par 60; 89 slope; 57.9 rating. Clubhouse, driving range, golf shop, golf pro, clubs, power golf carts; restaurant, snack bar, cocktails, coffee shop, beer, wine.

HIGHLAND FALLS GOLF CLUB Semi-Private

5 miles NW of US 95 via Lake Mead Blvd; 10201 Sun City Blvd. (702) 254-7010. Rate range including mandatory golf cart: $65-85. Beginning tee time: 7:30 a.m. The course is 18 holes; 6017 yards; par 72; 116 slope; 68.6 rating. Clubhouse, driving range, golf shop, golf pro, clubs, power golf carts; restaurant, snack bar, cocktails, beer, wine.

LAS VEGAS COUNTRY CLUB Private

LAS VEGAS GOLF CLUB Public

1½ miles N of US 95 via Decatur Blvd; 4300 Washington Ave. (702) 646-3003. Rate range including mandatory golf cart: $69-89. Beginning tee time: 5:30 a.m. The course is 18 holes; 5918 yards; par 72; 105 slope; 68.1 rating. Clubhouse, driving range, golf pro, golf shop, locker room, night lighting on driving range, clubs, power and hand golf carts; restaurant, cocktails, beer, wine.

LAS VEGAS NATIONAL GOLF CLUB Public

3 miles E of I-15 via Spring Mountain Rd, Sands Ave, Twain Ave and Maryland Pkwy; 1911 E Desert Inn Rd. (702) 734-1796. Rate range including mandatory golf cart: $99-150. The course is 18 holes; 6418 yards; par 71; 121 slope; 70.2 rating. Clubhouse, driving range, golf shop, golf pro, locker room, night lighting on driving range, clubs, power golf carts; restaurant, snack bar, cocktails, beer, wine.

LAS VEGAS PAIUTE RESORT Public

18 miles NW of Las Vegas via US 95; 10325 Nu-Wav Kaiv Blvd. (702) 658-1400. Rate range including mandatory golf cart: $125-195. Beginning tee time: 6 a.m. The **Snow Mountain** course is 18 holes; 6035 yards; par 72; 112 slope; 68.6 rating. The **Sun Mountain** course is 18 holes; 6074 yards; par 72; 116 slope; 68.8 rating. The **Wolf** course is 18 holes; 6483 yards; par 72; 130 slope; 71.4 rating. Clubhouse, driving range, golf shop, golf pro, locker room, clubs, power golf carts; restaurant, snack bar, cocktails, beer, wine.

LOS PRADOS GOLF COURSE Semi-Private

½ mile E of US 95 via Lone Mountain Rd and Los Prados Blvd; 5150 Los Prados Cir. (702) 645-5696. Rate range including mandatory golf cart: $40-65. Beginning tee time: sunrise. The course is 18 holes; 4937 yards; par 70; 101 slope; 62.2 rating. Clubhouse, golf shop, golf pro, clubs, power golf carts; restaurant, snack bar, cocktails, coffee shop, beer, wine.

NORTH LAS VEGAS COMMUNITY 3 PAR GOLF COURSE Public

1 mile W of I-15 via Cheyenne Ave; 324 E Brooks Ave. (702) 633-1833. Rate range: $6.50-8.50. Beginning tee time: sunrise. The course is 9 holes; 1086 yards; par 27. Clubhouse, golf shop, night lighting on golf course, clubs, hand golf carts; restaurant, coffee shop.

PAINTED DESERT GOLF CLUB Public

¼ mile W of US 95 via Ann Rd; 5555 Painted Mirage Way. (702) 645-2570. Rate range including mandatory golf cart: $79-109. Beginning tee time: 6 a.m. The course is 18 holes; 6323 yards; par 72; 128 slope; 71 rating. Clubhouse, driving range, golf shop, golf pro, clubs, power golf carts; snack bar, cocktails, beer, wine.

PALM VALLEY GOLF CLUB Semi-Private

4 miles W of US 95 via Lake Mead Blvd; 9201-B Del Webb Blvd. (702) 363-4373. Rate including mandatory golf cart: $60. Beginning tee time: 6 a.m. The course is 18 holes; 6341 yards; par 72; 124 slope; 69.8 rating. Driving range, golf shop, golf pro, clubs, power golf carts; restaurant, cocktails, beer, wine.

RED ROCK COUNTRY CLUB Public

10 miles W of I-15 off Sahara Ave via Red Rock Ranch Rd; 2250 Red Springs Dr. (702) 258-2300. Rate range including mandatory golf cart: $155-189. Beginning tee time: 7 a.m. The **Arroyo** course is 18 holes; 6634 yards; par 0; 0 slope; 0 rating. The **Mountain** course is 18 holes; 6651 yards; par 0; 0 slope; 0 rating. Clubhouse, driving range, golf shop, golf pro, locker room, clubs, power golf carts; restaurant, snack bar, beer, wine.

RHODES RANCH GOLF CLUB Public

8 miles SW of I-15 via Tropicana Ave and Durango Dr; 20 Rhodes Ranch Pkwy. (702) 740-4114. Rate range including mandatory golf cart: $130-160. Beginning tee time: sunrise. The course is 18 holes; 6009 yards; par 72; 120 slope; 71.1 rating. Clubhouse, driving range, golf shop, golf pro, locker room, clubs, power golf carts; restaurant, snack bar, cocktails, beer, wine.

THE ROYAL LINKS Public

6 miles E of Las Vegas Blvd via Flamingo Blvd; 5995 E Vegas Valley Dr. (702) 450-8123. Rate range including mandatory golf cart: $225-250. The course is 18 holes; 6602 yards; par 72; 131 slope; 71.2 rating. Clubhouse, driving range, golf shop, golf pro, locker room, clubs, power golf carts; restaurant, snack bar, cocktails, coffee shop, beer, wine.

SHADOW CREEK GOLF COURSE Private

SIENA GOLF CLUB Public

10 miles W of I-15 via Sahara Ave W and Town Center Dr; 10575 Siena Monte Ave. (702) 341-9200. Rate range including mandatory golf cart: $139-169. The course is 18 holes; 5639 yards; par 72; 115 slope; 66.3 rating. Clubhouse, driving range, golf shop, golf pro, locker room, night lighting on golf course, clubs, power golf carts; restaurant, snack bar, cocktails, beer, wine.

♠ Spa Facilities

After a long day of exploring the diverse offerings of Las Vegas, your tired and aching muscles may be screaming out for a relaxing massage, facial or an herbal wrap. On the other hand, your body may be used to a regular workout and you feel guilty about lounging around the hotel pool or casino all day, or worse, the number of buffets you've been frequenting. Alas, help is readily available. Many of the large resort hotels feature complete spa facilities, including whirlpool, sauna, massage, exercise programs (aquatic, aerobic), gym equipment, and more. Hotel spa and health club privileges often carry a fee; policies vary at each establishment. Some health clubs in hotels admit only registered guests. Public health clubs are numerous in the city, and most of the larger ones offer daily passes; check the local telephone directory yellow pages under "Health Clubs" for further information.

SILVERSTONE GOLF CLUB Public

3 miles NE of US 95 via Durango Dr and Grand Teton; 8600 Cupp Dr. (702) 562-3770. Rate range including mandatory golf cart: $120-175. The **Desert/Valley** course is 18 holes; 6380 yards; par 72; 132 slope; 69.4 rating. The **Mountain/Desert** course is 18 holes; 6552 yards; par 72; 128 slope; 70.2 rating. The **Valley/Mountain** course is 18 holes; 6316 yards; par 72; 121 slope; 69.3 rating. Clubhouse, driving range, golf shop, golf pro, locker room, clubs, power golf carts; restaurant, snack bar, cocktails, beer, wine.

SOUTHERN HIGHLANDS GOLF CLUB Private

SPANISH TRAIL GOLF AND COUNTRY CLUB Private

STALLION MOUNTAIN COUNTRY CLUB Semi-Private

2 miles E of US 95; 5500 E Flamingo Rd. (702) 450-8000. Rate range including mandatory golf cart: $115-195. Beginning tee time: 6:30 a.m. The **Citation** course is 18 holes; 6079 yards; par 72; 106 slope; 67.3 rating. The **Man O' War** course is 18 holes; 6474 yards; par 72; 117 slope; 69.3 rating. The **Secretariat** course is 18 holes; 6579 yards; par 72; 121 slope; 70.2 rating. Clubhouse, driving range, golf shop, golf pro, locker room, clubs, power golf carts; restaurant, snack bar, cocktails, coffee shop, beer, wine.

SUNRISE VISTA GOLF COURSE Military

TOURNAMENT PLAYERS CLUB AT THE CANYONS Public

4 miles W of US 95 via Summerlin Pkwy, Town Center and Village Center drs; 9851 Canyon Run Dr. (702) 256-2000. Rate range including mandatory golf cart: $95-250. The course is 18 holes; 6110 yards; par 71; 118 slope; 67.7 rating. Clubhouse, driving range, golf shop, golf pro, locker room, night lighting on driving range and golf course, clubs, power and hand golf carts; restaurant, snack bar, cocktails, beer, wine.

TOURNAMENT PLAYERS CLUB AT SUMMERLIN Private

CHAPARRAL COUNTRY CLUB Semi-Private

5 miles S of Bullhead City on AZ SR 95; 1260 E Mohave Dr, Bullhead City, AZ. (928) 758-3939. Rate range: $10-18. The course is 18 holes; 4626 yards; par 64; 100 slope; 62.1 rating. Clubhouse, golf shop, clubs, power and hand golf carts; restaurant, beer, wine.

DESERT LAKES GOLF COURSE Public

US Hwy 95, 13 miles from bridge to Laughlin, E on Joy Ln 1 mile; 5835 Desert Lakes Dr, Bullhead City, AZ. (928) 768-1000. Rate range including mandatory golf cart: $15-76. The course is 18 holes; 6600 yards; par 72; 119 slope; 70.5 rating. Clubhouse, driving range, golf shop, golf pro, clubs, power golf carts; snack bar, cocktails, coffee shop, beer, wine.

EMERALD RIVER GOLF COURSE Public

1½ miles E of Needles Hwy via Casino Dr; 1155 W Casino Dr, Laughlin, NV. (702) 298-4653. Rate range including mandatory golf cart: $80-90. Beginning tee time: 6 a.m. The course is 18 holes; 6048 yards; par 72; 131 slope; 69.1 rating. Driving range, golf shop, clubs, power golf carts; snack bar, beer, wine.

MOJAVE RESORT GOLF CLUB Public

9 miles S of Laughlin via Needles Hwy; 9905 Aha Macav Pkwy, Laughlin, NV. (702) 535-4653. Rate range including mandatory golf cart: $89-99. Beginning tee time: sunrise. The course is 18 holes; 6435 yards; par 72; 122 slope; 70.9 rating. Clubhouse, driving range, golf shop, golf pro, night lighting on golf course, clubs, power golf carts; snack bar, cocktails, beer, wine.

RIVERVIEW GOLF COURSE Public

2000 Ramar Rd, Bullhead City, AZ. (928) 763-1818. Rate range: $8-20. The course is 9 holes; 1160 yards; par 27. Clubhouse, golf shop, golf pro, clubs, power and hand golf carts; snack bar.

Primm

PRIMM VALLEY GOLF CLUB Public

8 miles S of Primm via I-15; 1 Yates Well Rd. (702) 256-8993. Rate including mandatory golf cart: $155. The **Desert** course is 18 holes; 6540 yards; par 72; 124 slope; 71.7 rating. The **Lakes** course is 18 holes; 6444 yards; par 71; 120 slope; 71.5 rating. Clubhouse, driving range, golf shop, golf pro, locker room, clubs, power golf carts; restaurant, snack bar, cocktails, beer, wine.

HORSEBACK RIDING

Las Vegas

COWBOY TRAIL RIDES, INC. *(702) 387-2457. Open daily. Guided rides ranging from 1 hour to overnight; prices $45 and up, depending on length of ride. Reservations recommended.* Riders traverse scenic Red Rock Canyon and Mount Charleston on trips that contain mustang viewing and twilight barbecues; the company also offers a Grand Canyon combo helicopter ride package.

SAGEBRUSH RANCH ADVENTURES *4 miles W of SR 95 at 12000 W Ann Rd. (702) 641-5536. Open daily. $25 per hour. Reservations required.* Rides may include breakfast, lunch or dinner.

Oatman

OATMAN STABLES *Oatman, Ariz. (928) 768-3257. Open daily. $25 per hour. Guided rides, 1 and 2 hours.* The route takes riders through the ruins of the Gold Roads.

Red Rock Canyon National Conservation Area

Ready to ride in Red Rock Canyon.

BONNIE SPRINGS OLD NEVADA *Off SR 159/W Charleston Blvd, 5½ miles S of Red Rock Canyon Visitor Center; 1 Gun Fighter Ln. (702) 875-4191. Open daily; first ride departs at 9 am; last at 3:15 pm, Jun-Oct at 5:45 pm. $25 per person; ages 5 and younger not admitted. No reservations.* One-hour guided rides traverse scenic Red Rock Canyon.

ROCK CLIMBING

Red Rock Canyon National Conservation Area

SKY'S THE LIMIT *(702) 363-4533, (800) 733-7597. Half-day rock-climbing lessons, $200; day hikes also available. Reservations recommended.* Participants learn climbing and rappelling fundamentals from experienced instructors amid the scenery of Red Rock Canyon. Climbing shoes and equipment are provided.

TENNIS & RACQUETBALL

Tennis and racquetball players will find plenty of places to hone their skills in Las Vegas. A number of publicly maintained parks have courts, as do many of the resort hotels and private clubs. Most of the courts are lighted for nighttime play. The hotels that allow visitors to use their facilities often give priority to their regis-

A little outdoor recreation.

tered guests, restricting others to open courts. Hotels whose courts are restricted to guests only are not listed here. It is always a good idea to phone ahead, since hours and regulations governing play are subject to change. Some public-use swimming pools have been included for convenience.

Public courts operate on a first-come, first-served basis and are open daily, generally from 6 a.m. to 11 p.m. For information about public courts, call (702) 455-8241.

Las Vegas

BALLY'S LAS VEGAS Semi-Private
3645 Las Vegas Blvd S. (702) 967-4598. Open daily 7 am-5 pm. Hotel guests, $10 per hour; nonguests, $15 per hour. Reservations required for play between 8:30 am and 5:30 pm. Eight lighted outdoor tennis courts.

DUCK CREEK PARK Public
8650 Pollock Dr. Two lighted tennis courts.

FLAMINGO LAS VEGAS Semi-Private
3555 Las Vegas Blvd S. (702) 733-3444. Open daily at 8 am; Mon-Thu to 7 pm; closing hour varies on weekends. $12 per hour for hotel guests, $20 for nonguests. Reservations required. Four lighted tennis courts.

HIDDEN PALMS PARK Public
8855 Hidden Palms Pkwy. Two lighted tennis courts.

LAS VEGAS ATHLETIC CLUB-MARYLAND PARKWAY Semi-Private
2655 S Maryland Pkwy. (702) 734-5822. Open 24 hours. Guest pass, $15. Reservations available. Five racquetball courts, 25-meter lap pool.

LAS VEGAS ATHLETIC CLUB-WEST SAHARA Semi-Private
5200 W Sahara Ave. (702) 364-5822. Open 24 hours. Guest pass, $15. Reservations available. Two racquetball courts, 25-meter lap pool.

LAURELWOOD PARK Public
4300 Newcastle Rd. Two lighted tennis courts.

MONTE CARLO RESORT & CASINO Semi-Private
3770 Las Vegas Blvd S. (702) 730-7411. Open daily 7 am-11 pm. Hotel guests $12, nonguests $18. Reservations required. Three lighted tennis courts.

PAUL MEYER PARK Public
4525 New Forest Dr. Two lighted tennis courts.

SUNRISE PARK AND COMMUNITY CENTER Public
2240 Linn Ln. Two lighted tennis courts.

SUNSET PARK Public
2601 E Sunset Rd. (702) 260-9803. Eight lighted tennis courts.

UNIVERSITY OF NEVADA, LAS VEGAS Semi-Private
McDermott Complex, on campus near Harmon Ave and Swenson St. Tennis reservations (702) 895-4489; racquetball reservations (702) 895-3150. Tennis courts open daily; times and rates vary. Reservations advised. Twelve lighted tennis courts; eight indoor racquetball courts.

WHITNEY PARK AND COMMUNITY CENTER Public
5700 E Missouri Ave. Two lighted tennis courts.

WINCHESTER PARK AND COMMUNITY CENTER Public
3130 S McLeod Dr. Two lighted tennis courts.

WINTERWOOD PARK Public
5310 Consul Ave. Two lighted tennis courts.

Laughlin

MOUNTAIN VIEW PARK Public
Needles Hwy, S of Desert Rd. Two lighted tennis courts.

WATER RECREATION

Entries for this section are listed north to south in three regions along the Colorado River: **Lake Mead**, **Lake Mohave** and **Below Davis Dam**. The first two fall within the Lake Mead National Recreation Area, which stretches from the upper reaches of Lake Mead to Davis Dam at the southern tip of Lake Mohave. The river below Davis Dam includes the Laughlin/Bullhead City area and southward from there toward Needles, California.

Jetting on Lake Mohave.

Lake Mead

25 miles SE of Las Vegas; 4 miles NE of Boulder City. Information available through the Lake Mead NRA at either the Alan Bible Visitor Center on US 93, by phone at (702) 293-8990 or (702) 293-8906, or at any park ranger station. Elevation 1200. This 110-mile-long lake on the Colorado River extends from Hoover Dam to the Grand Canyon. The shoreline offers sandy beaches and sheltered coves, while the rugged desert terrain invites hiking and climbing. Lake activities encompass boating, swimming, sailing, water-skiing, scuba diving, sailboarding and fishing. Complete recreation facilities are available at six sites operated by concessionaires of the National Park Service. Boaters should beware of sudden winds, floating debris, and underwater rocks and shoals caused by fluctuating water levels.

♠ Houseboating

Houseboats are permitted on Lake Mead, Lake Mohave and on the 75-mile stretch of the Colorado River from Davis Dam south to Parker Dam. The mild winter weather and hot summer days make houseboating popular all year in each of these areas; however, summer thunderstorms are common. Reservations should be made well in advance.

Houseboating on Lake Mead.

There are 246 square miles of uncrowded, open waters for house boaters on **Lake Mead.** The numerous secluded coves and scenic steep-walled canyons along its 550 miles of shoreline make the area popular with boaters. **Rentals:** Callville Bay Resort and Marina, (702) 565-8958; Temple Bar Resort and Marina, and Echo Bay Resort and Marina, (928) 767-3211.

Lake Mohave has numerous coves and inlets to explore at the south end of the lake, including many sandy coves. **Rentals:** Cottonwood Cove Resort and Marina, (702) 297-1464; Lake Mohave Resort and Marina, (928) 754-3245.

The **Colorado River from Davis Dam south** offers varied scenery, including rugged mountains, marshes, a narrow canyon (south of Needles) and the wide expanse of Lake Havasu. **Rentals:** Katherine Landing, (800) 752-9669; Cottonwood Cove Resort and Marina, (800) 255-5561.

Boating

CALLVILLE BAY RESORT AND MARINA *22 miles NE of Henderson on SR 167, 4 miles S of Northshore Rd.* (702) 565-8958. *Open daily.* Paved launch ramp, temporary mooring, slips, dry storage, auto/boat fuel, engine repairs, marine waste station. **Rentals:** Houseboats, motorboats (15 to 250 hp), fishing boats, personal watercraft. Marine hardware, campground, picnic area.

ECHO BAY RESORT AND MARINA *30 miles S of Overton off Northshore Rd.* (702) 394-4066. *Open daily.* Paved launch ramp, temporary mooring, slips, dry storage, auto/boat fuel, engine and hull repairs, marine waste station. **Rentals:** Houseboats, motorboats (15 to 150 hp), fishing tackle, water skis, personal watercraft. Marine hardware, bait, groceries, ice, snack bar, restaurant, lodging, campground with hookups, picnic area.

LAS VEGAS BOAT HARBOR *5 miles NE of Boulder City off Lakeshore Rd; Lake Mead NRA.* (702) 293-1191. *Open daily.* Wheelchair-accessible fishing dock, temporary mooring, slips, dry storage, boat fuel, engine and hull repairs, marine waste station. **Rentals**: Motorboats (40 to 250 hp), pontoons (40 hp), water skis, personal watercraft. Marine hardware, bait, groceries, ice, restrooms, restaurant.

Hemenway Launch Ramp Paved launch ramp.

LAKE MEAD RESORT AND MARINA *7 miles NE of Boulder City; 322 Lakeshore Rd. (702) 293-3484. Open daily.* Slips, temporary mooring, dry storage, boat fuel. **Rentals**: Motorboats (140 hp). Lodging, public campgrounds, restaurant, store; picnic area nearby.

Boulder Harbor Launch Ramp Paved launch ramp.

LAS VEGAS BAY MARINA *8 miles NE of Henderson off Lakeshore Rd. (702) 565-9111. Temporarily closed.* Paved launch ramp, temporary mooring, slips, dry storage, auto/boat fuel, engine and hull repairs, marine waste station. **Rentals**: Motorboats (15 to 185 hp), water-skis, Waverunners. Marine hardware, bait, groceries, ice, restaurant, picnic area.

OVERTON BEACH RESORT AND MARINA *11 miles SE of Overton off Lakeshore Rd. (702) 394-4040. Open daily. Closed Dec 25.* Paved launch ramp, temporary mooring, slips, dry storage, auto/boat fuel, engine and hull repairs, marine waste station. **Rentals**: Fishing boat (50 hp), patio boat, personal watercraft. Marine hardware, bait, groceries, ice, snack bar, RV sites with hookups.

TEMPLE BAR RESORT AND MARINA *28 miles NE of US 93 at the end of Temple Bar Rd. (928) 767-3211. Open daily. Closed Dec 25.* Paved launch ramp, mooring, slips, dry storage, auto/boat fuel, engine/hull repairs, marine waste station. **Rentals**: Motorboats (15 to 150 hp), water skis, personal watercraft. Cocktail lounge, marine hardware, bait, groceries, ice, restaurant, lodging, public campground, picnic area.

Fishing

Lake Mead offers some of the country's best fishing. Unlike some bodies of water, Lake Mead (and nearby Lake Mohave) has an open season on all species of fish year round. Largemouth bass, striped bass, channel catfish, black crappie and bluegill are popular catches; rangers or marina personnel can help point out the best fishing areas. Striped bass are most popular; some have tipped the scales at 50 pounds or more.

Angling at Lake Mead.

A wheelchair-accessible fishing dock is located at Hemenway Fishing Point on Boulder Beach.

♠ Fishing Licenses

Anglers fishing from Arizona, California and Nevada must possess valid fishing licenses from the state concerned. The rules and regulations of each state must be strictly adhered to, including within the Lake Mead National Recreation Area. Licenses and further information are available from the marinas or at local bait and tackle shops.

In **Arizona**, persons age 13 and younger do not require a license.

A license is not required for persons age 15 and younger in **California**.

In **Nevada**, a junior permit is required for anglers 12 to 15 years old.

Fishing on the **Colorado River** or **Lake Mead** requires a "special use" stamp affixed to a state fishing license. An additional stamp is required for trout fishing. A special fishing permit is required for fishing from shore on an **Indian reservation**.

Swimming

Clear and clean water ideal for swimming, snorkeling and diving can be found at Lake Mead. The best seasons are spring, summer and fall, when water temperatures average about 78 degrees. Boulder Beach is a designated swimming area. Swim with caution and with a buddy, as no lifeguard services are provided. The scuba diving trail at north Boulder Beach provides a protected dive area.

Water-skiing

The lake's wide basins offer perfect conditions for water-skiing. The sport is allowed on most of Lake Mead, except in the side canyons and for a few hundred feet north of Hoover Dam.

Lake Mojave

Accessible via US 95 and US 93. Information available through the Lake Mead NRA at either the Alan Bible Visitor Center (near Lake Mead on US 93), phone (702) 293-8990 or (702) 293-8906, or at any park ranger station. Elevation 675. This narrow lake, which stretches for 67 miles from below Hoover Dam to Davis Dam, is lined by rock canyon walls, and has numerous coves and sandy beaches. Activities include boating, swimming, water-skiing, skin diving, sailboarding, use of personal watercraft and fishing. Boating facilities are located at three points along the lake. Boaters should beware of sudden winds and flash floods.

Boating

COTTONWOOD COVE RESORT AND MARINA *14 miles E of Searchlight at the end of Cottonwood Cove Rd. (702) 297-1464. Open daily. Closed Dec 25.* Paved launch ramp, slips, dry storage, auto/boat fuel, engine repairs, temporary mooring, marine waste station. **Rentals:** Houseboats, motorboats (25 to 150 hp), personal watercraft, water skis. Bait, groceries, ice, clothing, restaurant, lodging, RV sites with hookups, picnic and swimming areas.

LAKE MOHAVE RESORT AND MARINA *At Katherine Landing, 6 miles N of Bullhead City via Ariz SR 95 and Katherine Landing Rd, Bullhead City, Ariz. (928) 754-3245. Open daily.* Paved launch ramp, slips, temporary mooring, dry storage, boat fuel, engine repairs, marine waste station. **Rentals:** Houseboats, motorboats (15 to 150 hp), fishing tackle, water skis, personal watercraft, houseboats. Marine hardware, bait, groceries, ice, snack bar, restaurant, lodging, RV sites with hookups, picnic area. Wheelchair-accessible fishing dock nearby.

PRINCESS COVE LAUNCH RAMP
Follow a graded dirt road 5 miles N of Katherine Landing, Bullhead City, Ariz. (928) 754-3272. Paved launch ramp.

WILLOW BEACH HARBOR *14 miles S of Hoover Dam via US 93 and Willow Beach Rd; Willow Beach, Ariz. (928) 767-4747. Open daily. Closed Dec 25.* Paved launch ramp, slips, boat fuel. **Rentals:** Motorboats (25 to 150 hp), personal watercraft. Bait, groceries, ice, picnic area.

Preparing for a cruise.

Fishing

Noted for its rainbow trout and bass fishing, Lake Mohave offers an open season on all species of fish year round. Trout spend the summer north of Willow Beach and migrate south from October through January; a fish hatchery at Willow Beach provides trout for planting in the lake. Rainbow trout are popular in the cold waters of upper Lake Mohave from Hoover Dam to Willow Beach, but the record sizes of the past have diminished to an occasional five pounds.

Large-mouth bass prefer the deep water at the south end of the lake and only move into shallow water to spawn. The best catches are taken from October to May. Trolling live bait at depths of 10 to 30 feet works well to lure them. Fishing the coves with floating minnow-shaped lures is also effective during midday. Striped bass have become an increasingly common catch throughout much of the lake in recent years.

July and August are the best months for finding catfish in the lake's small coves and inlets. February through April is crappie season; they can be found along the lower half of the lake. Mini-jigs, worms and minnows are the ticket for catching them.

A wheelchair-accessible fishing dock is located at Katherine Landing.

Note: There is a multi-agency effort under way to protect endangered species of the Colorado River. Fishermen should identify and immediately release hump-back chubs, bonytail chubs, razorback suckers and Colorado squawfish that they hook. Anglers who are unfamiliar with these species will find descriptions in the California and Arizona fishing regulations booklets that are available where licenses are sold.

Swimming

Lake Mohave offers swimming, snorkeling and diving in clear waters. Except for the northern reaches of the lake, where the water is quite cold, the water averages about 78 degrees during spring, summer and fall.

Water-skiing

Water-skiing is permitted on all of Lake Mohave except along a 21-mile stretch of the Colorado River extending south from Hoover Dam to Chalk Cliffs.

Below Davis Dam

Accessible via Ariz SR 95. El 550. This stretch of the Colorado River is bordered by mobile home parks and the many casinos of Laughlin, Nevada. Activities include swimming, water-skiing, sailboarding, use of personal watercraft and fishing. Supplies and tourist facilities are available in Bullhead City and Laughlin, and boat-launching ramps are scattered along the shoreline.

Boating

BULLHEAD CITY ROTARY PARK *Off Riverview Dr; 2315 Balboa Dr, Bullhead City, AZ. (928) 763-0184. Mid-May through Labor Day open till 5 pm, Fri-Sat from 8 am, Sun-Thu from 9 am; after Labor Day-early Oct open Sat-Sun only, 8 am-6 pm. Closed mid-Oct to mid-May. $15 entry fee May 26-Sep 30.* Paved launch ramp. Picnic area.

DAVIS CAMP COUNTY PARK *Mohave County Park, Bullhead City, AZ. Reservations at (877) 757-0915 or (928) 754-7250. Open daily at 7 am, Sun-Thu to 7 pm, Fri-Sat to 8 pm. $5 per vehicle entry fee.* Paved launch ramp, dry storage. Ice, tent and RV sites, picnic area.

LAZY HARRY'S *Off Whitewater Dr; 2170 Rio Grande Rd, Bullhead City, AZ. (928) 758-6322. Open daily 8 am-9 pm.* Paved launch ramp. Ice, restaurant, picnic area.

Fishing

Rainbow trout are the most popular catch along this stretch of the river; they inhabit the cold water along the gravel beds below Davis Dam (no fishing in posted areas). Trout are also planted south of Laughlin-Bullhead City near the California-Nevada state line from October to June. During warm weather, the fish are attracted to lures such as Super Dupers, Panther Martins, and spinners and spoons. In cooler weather, the best bet is live bait, mostly night crawlers and marshmallow combos. The fish stay in deep water during the day and move toward shore at night.

Anglers can also fill their creels with good-sized catfish, largemouth bass, and plenty of bluegill and crappie. Bass prefer the cooler deep water and will hit on live bait or floating lures. Catfish like stink baits (garlic cheese), dough balls, anchovies and night crawlers. Bluegill and crappie hit on almost anything that moves—try worms for bluegill, and minnows or mini-jigs for crappie.

Striped bass are a popular game fish, and they often tip the scales at around 30 pounds. The largest striper ever caught in an inland habitat was landed at Bullhead City and weighed in at 59 pounds, 12 ounces. These fish winter at Lake Havasu and start moving north in the spring, hitting the Laughlin-Bullhead City area in May; common baits are shad, frozen anchovies or sardines, with sinkers to keep the bait below the surface of the water.

Inner Tubing

Inner tubing is a popular sport along the Colorado River. For easy pickup and parking, swimmers usually launch their inner tubes from Davis Camp County Park, north of Bullhead City, Arizona, and float four or five miles south along the river, disembarking at Bullhead Community Park.

Swimming

Swimming in the river should not be attempted except from designated beach areas. A public beach is located at Davis Camp County Park on the Arizona side of the river (north of Bullhead City on SR 95). The best swimming in the area is at Lake Mohave. In the summer, the lake water can get as warm as 80 degrees. *Note:* A word of caution to river swimmers south of Davis Dam—the water released from the dam is very cold, sometimes below 60 degrees.

Water-skiing

Water-skiing is allowed along the Colorado River from Bullhead City south to Needles. A sparsely populated area just south of Bullhead City is usually the best location for the sport.

Transportation

A variety of transportation choices to Las Vegas and Laughlin makes getting there easy for conventioneers, families and groups of singles. Both desert cities boast international airports, convenient bus service and well-maintained roads.

AIR

For complete schedule information and help arranging flights from cities with direct or connecting service, contact **any AAA Travel Agency** office. Members in Southern California can call (800) 222-5000, Monday through Friday from 8 a.m. to 6 p.m., and Saturday from 9 a.m. to 1 p.m.

LAUGHLIN/BULLHEAD INTERNATIONAL AIRPORT *2550 Laughlin View Dr, Bullhead City, Ariz. (928) 754-2134.* This airport is located in Arizona just minutes from the casino gaming action across the river. The 7500-foot-by-150-foot runway accommodates aircraft as large as DC-10s, and is served by two commuter airlines and three charter carriers. About 100 flights are logged each week, serving more than 230,000 passengers a year. Taxis and free hotel shuttles serve the airport, and several car rental agencies have offices here.

McCARRAN INTERNATIONAL AIRPORT *E of the Strip; 5757 Wayne Newton Blvd off Paradise Rd, Las Vegas. (702) 261-5211; TDD (702) 261-3111. Online at www.mccarran.com.* McCarran is among the 10 busiest airports in North America, with more than 35 million passengers passing through it each year. More than 60 air carriers serve Las Vegas, among them 23 scheduled airlines, two commuter lines and up to 20 charter airlines (depending on the season). The airport also provides international service to Belgium, Canada, Germany, Japan, Mexico and the United Kingdom, all of which adds up to some 800 commercial and chartered flights a day.

Private shuttle buses, taxis, limousines and public buses make pickups at McCarran. Citizens Area Transit (CAT) buses 108 and 109 serve the airport; call (702) 228-7433 for further details. Ground transportation services at McCarran are abundant; see the Las Vegas telephone directory yellow pages under "Airport Transportation & Parking Services." All major car rental companies have offices at McCarran; refer to the yellow pages under "Automobile Renting and Leasing." Any AAA Travel Agency can reserve a rental car.

AUTOMOBILE

Las Vegas entertains millions of visitors each year, and not surprisingly more than half of them arrive by automobile. Southern Californians account for most of that automobile traffic, with more than 4 million people a year driving to Las Vegas. With the 70-mph speed limit in effect on I-15, Las Vegas is only about a five-hour drive from Los Angeles under optimum conditions; from San Diego it is about an

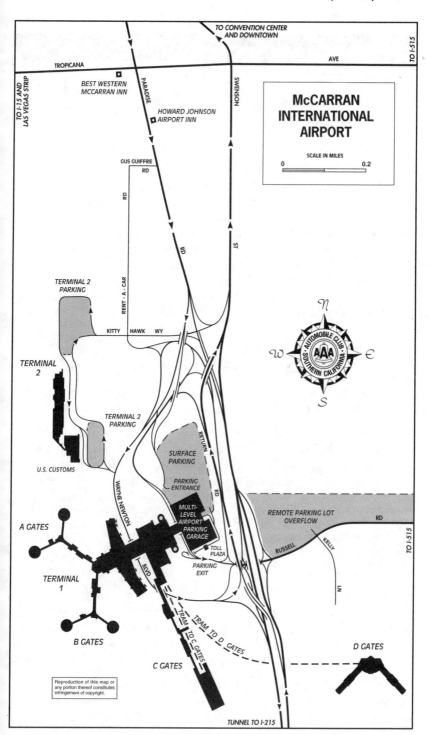

♠ Desert Driving Hints

Any automobile trip from California to Las Vegas will involve desert driving. At all times, but especially during the summer months, basic precautions should be taken when planning to cross the Mojave Desert.

- Check your car's engine and cooling systems and make sure they're in good working order. Look for radiator leaks, worn fan belts and cracked hoses.

- Take about five gallons of water in a clean container for emergency purposes—both for the car's radiator and for drinking. If your car overheats, do not remove the radiator cap immediately because of the risk of explosion. After the engine has cooled, slowly remove the cap and add water, leaving about an inch of air space between the water level and the top of the radiator. If an older model car experiences vapor lock, wrap a wet towel around the gas line between the fuel pump and the carburetor. Insure that the towel doesn't become entangled in moving parts (belts). This may cool the line and allow the car to start.

- Make certain that your car's tires are properly inflated before starting out. If the tires become overly hard while crossing the desert, do not release any air. Instead, stop the car and allow the tires to cool, then proceed.

- Watch the gas gauge; buy fuel when possible. Gas stations in the desert are few and far between; it can be miles to the next fuel stop.

- If your car becomes disabled, once safely out of the traffic lane activate the hazard warning lights and raise your hood. Do not abandon the car to go for help. Not only is it often a long walk to the nearest town or telephone, but extreme desert temperatures in the summer months bring a real threat of heat stroke—even a short walk could become dangerous.

Note: Desert driving often means that travelers must take "out of the ordinary" precautions in an emergency. For instance, pulling your car as far off the road as possible in an emergency is usually the most desirable action to take.

hour farther. The San Francisco Bay Area is roughly 11 hours away by car, exclusive of stops. Although the 70 mph speed limit is in effect for almost all of the driving along I-15 in both California and Nevada, weather and road conditions often dictate a lower speed. For current highway conditions, call the Nevada Department of Transportation at (702) 486-3116 (recording); in California call (800) 927-7623. Drivers should also be alert to posted lower speed limits in populated areas.

Laughlin is approximately the same distance from Los Angeles as Las Vegas. The routes from Los Angeles to both Las Vegas and Laughlin begin in a similar man-

♠ Desert Driving Hints

Many areas of desert terrain do not offer a firm gravel surface off the asphalt shoulder, however, so be aware that driving onto a shoulder of soft sand may mean a tow truck will be required to get your car back onto the road.

When weather permits, motorists should follow normal emergency procedures: remain in your car, in the seat that is the farthest from moving traffic, keep the seat belt fastened and headrest properly positioned, keep doors locked and wait for assistance. In extreme desert heat these procedures will not be possible—even with the windows rolled down, the car will become unbearably hot. In such cases, seek out a shady area to wait for highway assistance, either in the shadow of the vehicle itself or in the shade of nearby vegetation. Do not leave pets or children in the car—they suffer the effects of the heat even more quickly than adults can.

Driving near Red Rock Valley.

When faced with a disabled car, the Auto Club recommends waiting for Highway Patrol assistance. Emergency call boxes are numerous along well-traveled highways, and cellular phones can be convenient tools for getting swift assistance. Highway Patrol officers routinely patrol desert highways. Motorists should use extreme caution in accepting help from strangers.

ner: I-10 east past Ontario, then north on I-15 to Barstow. At Barstow, those bound for Las Vegas continue on I-15. For Laughlin, motorists take I-40 east across the Mojave Desert toward Needles. Near Needles, there are two possible routes for the remainder of the drive to Laughlin. One is about 10 miles west of Needles, where motorists can take US 95 north 24 miles, then take SR 163 east 18 miles to Laughlin Civic Drive; the other is about four miles west of Needles, where there's an alternate route along Needles Highway (River Road) north to Laughlin. To get to the Arizona side of the river, Arizona SR 95 and Bullhead City, there's a choice of three bridges (listed south to north): Needles, Veterans and Laughlin. For emer-

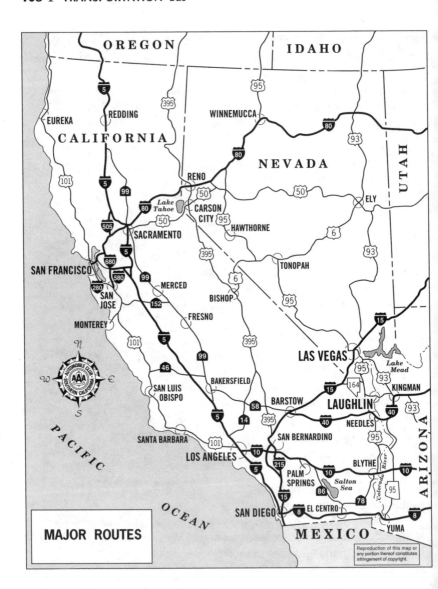

gency roadside assistance, AAA members may call (800) AAA-HELP in the USA and Canada; hearing impaired call (800) 464-0889.

BUS

Greyhound/Trailways offers service to Las Vegas from most towns in California and Nevada. Reservations are not accepted, and tickets can usually be purchased just prior to departure. Purchase of a return ticket does not guarantee passage. In

Las Vegas, Greyhound/Trailways uses the downtown bus terminal building at 200 South Main Street (at Carson Avenue); phone (800) 231-2222.

The route for bus travelers to Laughlin-Bullhead City is through Needles, California, or Las Vegas, Nevada. From there, both Greyhound/Trailways and K-T Services bus lines provide daily service to Laughlin; the trip takes about 2½ hours. Don Laughlin's Riverside Resort Hotel & Casino, South Tower, is the terminus in Laughlin for both bus lines. Both companies also serve Bullhead City, with pick-ups and drop-offs at the River Queen Motel, 125 Long Street. For more information, phone Greyhound/Trailways at (702) 298-1934 or (800) 231-2222, or K-T Services at (702) 644-2233.

TRAIN

As of press time, Amtrak's long-delayed plan to start daily, round-trip service along the Los Angeles-Las Vegas route was still under review. Custom-designed trains would make the 340-mile trip in approximately 5½ hours. There is no definite timetable for this service and prices have not been established. For current information, call Amtrak at (800) 872-7245. For reservations and help in arranging connecting trains or buses, contact any AAA Travel Agency.

Tourist Information Services

The chambers of commerce and visitor information bureaus listed below are resources for obtaining additional information about Las Vegas, Laughlin and the surrounding areas. AAA/CSAA district offices provide travel services and publications, and highway information to Auto Club members.

CHAMBERS OF COMMERCE & VISITOR INFORMATION BUREAUS

Boulder City Chamber of Commerce
465 Nevada Way, Boulder City
(702) 293-2034
Office hours: Mon-Fri 9 am-5 pm, Sat 9 am-4 pm

Bullhead Area Chamber of Commerce
1251 Hwy 95, Bullhead City, AZ
(928) 754-4121
Office hours: Mon-Fri 8 am-5 pm, Sat 9 am-5pm

Las Vegas Convention and Visitors Authority
3150 Paradise Rd, Las Vegas
(702) 892-0711
Office hours: Mon-Fri 8 am-5 pm

Laughlin Visitors Bureau
1555 S Casino Dr, Laughlin
(702) 298-3321
Office hours: Mon-Fri 8 am-5 pm, Sat-Sun 8:30 am-5 pm

Nevada Welcome Center
100 Nevada Hwy, Boulder City, NV
(702) 294-1252
Office hours: Daily 8:00 am-4:30 pm

AAA DISTRICT OFFICES

AAA Travel Agencies can help members in preparing a trip to anywhere in the world. For travel within the United States, Canada and Mexico, the Club can make reservations for lodging and transportation, and provide weather, routing and emergency road service information. They can also make airline, train and package tour reservations for travel throughout the world.

♠ Show Your Card & Save™

Certain attractions offer AAA members a special discount. The discount is given to both adults and children and applies to the member and his or her family traveling together, usually up to six people. The discount may not apply if any other gate reduction is offered or if tickets are purchased through an agent rather than the attraction's ticket office. Because such discounts change frequently, they are not listed here. For current information on such attractions and discounts, check the most recent edition of the AAA *Southern California & Las Vegas TourBook*. When in doubt, ask if a discount is available at the time of your visit.

Auto Club members can also take advantage of discounts on lodging, as indicated in the AAA *Southern California & Las Vegas TourBook*, available free to members. Auto Club members in Southern California can take advantage of the *Member Saver*, which is published monthly and is a valuable source for seasonal discounts on events and points of interest.

The following AAA/California State Automobile Association district offices are located in the Las Vegas region.

Henderson

601-A Whitney Ranch Dr, Henderson

(702) 458-2323

Office hours: Mon-Fri 8:30 am- 5:30 pm

Las Vegas

3312 W Charleston Blvd, Las Vegas

(702) 870-9171

Office hours: Mon-Fri 8:30 am-5:30 pm

Summerlin

8440 W Lake Mead, Ste 203, Las Vegas

(702) 360-3151

Office hours: Mon-Fri 8:30 am-5:30 pm

Lodging & Restaurants

Despite the fact that Las Vegas has more than 125,000 rooms, it is advisable to make reservations as far in advance as possible. "No vacancy" signs are constant reminders that the town generally operates at near capacity all year. Although economic and travel uncertainties can take their toll here the same as anywhere, under normal conditions a one-night reservation for Friday or Saturday night is difficult to obtain.

There are several things to be considered in addition to price when staying in **Las Vegas**. It is easier to obtain reservations to sell-out celebrity shows when staying at the hotel where the performer is appearing. Golf privileges, tennis and spa facilities may also be a consideration.

Laughlin draws more than 50,000 visitors to its casinos on an average weekend, and holiday crowds can be even larger. While space is limited in Laughlin, additional lodging can also be found across the river in Bullhead City, Arizona (listings follow Nevada cities). Passenger ferries provide frequent service from parking lots on the Arizona side of the river to the various casinos on the Nevada side, and 24-hour shuttle bus service is available between the two cities.

Properties are listed alphabetically under the nearest town, with lodging facilities first and restaurants second. Each facility's location is given from the center of town or from the nearest major highway. Lodgings and restaurants are also shown for the communities of **Boulder City**, **Cottonwood Cove**, **Echo Bay-Lake Mead**, **Henderson**, **Overton** and **Primm**.

A trained representative of AAA has inspected the properties listed in these pages at least once in the past year. In surprise inspections, each property was found to meet AAA's extensive and detailed requirements for approval. These requirements are reflective of current industry standards and the expectations of the traveling public.

Most listings include AAA's "diamond" rating, reflecting the overall quality of the establishment. Many factors are considered in the process of determining the diamond rating. In lodging properties, the facility is first "classified" according to its physical design—is it a motel, a hotel, a bed & breakfast, condominium, etc. Since the various types of lodging establishments offer differing amenities and facilities, rating criteria are specific for each classification. For example, a motel, which typically offers a room with convenient parking and few if any recreational or public facilities, is rated using criteria designed only for motel-type establishments—it is not compared to a hotel with its extensive public and meeting areas, or to a resort-type property with its wide range of recreational facilities and programs. The diamonds do, however, represent standard levels of quality in all types of establishments.

There is no charge for a property to be listed in AAA publications. However, many lodgings and restaurants have expressed a special desire to attract the AAA member's business. In order to communicate this interest to the traveling public, these facilities have purchased the right to display the Ⓐ emblem.

Nearly all lodging and restaurant facilities accept credit cards as forms of payment for services rendered. The following symbols are used to identify the specific cards accepted by each property:

AX=American Express	MC=MasterCard
CB=Carte Blanche	C=Japan Credit Bureau
DC=Diners Club	VI=Visa
DS=Discover	

Listings which denote "laundry" may offer a coin laundry, valet laundry and/or dry cleaning service. The term "business services" indicates that any of these are available: personal computers, administrative or secretarial services, and meeting rooms and/or conference facilities. Call the establishment to determine if the services and/or facilities you require are offered.

Some lodgings and restaurants listed in Auto Club publications have symbols indicating that they are accessible to individuals with disabilities. The criteria used in qualifying these listings are consistent with, but do not represent the full scope of, the Americans with Disabilities Act of 1990 Accessibility Guidelines (ADAAG). AAA does not evaluate recreational facilities, banquet rooms, or convention and meeting facilities for accessibility. Individuals with disabilities are urged to phone ahead to fully understand an establishment's accessibility options.

In accommodation listings, 🚹 indicates that the property has at least one guest room offering some accessibility features for mature travelers or those who are disabled. In addition to designated criteria, an individual will find accessible parking and restrooms. For restaurants, the symbol indicates that parking, dining rooms and restrooms are accessible.

The 🚻 in a lodging listing means that the following in-room elements are provided: closed-captioned decoders; text telephones; visual notification for fire alarms, incoming phone calls and door knocks; and phone amplification devices.

Lodging

The following accommodations classifications may appear in this book.

Large Hotel—A multistory establishment with interior room entrances and a variety of guest unit styles. Public areas are spacious and include supplemental facilities such as a restaurant, shops, fitness center, spa, business center or meeting rooms.

Small Hotel—A multistory establishment, typically with interior room entrances. A variety of guest unit styles are offered. Public areas are limited in size and/or the types of facilities available.

Motel—A one- to three-story establishment, typically with exterior room entrances facilitating convenient access to parking. The standard guest units have one bedroom with a bathroom and are typically similar in decor and design throughout. Public areas are limited in size and/or the variety of facilities available.

Condos—Vacation-oriented or extended-stay, apartment-style accommodations that are routinely available for rent through a management company. Units vary in design and decor and often contain one or more bedrooms, living room, full kitchen and an eating area. Studio-type models combine the sleeping and living areas into one room. Typically, basic cleaning supplies, kitchen utensils and complete bed and bath linens are supplied. The guest registration area may be located off-site.

A property's diamond rating is not based on the room rate or any one specific aspect of its facilities or operations. Many factors are considered in calculating the rating, and certain minimum standards must be met in all inspection categories. If a property fails approval in just one category, it does not receive a AAA diamond rating. The inspection categories include housekeeping, maintenance, service, furnishings and decor. Guest comments received by AAA may also be reviewed in a property's approval/rating process.

These criteria apply to all properties listed in this publication:

- Clean and well-maintained facilities

- Hospitable staff

- Adequate parking

- A well-kept appearance

- Good quality bedding and comfortable beds, with adequate illumination

- Good locks on all doors and windows

- Comfortable furnishings and decor

- Smoke detectors

- Adequate towels and supplies

- At least one comfortable easy chair with adequate illumination

- A desk or other writing surface with adequate illumination

Lodging ratings range from one to five diamonds and are defined below:

♦—These unpretentious establishments target the needs of a budget-oriented traveler. With a focus on functionality, the properties' rooms are clean and comfortable, meeting the basic needs of privacy and cleanliness.

♦♦—Featuring both modest prices and enhancements to physical attributes, design elements and amenities, these properties provide travelers with more than just basic lodging.

♦♦♦—With noticeably upgraded amenities, physical attributes and comfort, three-diamond properties are multifaceted and have a distinct style.

◆◆◆◆—Showing style and refinement, these upscale properties feature obviously enhanced physical attributes in addition to extensive amenities and high levels of hospitality, service and attention to detail.

◆◆◆◆◆—Luxury and sophistication are the hallmarks of five-diamond lodgings, reflecting impeccable service, amenities and comfort in all aspects of the facility and operations.

The diamond ratings shown in this publication are based on inspections done in 2003-04. Occasionally a property is listed without a rating, for example when an establishment was under construction or undergoing renovations at press time and a rating could not be determined.

Room rates shown in these listings were provided by each establishment's management for publication by AAA. Rates range from the minimum off-season rate to the maximum high-season rate, for one or two persons occupying a typical room as opposed to a special unit. Taxes are not included. ***All rates are subject to change.*** During special events or holiday periods, rates may exceed those published, and special discounts or savings programs may not be honored.

Inquire as to whether a lodging's rates include breakfast or continental breakfast. Our listings do not indicate the availability of special meal plans, such as American Plan, which includes three meals, or Modified American Plan, which offers two meals, usually breakfast and dinner.

Many properties make special and discounted rates available exclusively to AAA members. Two publications list these rates: the AAA *TourBook*, which is published annually, and the Auto Club's *Member Saver*, a monthly newsletter featuring short-term rates and packages that offer discounts for reservations made through the Auto Club. AAA *TourBooks* are available to AAA members at no charge through AAA offices; the *Member Saver* is available to AAA members at no charge through all Automobile Club of Southern California district offices.

Some properties offer discounts to senior citizens, or special rate periods such as weekly or monthly rentals. Inquiries as to the availability of any special discounts should be made at the time of registration. Typically, a property will allow a guest to take advantage of only one discount during his or her stay (i.e., a guest staying at a property offering both a AAA discount and a senior discount may choose only one of the two savings plans).

Since nearly all establishments have air conditioning, telephones and color cable TV, only the absence of any of these items is noted in the listing. Other facilities, amenities and services, movies, in-room whirlpool, child care, massage and recreational activities, may have extra fees associated with them. It is best to inquire about these fees when making reservations. Check-in time is shown only if it is after 3 p.m.; check-out time is shown only if it is before 10 a.m. Service charges are not shown unless they are $1 or more, or at least 5 percent of the room rate. If the pet acceptance policy varies within the establishment, no mention of pets is made; it is best to call ahead to verify specifics. By U.S. law, pet restrictions do not apply to service animals. Outdoor pools may or may not be heated, and may not be open in winter.

Reservations are always advisable in resort areas and may be the only way to obtain the type of accommodations desired. Deposits are almost always required. Should plans change and reservations need to be canceled, be aware of the amount of notice required to receive a deposit refund.

Many properties welcome children in the same room with their parents at no additional charge; individual listings indicate if there is an age limit. There may be charges for additional equipment, such as roll-aways or cribs. Many establishments have a minimum age requirement for renting rooms; in most cases the minimum age is 18, but at some properties the minimum age is 21.

In order to be listed, facilities must have smoke detectors and may have additional fire safety equipment. Listings here do not reference these items. Members should call the facility in order to obtain more detailed fire-safety information. Many properties have reserved rooms for nonsmokers; look for the ☻ symbol in the listing. If a smoke-free room is desired, be sure to request it when making a reservation and upon registration.

Restaurants

Restaurants listed in this publication have been found to be consistently good dining establishments. In metropolitan areas, where many restaurants are above average, some of those known for the superiority of their food, service and atmosphere are selected, as well as those offering a selection of quality food at moderate prices (including some cafeterias and family restaurants). In smaller communities, the restaurants considered to be the best in the area may be listed.

The type of cuisine featured at a dining establishment is used as a means of classification for restaurants. There are listings for Steakhouses and Continental cuisine as well as a range of ethnic foods, such as Brazilian, French, Italian and yes, American. Special menu types, such as early bird, a la carte, children's or Sunday brunch, are also listed. In many cases, something is indicated about each restaurant's atmosphere and appropriate attire. The availability of alcoholic beverages is shown, as well as entertainment and dancing.

Price ranges are for an average, complete meal without alcoholic beverage. Taxes and tips are not included.

Restaurant ratings are applied to two categories of operational style—full-service eating establishments, and self-service, family-dining operations such as cafeterias or buffets.

◆—Good but unpretentious dishes. Table settings are usually simple and may include paper place mats and napkins. Alcoholic beverage service, if any, may be limited to beer and wine. Ambience is typically informal with an atmosphere conducive to family dining.

◆◆—More extensive menus represent more complex food preparation and, usually, a wider variety of alcoholic beverages. The atmosphere is appealing and suitable for either family or adult dining. Service may be casual, but host or hostess seating can be expected. Table settings may include tablecloths and cloth napkins.

♠ Dining Out

Dining options in Las Vegas are as varied as accommodations. Prices range from about $2 for breakfast to more than $100 for gourmet dinners. All the large hotels have numerous places to eat, and most have themed dining rooms that feature regional or ethnic decor and food. Many coffee shops are open 24 hours. Buffets are available at almost every major hotel and offer diners a choice of three or more entrees, plus vegetables, salads, desserts and beverages for one price; buffet-style champagne brunches are offered at numerous hotels on weekends.

Similarly, all the large casino/hotels in Laughlin have several restaurants, some with themed dining rooms overlooking the river, that feature regional or ethnic foods. Also, a number of restaurants and major fast-food franchise outlets can be found across the river in Bullhead City. Prices in Laughlin range from a low of about $2 for breakfast to a high of $70 for a gourmet dinner. Buffets are common and range in price from $5 to $7, with buffet breakfasts priced from $2 to $3.50 and lunches priced similarly.

◆◆◆—Extensive or specialized menus and more complex cuisine preparation requiring a professional chef contribute to either a formal dining experience or a special family meal. Cloth table linens, above-average quality table settings, a skilled service staff and an inviting decor should all be provided. Generally, the wine list includes representatives of the best domestic and foreign wine-producing regions.

◆◆◆◆—An appealing ambiance is often enhanced by fresh flowers and fine furnishings. The overall sophistication and formal atmosphere visually create a dining experience more for adults than for families. The wine list, as well as the staff's knowledge about wine, is more extensive than that of a three-diamond restaurant. A smartly attired, highly skilled staff is capable of describing how any dish is prepared. Elegant silverware, china and correct glassware are typical. The menu includes creative dishes prepared from fresh ingredients by a chef who frequently has international training. Eye-appealing desserts are offered at tableside.

◆◆◆◆◆—A world-class operation presents even more luxury and sophistication than four-diamond restaurants. A proportionally large staff, expert in preparing tableside delicacies, provides flawless service. Tables are set with impeccable linens, silver and crystal glassware.

Boulder City

Lodging

BOULDER DAM HOTEL
◆◆ Historic Small Hotel

(702) 293-3510
$89-159
1305 Arizona St.

XP $10. Breakfast. Complimentary evening beverages. Senior discount. Package plans. AX, DC, DS, MC, VI. Gift shop, museum. 3 stories; interior corridors. **Rooms:** 21; 3 1-bedroom suites. Some shower baths, hair dryers, some microwaves, some refrigerators, some VCRs, data ports, voice mail, ⊛. Roll-in showers. **Dining:** Matteo's, see separate listing.

EL RANCHO BOULDER MOTEL ⒶⒶ
◆◆ Motel

(702) 293-1085
$65-105
On US 93; 725 Nevada Hwy.

7-day cancellation notice. Dogs, $10 extra charge. AX, DS, MC, VI. Video library. 2 stories, no elevator; exterior corridors. **Rooms:** 39. Some efficiencies, some coffeemakers, some microwaves, refrigerators, movies, some VCRs, some ⊛. **Recreation:** Pool. **Dining:** Restaurant nearby.

SANDS MOTEL ⒶⒶ
◆ Motel

(702) 293-2589
$59-110
On US 93; 809 Nevada Hwy.

Senior discount. Weekly rates, continental breakfast and package plans available. AX, DC, DS, MC, VI. 1 story; exterior corridors. **Rooms:** 26. Some shower baths, some kitchens, some microwaves, refrigerators, movies, voice mail, some ⊛. **Dining:** Restaurant nearby.

SUPER 8 MOTEL
◆ Motel

(702) 294-8888
$59-128
On US 93; 704 Nevada Hwy.

XP $7; ages 12 and younger, free. Small pets, $10 extra charge. 3 stories; exterior corridors. **Rooms:** 114. Some shower baths, some whirlpools, some microwaves, refrigerators, movies, data ports, voice mail, some ⊛. Roll-in showers. **Recreation:** Pool, whirlpool. **Services:** Laundry, business services. **Dining:** Restaurant nearby; cocktails.

Restaurant

MATTEO'S
◆◆ Italian

(702) 293-0098
Lunch $6-9, dinner $10-25
Center, in Boulder Dam Hotel; 1305 Ariona St.

AX, DC, MC, VI. Open daily 7 am-8 pm, Sat to 9 pm. Closed 12/25. Patio or indoor dining. Casual attire. ⊛ Cocktails.

Cottonwood Cove

Lodging

COTTONWOOD COVE MOTEL ⚫⚫⚫   ◆◆ Motel

(702) 297-1464   *$60-108*

Between Las Vegas and Needles; 14 mi E of Searchlight, off US 95; 10000 Cottonwood Cove Rd.

XP $10. 14-day cancellation notice. AX, DS, MC, VI. Gift shop. 1 story; exterior corridors. **Rooms:** 24. Refrigerators, movies, some data ports. **Recreation:** Marina, houseboats, powerboats and equipment, fishing, water-skiing, shuffleboard, horseshoes, volleyball. **Services:** Laundry, business services. **Dining:** Restaurant; 7 am-8 pm, 11/1-4/1 to 6 pm.

Echo Bay-Lake Mead

Lodging

ECHO BAY RESORT AND MARINA ⚫⚫⚫   ◆◆ Motel

(702) 394-4000   *$60-115*

On Lake Mead; 4 mi E of SR 167.

XP $10; ages 5 and younger, free. $2 service charge. 3-night minimum stay in season. 3-day cancellation notice. DS, MC, VI. Pets, $10 extra charge; $50 deposit. Gift shop. 2 stories, no elevator; interior corridors. **Rooms:** 52. Some shower baths, hair dryers, coffeemakers, some ⊛. Ⓖ, roll-in showers. **Recreation:** Marina, houseboats, rental boats, fishing, water-skiing. **Services:** Laundry, business services. **Dining:** Restaurant; 7 am-9 pm, 10/1-4/5 10 am-4 pm; cocktails.

Henderson

Lodging

COURTYARD BY MARRIOTT   ◆◆◆ Small Hotel

(702) 434-4700   *$99-169*

I-215, exit Green Valley Pkwy, 2½ mi N; near Sunset Rd; 2800 N Green Valley Pkwy.

Senior discount. Package plans. AX, CB, DC, DS, JC, MC, VI. 3 stories; interior corridors. **Rooms:** 155. Some shower baths, some whirlpools, hair dryers, coffeemakers, some microwaves, some refrigerators, movies, data ports, voice mail, irons, some ⊛. Ⓖ, roll-in showers. **Recreation:** Pool, whirlpool, exercise rm. **Services:** Area and airport transportation, laundry, business services. **Dining:** Restaurant nearby; cocktails.

FIESTA-HENDERSON ⚫⚫⚫   ◆◆◆ Small Hotel

(702) 558-7000   *$69-139*

I-515, exit Lake Mead Dr; 777 W Lake Mead Dr.

XP $15; ages 12 and younger, free. $5 service charge. Senior discount. AX, DC, DS, MC, VI. Casino, gift shop. 9 stories; interior corridors. **Rooms:** 224. Some shower baths, some whirlpools, hair dryers, coffeemakers, some refrigerators,

movies, data ports, video games, voice mail, some ⊛. ♿, roll-in showers, ▨.
Recreation: Pool, whirlpool. **Services:** Valet parking available, laundry, business
services. **Dining:** 3 restaurants; buffet, $7-10; 24 hrs; cocktails.

GREEN VALLEY RANCH ⏦ ◆◆◆◆ Large Hotel
(702) 617-7777 *$250-500*
I-215, exit Green Valley Pkwy, just S; 2300 Paseo Verde Pkwy.
XP $20; ages 18 and younger, free. Pets, $20 extra charge. Casino, gift shop,
movie theater, entertainment. 5 stories. **Rooms:** 201; 8 1-, 8 2- and 1 3-bed-
room suites with whirlpools. Some shower baths, hair dryers, coffeemakers,
honor bars, movies, CD players, data ports, high-speed Internet access, dual
phone lines, voice mail, irons, safes, some ⊛. ♿, roll-in showers. **Recreation:**
Pool, wading pool, whirlpool, spa, exercise rm, game rm. **Services:** Valet parking
available, area and airport transportation, laundry, business services. **Dining:** 6
restaurants, including Bullshrimp, China Spice and Fado Irish Pub & Restaurant,
see separate listings; buffet, $6-19; 24 hrs; 24-hr room service; cocktails.

HAMPTON INN HOTEL & SUITES ◆◆◆ Motel
(702) 992-9292 *$99-149*
I-215 exit Stephanie St, 1¾ mi N, E on Warm Springs Rd; 421 Astaire Dr.
Small pets in selected units. 3 stories; interior corridors. **Rooms:** 99. Some
shower baths, hair dryers, coffeemakers, some microwaves, some refrigerators,
movies, video games, data ports, high-speed Internet access, dual phone lines,
voice mail, irons, some ⊛. ♿, roll-in showers. **Recreation:** Pool, whirlpool, exercise rm. **Services:** Laundry, business services. **Dining:** Restaurant nearby.

HAWTHORN INN & SUITES ⏦ ◆◆◆ Motel
(702) 568-7800 *$99-199*
S of Lake Mead Dr; 910 S Boulder Hwy.
3-day cancellation notice; fee. Senior discount. AX, DC, DS, MC, VI. Pets, $25 extra
charge. 3 stories; interior corridors. **Rooms:** 71. Some shower baths, some
whirlpools, hair dryers, some microwaves, some refrigerators, movies, some VCRs,
data ports, voice mail, irons, some ⊛. Roll-in showers. **Recreation:** Pool, whirlpool,
exercise rm. **Services:** Laundry, business services. **Dining:** Restaurant nearby.

HOLIDAY INN EXPRESS & SUITES ◆◆◆ Motel
(702) 990-2323 *$89-199*
I-215 exit Stephanie St, 1¾ mi N, E on Warm Springs Rd; 441 Astaire Dr.
Senior discount. AX, DC, MC, VI. Small pets, selected units. 3 stories; interior/exte-
rior corridors. **Rooms:** 101. Some shower baths, hair dryers, coffeemakers, some
microwaves, some refrigerators, movies, data ports, high-speed Internet access,
dual phone lines, voice mail, irons, some ⊛. **Recreation:** Pool, whirlpool, exercise
rm. **Services:** Laundry, business services. **Dining:** Restaurant nearby.

HYATT REGENCY LAKE LAS VEGAS RESORT ⏦ ◆◆◆◆ Large Hotel
(702) 567-1234 *$99-299*
I-215 E to Lake Las Vegas Pkwy, then N; 101 MonteLago Blvd.
3-day cancellation notice, fee. AX, CB, DC, DS, JC, MC, VI. Casino, gift shop. 9
stories; interior corridors. **Rooms:** 493; 21 1-bedroom suites, some with

whirlpools. Some shower baths, hair dryers, coffeemakers, refrigerators, movies, video games, data ports, high-speed Internet access, dual phone lines, irons, safes, some ⊛. ⬕, roll-in showers. **Recreation:** 2 pools, whirlpool, health club, exercise rm, massage, putting green, marina, canoe and paddleboat rentals, fishing, bikes. **Services:** Valet parking available, area transportation, laundry, childcare, business services. **Dining:** 2 restaurants, including Japengo, see separate listing; 24 hrs; 24-hr rm service; cocktails.

LAKE MEAD INN
♦♦ Motel

(702) 564-1712   *$56-79*

US 93/95 exit Lake Mead Dr; 1½ mi E on SR 146; 85 W Lake Mead Dr.
XP $10; ages 13 and younger, free. Cancellation fee. Senior discount. Weekly rates available. AX, MC, VI. 2 stories; exterior corridors. **Rooms:** 59. Some shower baths, hair dryers, coffeemakers, refrigerators, movies, data ports, irons, some ⊛. Roll-in showers. **Recreation:** Pool. **Services:** Laundry. **Dining:** Restaurant nearby.

RESIDENCE INN-GREEN VALLEY
♦♦♦ Motel

(702) 434-2700   *$139*

I-215 exit Green Valley Pkwy, N to Sunset Rd; 2190 Olympic Ave.
Complimentary evening beverages Mon-Thu. AX, CB, DC, DS, JC, MC, VI. Pets, $10 extra charge, $50 fee. Extended continental breakfast plan available. 3 stories; interior corridors. **Rooms:** 126; 36 1- and 27 2-bedroom suites with kitchens, $180. Some shower baths, hair dryers, kitchens, coffeemakers, microwaves, refrigerators, movies, data ports, voice mail, irons, some ⊛. ⬕, roll-in showers. **Recreation:** Pool, whirlpool, exercise rm, sports court. **Services:** Airport transportation, laundry, business services. **Dining:** Restaurant nearby.

THE RITZ-CARLTON, LAKE LAS VEGAS ⒶⒶⒶ
♦♦♦♦♦ Large Resort Hotel

(702) 567-4700   *$199-589*

I-215 E to Lake Las Vegas Pkwy, then N; 1610 Lake Las Vegas Pkwy.
2/1-3/2 XP $75, children free. Pay parking. Small pets, $125 extra charge. Gift shop. 8 stories; interior corridors. **Rooms:** 349; 38 1-bedroom suites, some with whirlpools. Some shower baths, hair dryers, coffeemakers, honor bars, movies, video games, CD players, data ports, high-speed Internet access, dual phone lines, voice mail, irons, safes, some ⊛. ⬕, roll-in showers, ▨. **Recreation:** Pool, whirlpool, health club, spa, 4 lighted tennis courts, 54 holes golf, volleyball. **Services:** Valet parking available, area and airport transportation, laundry, business services. **Dining:** 2 restaurants, including Medici Cafe and Terrace, see separate listing; 7 am-11 pm; 24-hr room service; cocktails.

SUNSET STATION HOTEL & CASINO ⒶⒶⒶ
♦♦♦ Large Hotel

(702) 547-7777   *$50-300*

I-15 exit I-215 to Warm Springs Rd; 7 mi E to Stephanie St and Sunset Rd; 1301 W Sunset Rd.
XP $20; ages 12 and younger, free. AX, CB, DC, DS, MC, VI. Casino, gift shop, movie theaters, nightclub, entertainment. 21 stories; interior corridors. **Rooms:** 457; 19 1-bedroom suites with whirlpools. Some shower baths, hair dryers, movies, data ports, high-speed Internet access, voice mail, irons, some ⊛. ⬕, roll-in showers, ▨. **Recreation:** Pool, exercise rm, game rm. **Services:** Valet park-

ing, area and airport transportation, laundry, childcare, business services. **Dining:**
8 restaurants, including Guadalajara, Sonoma Cellar and Sunset Cafe, see separate listings; 24 hrs; cocktails.

Restaurants

BULLSHRIMP
♦♦♦ Steak & Seafood
(702) 942-4110   *Lunch $8-18, dinner $19-46*
I-215 exit Green Valley Pkwy, just S; at Green Valley Ranch, 2300 Paseo Verde Pkwy.
AX, CB, DC, DS, JC, MC, VI. Open Mon-Fri 11:30 am-3 and daily 5-10:30 pm.
Dressy casual attire. ⊗ Cocktails. **Reservations:** Suggested. **Services:** Valet park-
ing available.

CHINA SPICE
♦♦♦ Chinese
(702) 617-7001   *Dinner $9-25*
I-215 exit Green Valley Pkwy, just S; at Green Valley Ranch, 2300 Paseo Verde Pkwy.
AX, CB, DC, DS, JC, MC, VI. Open daily 5-10 pm, Fri-Sat to 11 pm. Casual attire.
⊗ Cocktails. **Services:** Valet parking available.

COMO'S
♦♦♦ Steak & Seafood
(702) 567-9950   *Lunch $10-20, dinner $15-40*
*I-215 E to Lake Las Vegas Pkwy, then N; at Lake Las Vegas Resort Village
MonteLago; 10 Via Brianza.*
AX, MC, VI. Open daily 11 am-2:30 and 5-10 pm. Dressy casual attire. ⊗ Cocktails.
Reservations: Suggested. **Menu:** Wide variety of upscale menu choices.

FADO IRISH PUB & RESTAURANT
♦♦ Irish
(702) 407-8691   *Lunch $7-10, dinner $10-15*
I-215 exit Green Valley Pkwy, just S; at Green Valley Ranch, 2300 Paseo Verde Pkwy.
AX, CB, DC, DS, JC, MC, VI. Open daily 11 am-11 pm. Casual attire. ⊗ Cocktails.
Reservations: Accepted. **Services:** Valet parking available. **Menu:** Wide variety of
menu choices.

FANNY'S BISTRO & DELI
♦♦♦ Deli/Subs & Sandwiches
(702) 269-1699   *Lunch $5-8*
I-215 exit Pecos Rd, ¾ mi N; 80 N Pecos Rd.
AX, MC, VI. Open Mon-Sat 7 am-3 pm, Sun 8 am-1 pm. Casual attire. ⊗ **Menu:**
Variety breakfast and lunch choices in generous portions.

GUADALAJARA
♦♦ Mexican
(702) 547-7777   *Dinner $8-20*
*I-15 exit I-215 to Warm Springs Rd; 7 mi E to Stephanie St and Sunset Rd; at Sunset
Station Hotel & Casino, 1301 W Sunset Rd.*
AX, CB, DC, DS, JC, MC, VI. Open daily 5-10 pm. Casual attire. ⊗ Cocktails.
Reservations: Accepted. **Services:** Valet parking available. **Menu:** Varied menu.

HOT ROD GRILLE
♦♦ American
(702) 567-5659   *Lunch and dinner $7-17*
I-215 exit Stephanie St, N ½ mi, then ⅓ mi E; 1231 American Pacific Dr.
MC, VI. Open 24 hrs. Casual attire. ⊗ Cocktails. **Reservations:** Accepted.

JAPENGO
◆◆◆◆ Pacific Rim

(702) 567-6125
$22-46

I-215 E to Lake Las Vegas Pkwy, then N; at Hyatt Regency Lake Las Vegas Resort, 101 MonteLago Blvd.

AX, DC, DS, MC, VI. Open Tue-Sun 6-10:30 pm. Closed Mon. Dressy casual attire. ⊗ Cocktails. **Reservations:** Suggested. **Services:** Valet parking available. **Menu:** Asian-fusion cuisine.

MEDICI CAFE AND TERRACE
◆◆◆◆ Mediterranean

(702) 567-4700
Lunch $10-20, dinner $15-50

I-215 E to Lake Las Vegas Pkwy, then N; at The Ritz-Carlton, Lake Las Vegas, 1610 Lake Las Vegas Pkwy.

AX, CB, DC, DS, JC, MC, VI. Open daily 7 am-11, noon-3 and 6-10 pm. Patio or indoor dining. Dressy casual attire. ⊗ Cocktails. **Reservations:** Suggested. **Services:** Valet parking available. **Menu:** Spanish, French and Italian cuisine prepared in an exhibition kitchen.

SONOMA CELLAR
◆◆◆ Steakhouse

(702) 547-7777
Dinner $18-35

I-15 exit I-215 to Warm Springs Rd; 7 mi E to Stephanie St and Sunset Rd; at Sunset Station Hotel & Casino, 1301 W Sunset Rd.

AX, CB, DC, DS, JC, MC, VI. Open daily 5-10 pm. Dressy casual attire. ⊗ Cocktails. **Reservations:** Suggested. **Services:** Valet parking available.

SUNSET CAFE
◆◆ American

(702) 547-7777
Lunch & dinner $4-14

I-215 exit Warm Springs Rd; 7 mi E to Stephanie St and Sunset Rd; at Sunset Station Hotel & Casino, 1301 W Sunset Rd.

AX, CB, DC, DS, JC, MC, VI. Open 24 hrs. Casual attire. ⊗ Cocktails. **Services:** Valet parking available. **Menu:** In addition to a variety of lunch and dinner entrees, breakfast is served anytime.

TENUTA
◆◆ American

(702) 939-8888
Lunch $8-15, dinner $12-25

I-215 E to Lake Las Vegas Pkwy, then N; at Casino MonteLago; 8 Strada di Villaggio.

AX, CB, DC, DS, JC, MC, VI. Open daily 11 am-10 pm. Casual attire. ⊗ Cocktails. **Reservations:** Accepted.

Las Vegas

Lodging

ALEXIS PARK RESORT HOTEL
◆◆◆ Small Hotel

(702) 796-3300
$69-159

I-15 exit Tropicana Ave; E to Koval Ln, N to Harmon Ave, then E; 375 E Harmon Ave.

XP $20; ages 12 and younger, free. 2 stories; exterior corridors. Gift shop. **Rooms:** 496; 12 2-bedroom units. Some shower baths, some whirlpools, hair dryers, refrigerators, movies, data ports, high-speed Internet access, dual phone lines, voice mail, irons, some ⊗. ▨ **Recreation:** 2 pools, saunas, whirlpools, health club, massage. **Services:** Laundry, business services. **Dining:** Restaurant; 24-hr room service; cocktails.

AMBASSADOR STRIP INN TRAVELODGE ⚑   ◆◆ Motel
Formerly Airport Inn Travelodge
(702) 736-3600 $99-199
I-15 exit Tropicana Ave, ½ mi E, just S; 5075 S Koval Ln.
2 stories, no elevator; exterior corridors. **Rooms:** 106. Hair dryers, coffeemakers, movies, data ports, voice mail, safes, some ⊛. **Recreation:** Pool. **Services:** Area and airport transportation, laundry. **Dining:** Restaurant nearby.

AMERIHOST INN NORTH LAS VEGAS   ◆◆◆ Motel
(702) 644-5700 $69-179
I-15 exit Craig Rd, 2⅓ mi E, then just S; 4035 N Nellis Blvd.
XP $10; ages 17 and younger, free. Senior discount. AX, DC, DS, MC, VI. 3 stories; interior corridors. **Rooms:** 87. Some shower baths, hair dryers, coffeemakers, some microwaves, some refrigerators, movies, video games, data ports, voice mail, irons, some ⊛. **Recreation:** Pool, whirlpool, exercise rm. **Services:** Laundry, business services.

AMERISUITES (LAS VEGAS/PARADISE ROAD) ⚑   ◆◆◆ Small Hotel
(702) 369-3366 $69-159
Cross sts Harmon Ave and Paradise Rd, E of The Strip; 4520 Paradise Rd.
XP $10; ages 17 and younger, free. Expanded continental breakfast. 4 pm check-in. Senior discount. AX, DC, DS, JC, MC, VI. Small pets only. 6 stories; interior corridors. **Rooms:** 202. Some shower baths, hair dryers, coffeemakers, microwaves, refrigerators, movies, VCRs, video games, data ports, high-speed Internet access, some dual phone lines, voice mail, irons, some ⊛. 🖂, roll-in showers, 🖾. **Recreation:** Pool, exercise rm. **Services:** Area and airport transportation, laundry, business services. **Dining:** Restaurant nearby.

ARIZONA CHARLIE'S DECATUR   ◆◆ Small Hotel
(702) 258-5200 $40-250
US 95 exit Decatur Blvd, ¾ mi S at Evergreen Ave; 740 S Decatur Blvd.
XP $10; ages 11 and younger, free. Cancellation fee; $2 service charge. Senior discount. AX, DC, DS, MC, VI. 3-7 stories; interior corridors. Casino, gift shop. **Rooms:** 257; 5 1- and 2 2-bedroom suites with whirlpools. Some shower baths, hair dryers, some refrigerators, movies, data ports, irons, some ⊛. 🖂, roll-in showers, 🖾. **Recreation:** Pool, whirlpool, game rm. **Services:** Valet parking available, laundry, business services. **Dining:** Restaurants, including Sourdough Cafe and Yukon Grille, see separate listings; cocktails.

ATRIUM SUITES HOTEL ⚑   ◆◆◆ Large Hotel
Formerly Crowne Plaza
(702) 369-4400 $99-259
I-15 exit Flamingo Rd, ½ mi E to Paradise Rd, then ⅓ mi S; 4255 S Paradise Rd.
XP $10; ages 12 and younger, free. 3-day cancellation notice. Senior discount. AX, CB, DC, DS, JC, MC, VI. 6 stories; interior corridors. **Rooms:** 201. Hair dryers, coffeemakers, refrigerators, movies, video games, data ports, some high-speed

Internet access, dual phone lines, voice mail, irons, some ⊛. 🖫, 🖾. **Recreation:** Pool, whirlpool, sauna, exercise rm. **Services:** Area and airport transportation, laundry, business services. **Dining:** Restaurant; 6 am-11:30 pm; cocktails.

BALLY'S LAS VEGAS
♦♦♦ Large Hotel
(702) 739-4111 $79-399
On The Strip; 3645 Las Vegas Blvd S.
XP $30; ages 18 and younger, free. 3-day cancellation notice. Senior discount. Package plans. AX, DC, DS, JC, MC, VI. 26 stories; interior corridors. Casino, gift shop. **Rooms:** 2814; 300 1-bedroom suites. Some shower baths, hair dryers, some refrigerators, movies, data ports, high-speed Internet access, some dual phone lines, voice mail, irons, safes, some ⊛. 🖫, roll-in showers, 🖾. **Recreation:** Pool, sauna, whirlpool, health club, steam rm, massage, 8 lighted tennis courts, game rm. **Services:** Valet parking available, laundry, business services. **Dining:** Al Dente, see separate listing; 24-hr room service; cocktails.

BARBARY COAST HOTEL ⏣
♦♦♦ Large Hotel
(702) 737-7111 $49-279
On The Strip; 3595 Las Vegas Blvd S.
XP $15; ages 12 and younger, free. AX, CB, DC, DS, JC, MC, VI. 5 stories; interior corridors. Casino, gift shop. **Rooms:** 200; 12 1-bedroom suites, some with whirlpools. Some shower baths, hair dryers, some coffeemakers, some refrigerators, movies, data ports, voice mail, some ⊛. 🖫, roll-in showers, 🖾. **Services:** Valet parking available, laundry. **Dining:** 2 restaurants including Michaels and the Victorian Room, see separate listings; 24 hrs; cocktails.

BARCELONA MOTEL ⏣
♦♦ Motel
(702) 644-6300 $65-125
I-15 exit 48 EB, 7 mi NE; ½ mi from Nellis AFB; 5011 E Craig Rd.
XP $10; ages 12 and younger, free. $2 service charge. Senior discount. Package plans. AX, DC, DS, MC, VI. 2 stories, no elevator; exterior corridors. Small casino, entertainment. **Rooms:** 172. Some shower baths, some microwaves, refrigerators, movies, data ports, some safes, some ⊛. 🖫, roll-in showers. **Recreation:** Pool, whirlpool. **Services:** Laundry, business services. **Dining:** 24 hrs; cocktails.

BELLAGIO ⏣
♦♦♦♦♦ Large Hotel
(702) 693-7111 $159-799
I-15 exit E Flamingo Rd, on The Strip; 3600 Las Vegas Blvd S.
XP $35. Cancellation fee. AX, CB, DC, DS, JC, MC, VI. 33-36 stories; interior corridors. Casino, gift shop, entertainment. **Rooms:** 3933; 250 1-, 68 2- and 11 3-bedroom suites with whirlpools, $450-5000. Some shower baths, some whirlpools, hair dryers, some refrigerators, honor bars, movies, some VCRs, CD players, data ports, high-speed Internet access, dual phone lines, voice mail, irons, safes, some ⊛. 🖫, roll-in showers, 🖾. **Recreation:** 6 pools, whirlpools, 58 pool cabanas, health club, spa, game rm. **Services:** Valet parking available, laundry, child care, business services. **Dining:** 11 restaurants, including Le Cirque, Olives at Bellagio, Picasso and Prime Steakhouse, see separate listings; buffet, $13-32; 24 hrs; 24-hr room service; cocktails.

BEST WESTERN MAIN STREET INN 🏧

◆◆ Motel

(702) 382-3455   *$49-159*
I-15 exit 43, just E; 1000 N Main St.

XP $7; ages 12 and younger, free. Senior discount. AX, CB, DC, DS, JC, MC, VI. Small pets only, $8 extra charge. 2-3 stories; exterior corridors. **Rooms:** 91. Hair dryers, coffeemakers, some refrigerators, movies, data ports, irons, some ⊛. **Recreation:** Pool. **Services:** Laundry, business services. **Dining:** Restaurant; 6 am-11 pm; cocktails.

BEST WESTERN MARDI GRAS INN & CASINO 🏧

◆◆ Motel

(702) 731-2020   *$59-139*
½ mi S of convention center; 3500 Paradise Rd.

XP $10; ages 12 and younger, free. Senior discount. AX, CB, DC, DS, JC, MC, VI. 3 stories; exterior corridors. Gift shop, video library. **Rooms:** 314. Hair dryers, coffeemakers, refrigerators, movies, video games, data ports, voice mail, irons, safes, some ⊛. 🖾 **Recreation:** Pool, whirlpool, sun deck. **Services:** Area and airport transportation, laundry, business services. **Dining:** Restaurant; 6:30 am-10 pm; cocktails.

BEST WESTERN MCCARRAN INN 🏧

◆◆ Motel

(702) 798-5530   *$59-229*
I-15 exit Tropicana Ave, E 5½ blks to Paradise Rd; 4970 Paradise Rd.

XP $10; ages 13 and younger, free. Expanded continental breakfast. Cancellation fee. Senior discount. AX, CB, DC, DS, MC, VI. 3 stories; interior corridors. **Rooms:** 100. Hair dryers, coffeemakers, some microwaves, some refrigerators, some VCRs, data ports, irons, some ⊛. 🖾 **Recreation:** Pool. **Services:** Area and airport transportation, laundry.

BEST WESTERN NELLIS MOTOR INN 🏧

◆◆ Motel

(702) 643-6111   *$55-200*
I-15 exit 48, 2½ mi E; ⅓ mi from Nellis AFB; 5330 E Craig Rd.

XP $5; ages 14 and younger, free. Breakfast. 4 pm check-in. Senior discount. AX, DC, DS, JC, MC, VI. Pets, $10 extra charge. 2 stories, no elevator; exterior corridors. **Rooms:** 52. Hair dryers, coffeemakers, refrigerators, movies, data ports, irons, some ⊛. **Recreation:** Pool. **Services:** Laundry. **Dining:** Restaurant nearby.

BEST WESTERN PARKVIEW INN 🏧

◆◆ Motel

(702) 385-1213   *$49-169*
I-15 exit Washington Ave, E to Las Vegas Blvd, just N; 921 Las Vegas Blvd N.

Continental breakfast. XP $7; ages 12 and younger, free. 14-day cancellation notice. Senior discount. AX, CB, DC, DS, JC, MC, VI. Small pets only, $8 extra charge. 2 stories, no elevator; exterior corridors. **Rooms:** 42. Hair dryers, coffeemakers, data ports, voice mail, irons, some ⊛. **Recreation:** Pool. **Services:** Laundry.

BOARDWALK HOTEL & CASINO 🏧

◆◆◆ Large Hotel

(702) 735-2400   *$49-350*
I-15 exit Flamingo Rd, S on The Strip; 3750 Las Vegas Blvd S.

XP $15; ages 12 and younger, free. 2-night minimum stay weekends.

Cancellation fee. Senior discount. AX, CB, DC, DS, MC, VI. 4-16 stories; interior/exterior corridors. Casino, gift shop. **Rooms:** 654; 3 2-bedroom standard units, some with whirlpools; 8 1-bedroom suites, $150-450. Some shower baths, hair dryers, some coffeemakers, some refrigerators, movies, data ports, voice mail, irons, some ⊗. 🅰, roll-in showers, 🔲. **Recreation:** 2 pools, exercise rm. **Services:** Laundry, business services. **Dining:** 2 restaurants; buffet, $7-10; 24 hrs; 24-hr room service; cocktails.

BOULDER STATION HOTEL CASINO ⨁
(702) 432-7777   ◆◆◆ Large Hotel
Just S of Sahara Ave; 4111 Boulder Hwy. $60-130
XP $12; ages 12 and younger, free. 2-night minimum stay weekends. $5 service charge. AX, CB, DC, DS, JC, MC, VI. Casino, gift shop, movie theaters, entertainment. 15 stories; interior corridors. **Rooms:** 300; 6 1-bedroom suites, some with whirlpools. Some shower baths, hair dryers, some coffeemakers, some refrigerators, movies, data ports, high-speed Internet access, voice mail, irons, some safes, some ⊗. Roll-in showers. **Recreation:** Pool, game rm. **Services:** Valet parking available, laundry, childcare, business services. **Dining:** 5 restaurants, including Guadalajara Bar & Grille and Pasta Palace, see separate listings; buffet, $5-12; 24 hrs; 24-hr room service; cocktails.

BUDGET INN HOTEL ⨁
(702) 385-5560   ◆ Motel
I-15 exit Charleston Blvd E, at Bridger Ave; 301 S Main St $39-139
XP $10; discount for ages 12 and younger. Package plans. AX, DS, MC, VI. 4 stories; interior corridors. **Rooms:** 81. Shower baths, some ⊗. **Dining:** Restaurant nearby.

CAESARS PALACE ⨁
(702) 731-7110   ◆◆◆◆ Large Hotel
I-15 exit Flamingo Rd E; on The Strip; 3570 Las Vegas Blvd S. $129-750
XP $30; ages 18 and younger stay free. 5 pm check-in. Cancellation fee. AX, DC, DS, MC, VI. Senior discount. Package plans. 14-29 stories; interior corridors. Casino, gift shop, name entertainment, art galleries, mall. **Rooms:** 2419; 212 1-bedroom suites with whirlpools, $350-4000. Some shower baths, some whirlpools, hair dryers, coffeemakers, some refrigerators, movies, some VCRs, data ports, high-speed Internet access, some dual phone lines, voice mail, irons, safes, some ⊗. 🅰, roll-in showers, 🔲. **Recreation:** 3 pools, whirlpools, massage. **Services:** Valet parking available, laundry, business services. **Dining:** 10 restaurants, including Bradley Ogden, Cafe Lago, Empress Court and Neros, see separate listings; buffet, $11-25; 24 hrs; 24-hr room service; cocktails.

CANDLEWOOD SUITES
(702) 836-3660   ◆◆◆ Small Hotel
I-15 exit Flamingo Rd E to Paradise Rd, just N; 4034 S Paradise Rd. $89-209
Senior discount. AX, CB, DC, DS, JC, MC. Pets, $75 fee. 4 stories; interior corridors. Sundries shop. **Rooms:** 276; 98 1-bedroom suites with efficiencies. Some shower baths, hair dryers, coffeemaker, microwaves, refrigerators, movies, VCRs, CD players, data ports, dual phone lines, voice mail, irons, some ⊗. 🅰, roll-in

showers. **Recreation:** Pool, whirlpool, exercise rm. **Services:** Laundry, business services. **Dining:** Restaurant nearby.

CARRIAGE HOUSE ⊕   ◆◆◆ Small Hotel
(702) 798-1020   *$145-500*
Just E off The Strip; 105 E Harmon Ave.
4 pm check-in. Senior discount. AX, CB, DC, DS, MC, VI. 9 stories; interior corridors. Video library, video games. **Rooms:** 155; 15 2-bedroom units. Some shower baths, hair dryers, some efficiencies or kitchens, coffeemakers, microwaves, refrigerators, movies, some VCRs, data ports, voice mail, irons, safes, some ⊛. ⬧, roll-in showers. **Recreation:** Pool, whirlpool, exercise rm, lighted tennis court, basketball. **Services:** Area and airport transportation, laundry, business services. **Dining:** Joey Bistro & Bar, see separate listing.

CASINO ROYALE AND HOTEL ⊕   ◆◆ Small Hotel
(702) 737-3500   *$49-150*
Center of The Strip; 3411 Las Vegas Blvd S.
XP $10; ages 18 and younger, free. 4 pm check-in. AX, MC, VI. 4 stories; interior corridors. Casino. **Rooms:** 151; 2 1-bedroom suites with whirlpools, $150-350. Coffeemakers, refrigerators, movies, some data ports, voice mail, safes, some ⊛. **Recreation:** Pool. **Services:** Laundry. **Dining:** 2 restaurants; 24 hrs; cocktails.

CIRCUS CIRCUS HOTEL, CASINO & THEME PARK   ◆◆◆ Large Hotel
(702) 734-0410   *$40-229*
On The Strip; 2880 Las Vegas Blvd S.
XP $12; ages 17 and younger, free. Cancellation fee. Service charge. Senior discount. AX, CB, DC, DS, JC, MC, VI. 3-35 stories; interior corridors. Casino, gift shop. **Rooms:** 3770. Some shower baths, some whirlpools, hair dryers, some refrigerators, movies, data ports, voice mail, safes, some ⊛. ⬧, roll-in showers, ⬚. **Recreation:** 3 pools, whirlpools, exercise rm, game rm. **Services:** Valet parking available, laundry, business services. **Dining:** Restaurants, including Blue Iguana, see separate listing; 24-hr room service; cocktails.

CLARION HOTEL & SUITES EMERALD SPRINGS   ◆◆◆ Small Hotel
Formerly Emerald Springs-Holiday Inn
(702) 732-9100   *$99-269*
I-15 exit Flamingo Rd E; 325 E Flamingo Rd.
XP $20; ages 16 and younger, free. 2-night minimum stay in season and on weekends. Senior discount. AX, CB, DC, DS, JC, MC, VI. 3 stories; interior corridors. **Rooms:** 150; 5 1-bedroom suites, some with whirlpools. Some whirlpools, hair dryers, coffeemakers, some microwaves, refrigerators, movies, some VCRs, video games, data ports, voice mail, irons, some ⊛. **Recreation:** Pool, whirlpool, exercise rm. **Services:** Area and airport transportation, laundry, business services. **Dining:** Restaurants; 24-hr room service; cocktails.

COMFORT INN   ◆◆◆ Motel
(702) 399-1500   *$69-299*
I-15 exit 46 (Cheyenne Ave), just W; 910 E Cheyenne Ave.
XP $10; children, free. Cancellation fee. Senior discount. AX, DS, MC, VI. Pets, $5

extra charge. 3 stories, no elevator; interior corridors. Sundries shop. **Rooms:** 59. Some shower baths, some whirlpools, hair dryers, coffeemakers, some microwaves, some refrigerators, movies, data ports, irons, some ⊛. ♿, roll-in showers. **Recreation:** Pool, whirlpool. **Services:** Laundry, business services. **Dining:** Restaurant nearby.

COMFORT INN ◆◆ Motel
(702) 938-2000 *$59-189*
I-15 exit Flamingo Rd E; 4350 Paradise Rd.
XP $10; ages 18 and younger, free. AX, CB, DC, DS, MC, VI. 2 stories, no elevator; exterior corridors. **Rooms:** 199 efficiencies. Some shower baths, hair dryers, coffeemakers, microwaves, refrigerators, data ports, voice mail, irons, some ⊛. ♿, roll-in showers. **Recreation:** Pool. **Services:** Airport transportation, laundry, business services. **Dining:** Restaurant nearby.

COURTYARD BY MARRIOTT-CONVENTION CENTER ◆◆◆ Small Hotel
(702) 791-3600 *$119-269*
Just E of The Strip; 1 blk to convention center; 3275 Paradise Rd.
Cancellation fee. Senior discount. Breakfast and package plans. AX, DC, DS, JC, MC, VI. 3 stories; interior corridors. Sundries shop. **Rooms:** 149. Some shower baths, hair dryers, coffeemakers, refrigerators, movies, data ports, high-speed Internet access, dual phone lines, voice mail, irons, some ⊛. ♿, roll-in showers, ▨. **Recreation:** Pool, whirlpool, exercise rm. **Services:** Laundry, business services. **Dining:** Restaurant.

COURTYARD BY MARRIOTT LAS VEGAS SOUTH ◆◆◆ Small Hotel
(702) 895-7519 *$99-249*
I-15 exit Russell Rd, just SW; 5845 Industrial Rd.
AX, CB, DC, DS, JC, MC, VI. 4 stories; interior corridors. Sundries shop. **Rooms:** 146; 7 1-bedroom suites, $149-299. Some shower baths, hair dryers, coffeemakers, movies, data ports, high-speed Internet access, voice mail, irons, some ⊛. ♿, roll-in showers. **Recreation:** Pool, whirlpool, exercise rm. **Services:** Area transportation, business services. **Dining:** Cocktails.

COURTYARD BY MARRIOTT LAS VEGAS-SUMMERLIN ◆◆◆ Small Hotel
(702) 646-4400 *$99-109*
US 95 exit Lake Mead Dr, just E; 1901 N Rainbow Blvd.
Senior discount. AX, CB, DC, DS, JC, MC, VI. 3 stories; interior corridors. **Rooms:** 154; 6 1-bedroom suites with whirlpools. Some shower baths, hair dryers, coffeemakers, some refrigerators, movies, data ports, dual phone lines, voice mail, irons, some ⊛. ♿, roll-in showers. **Recreation:** Pool, whirlpool, exercise rm. **Services:** Laundry, business services. **Dining:** Restaurant; cocktails.

DAYS INN DOWNTOWN ◆◆ Motel
(702) 388-1400 *$35-99*
On US 93/95 business route; 707 E Fremont St.
Senior discount. AX, CB, DC, DS, MC, VI. 3 stories; exterior corridors. **Rooms:** 147. Hair dryers, some data ports, some ⊛. ▨ **Recreation:** Pool.

DOUBLETREE CLUB HOTEL LAS VEGAS AIRPORT ◍   ◆◆◆ Small Hotel
(702) 948-4000   *$79-239*
I-215 exit 8 (Warm Springs Rd), just E; 7250 Pollock Dr.
XP $15; ages 18 and younger, free. Package plans. AX, CB, DC, DS, JC, MC, VI. 6 stories; interior corridors. **Rooms:** 190. Some shower baths, hair dryers, coffeemakers, some microwaves, some refrigerators, movies, video games, data ports, dual phone lines, voice mail, irons, some ⊛. ⓑ, roll-in showers, ◨. **Recreation:** Exercise rm. **Services:** Area and airport transportation, laundry, business services. **Dining:** Restaurant; 6 am-10 pm; cocktails.

ECONO LODGE ◍   ◆ Motel
(702) 382-6001   *$35-299*
I-15 exit Charleston Blvd E to Las Vegas Blvd, then S; 1150 Las Vegas Blvd S.
Senior discount. AX, CB, DC, DS, JC, MC, VI. 2 stories, no elevator; exterior corridors. **Rooms:** 121. Data ports, some ⊛. **Recreation:** Pool. **Dining:** Restaurant nearby.

EMBASSY SUITES CONVENTION CENTER   ◆◆◆ Large Hotel
(702) 893-8000   *79-269*
I-15 exit Sahara Ave E; ½ mi S of convention center; 3600 Paradise Rd.
XP $10; ages 18 and younger, free. Breakfast. Complimentary evening beverages. Senior discount. AX, CB, DC, DS, JC, MC, VI. 11 stories; interior corridors. Gift shop. **Rooms:** 286. Some shower baths, hair dryers, coffeemakers, microwaves, refrigerators, movies, video games, data ports, high-speed Internet access, dual phone lines, voice mail, irons, some ⊛. ⓑ, roll-in showers. **Recreation:** Pool, whirlpool, exercise rm. **Services:** Area transportation, laundry, business services. **Dining:** Restaurant; 24-hr room service; cocktails.

EMBASSY SUITES HOTEL LAS VEGAS   ◆◆◆ Large Hotel
(702) 795-2800   *$119-299*
I-15 exit Tropicana Ave E, then N; 4315 Swenson St.
XP $10; ages 18 and younger, free. Complimentary evening beverages. Senior discount. Package plans. AX, MC, VI. 6 stories; interior corridors. Gift shop. **Rooms:** 220. Some shower baths, hair dryers, coffeemakers, microwaves, refrigerators, movies, some VCRs, data ports, dual phone lines, voice mail, irons, some ⊛. ⓑ, roll-in showers. **Recreation:** Pool, whirlpools, exercise rm. **Services:** Area transportation, laundry, business services. **Dining:** Restaurant; cocktails.

EXCALIBUR HOTEL & CASINO   ◆◆◆ Large Hotel
(702) 597-7777   *$59-450*
I-15 exit Tropicana Ave E; 3850 Las Vegas Blvd S.
XP $15; ages 12 and younger, free. 2-night minimum stay in season and on weekends. AX, CB, DC, DS, JC, MC, VI. 28 stories; interior corridors. Casino, gift shop. **Rooms:** 3991; 30 1-bedroom suites. Shower baths, some whirlpools, hair dryers, some refrigerators, movies, video games, data ports, high-speed Internet access, voice mail, irons, some ⊛. ⓑ, roll-in showers, ◨. **Recreation:** 2 pools, whirlpool, spa, health club, game rm. **Services:** Valet parking available, laundry, business services. **Dining:** Restaurant, The Steakhouse at Camelot, see separate listing; 24-hr room service; cocktails.

FAIRFIELD INN & SUITES BY MARRIOTT SOUTH

◆◆◆ Small Hotel

(702) 895-9810
$89-229

I-15 exit Russell Rd, just W; 5775 Industrial Rd.

Expanded continental breakfast. Cancellation fee. Senior discount. AX, DC, DS, MC, VI. 4 stories; interior corridors. **Rooms:** 142. Some shower baths, hair dryers, coffeemakers, some microwaves, some refrigerators, movies, some CD players, data ports, high-speed Internet access, voice mail, irons, some ⊗. Ⓐ, roll-in showers. **Recreation:** Pool, whirlpool, exercise rm. **Services:** Area transportation, laundry, business services.

FIESTA CASINO HOTEL ⒶⒶ

◆◆ Small Hotel

(702) 631-7000
$29-99

3 mi NW of downtown; 2400 N Rancho Dr.

XP $10; ages 18 and younger, free. Cancellation fee. $5 service charge. Package plans. AX, DC, DS, MC, VI. 5 stories; interior corridors. Casino, gift shop. **Rooms:** 100. Some shower baths, hair dryers, movies, data ports, voice mail, irons, some ⊗. Ⓐ, roll-in showers. **Recreation:** Pool. **Services:** Valet parking available, business services. **Dining:** 2 restaurants, including Garduno's of Mexico, see separate listing; buffet, $5-9; 24 hrs; cocktails.

FITZGERALDS HOTEL & CASINO ⒶⒶ

◆◆◆ Large Hotel

(702) 388-2400
$39-195

In downtown casino center; 301 Fremont St.

XP $20; ages 17 and younger, free. 2-night minimum stay weekends. Cancellation fee. Senior discount. Package plans. AX, CB, DC, DS, JC, MC, VI. 34 stories; interior corridors. Casino, gift shop. **Rooms:** 640; 15 1-bedroom suites with whirlpools. Some shower baths, some whirlpools, hair dryers, some coffeemakers, some refrigerators, movies, data ports, irons, safes, some ⊗. **Recreation:** Pool, whirlpool. **Services:** Valet parking available, business services. **Dining:** 3 restaurants; buffet; 24 hrs; 24-hr room service; cocktails.

FLAMINGO LAS VEGAS ⒶⒶ

◆◆◆ Large Hotel

(702) 733-3111
$65-400

I-15 exit Flamingo Rd E, N on The Strip; 3555 Las Vegas Blvd S.

XP $20; ages 18 and younger, free. AX, CB, DC, DS, JC, MC, VI. 28 stories; interior corridors. Casino, gift shop, entertainment. **Rooms:** 3565; 30 1- and 24 2-bedroom suites, some with whirlpools, $495-1000. Some shower baths, hair dryers, some refrigerators, movies, video games, data ports, high-speed Internet access, voice mail, irons, safes, some ⊗. Ⓐ, roll-in showers, ⬚. **Recreation:** 2 pools, wading pool, waterslide, whirlpools, health club, massage, 4 lighted tennis courts. **Services:** Valet parking available, laundry, business services. **Dining:** 7 restaurants, including Conrad's and Ventuno Ristorante, see separate listings; buffet, $11-16; 24 hrs; 24-hr room service; cocktails.

FOUR SEASONS HOTEL LAS VEGAS ⒶⒶ

◆◆◆◆◆ Large Hotel

(702) 632-5000
$265-1815

I-15 exit Tropicana Ave E, S on The Strip; 3960 Las Vegas Blvd S.

XP $30; ages 18 and younger, free. Cancellation fee. Parking fee. Package plans. AX, DC, DS, JC, MC, VI. Small pets. 5 stories, on floors 35-39 of high-rise; interior corridors. Gift shop. **Rooms:** 424; 54 1- and 32 2-bedroom suites, some with whirlpools, $475-4150. Some shower baths, hair dryers, coffeemakers, honor bars, movies, VCRs, video games, CD players, data ports, high-speed Internet access, dual phone lines, voice mail, irons, safes, some ⊛. ♿, roll-in showers. **Recreation:** Pool, whirlpools, spa, health club, jogging. **Services:** Airport transportation, laundry, child care, business services. **Dining:** 2 restaurants, including Charlie Palmer Steak and Verandah, see separate listings; 6:30 am-10:30 pm; 24-hr room service; cocktails.

GOLD COAST HOTEL ⍟   ♦♦♦ Large Hotel
(702) 367-7111   *Property failed to provide current rates*
I-15 exit Flamingo Rd W, just W; 4000 W Flamingo Rd.
10 stories; interior corridors. Casino, gift shop, entertainment. **Rooms:** 711; 11 1-bedroom suites. Some shower baths, hair dryers, movies, data ports, voice mail, irons, some ⊛. **Recreation:** Pool, whirlpool, exercise rm, health club, bowling. **Services:** Valet parking available, area transportation, laundry, childcare, business services. **Dining:** 5 restaurants, including Monterey Room and Ping Pang Pong, see separate listings; buffet, $5-12; 24 hrs; 24-hr room service; cocktails.

THE GOLDEN NUGGET ⍟   ♦♦♦♦ Large Hotel
(702) 385-7111   *$69-299*
Downtown, casino center area; 129 E Fremont St.
XP $20. Cancellation fee. Package plans. AX, CB, DC, DS, JC, MC, VI. 10-22 stories; interior corridors. Casino, gift shop, entertainment. **Rooms:** 1907; 102 1-bedroom suites with whirlpools, $275-500. Some shower baths, hair dryers, movies, video games, data ports, high-speed Internet access, some dual phone lines, voice mail, irons, safes, some ⊛. ♿, roll-in showers, 🖵. **Recreation:** Pool, whirlpool, health club, massage. **Services:** Valet parking available, laundry, business services. **Dining:** 4 restaurants, including Lillie Langtry's and Stephano's, see separate listings; buffet, $7-14; 24 hrs; 24-hr room service; cocktails.

GOLDEN PALM CASINO HOTEL   ♦♦ Small Hotel
Formerly Howard Johnson Hotel & Casino
(702) 798-1111   *$29-189*
I-15 exit Tropicana Ave W; 3111 W Tropicana Ave.
XP $10; ages 12 and younger, free. Senior discount. AX, DC, DS, MC, VI. 6 stories; interior corridors. Casino. **Rooms:** 150. Hair dryers, coffeemakers, some microwaves, some refrigerators, movies, data ports, voice mail, some ⊛. **Recreation:** Pool, whirlpool. **Services:** Airport transportation, laundry. **Dining:** Restaurant; cocktails.

HAMPTON INN LAS VEGAS   ♦♦♦ Motel
(702) 360-5700   *$79-129*
US 95, exit W Cheyenne Ave, S on Tenaya Wy; 7100 Cascade Valley Ct.
Breakfast. Cancellation fee. Senior discount. AX, CB, DC, DS, JC, MC, VI. Small pets, $25 charge. 3 stories; interior corridors. **Rooms:** 127. Some shower baths, hair dryers, coffeemakers, microwaves, refrigerators, data ports, voice mail, irons, some ⊛. **Recreation:** Pool, whirlpool, health club. **Services:** Laundry, business services. **Dining:** Restaurant nearby.

HAMPTON INN TROPICANA
◆◆◆ Motel

(702) 948-8100   *$70-220*
I-15 exit Tropicana Ave W; 4975 S Industrial Rd.

2-night minimum stay weekends. Cancellation fee. Senior discount. AX, CB, DC, DS, JC, MC, VI. 6 stories; interior corridors. Sundries shop, video library. **Rooms:** 320; 12 1-bedroom suites, $240-300. Some shower baths, hair dryers, coffeemakers, some microwaves, some refrigerators, movies, some VCRs, video games, data ports, dual phone lines, voice mail, irons, some ⊗. ⬚, roll-in showers. **Recreation:** Pool, whirlpool, exercise rm. **Services:** Area and airport transportation, laundry, business services. **Dining:** Restaurant nearby.

HARRAH'S LAS VEGAS CASINO & HOTEL
◆◆◆ Large Hotel

(702) 369-5000   *Property failed to provide current rates*
I-15 exit E Flamingo Rd; 3475 Las Vegas Blvd S.

4 pm check-in. 15-35 stories; interior corridors. Casino, gift shop, name entertainment. **Rooms:** 2526; 190 1-bedroom suites with whirlpools. Some shower baths, hair dryers, some refrigerators, honor bars, movies, video games, data ports, voice mail, irons, some ⊗. ⬚, roll-in showers, ⬚. **Recreation:** Pool, whirlpools, health club, massage. **Services:** Valet parking available, area transportation, laundry, business services. **Dining:** Restaurants, including Garden Room and Range Steakhouse at Harrah's, see separate listings; 24-hr room service; cocktails.

HAWTHORN SUITES-LAS VEGAS
◆◆◆ Motel

(702) 739-7000   *$79-169*
I-15 exit Tropicana Ave E ¾ mi to Duke Ellington Wy, just S; 5051 Duke Ellington Wy.

4 pm check-in. Complimentary evening beverages Mon-Thu. 3-day cancellation notice; fee. Senior discount. AX, DC, DS, MC, VI. Small pets, $50 extra charge. 3 stories; exterior corridors. Sundries shop. **Rooms:** 207; 49 2-bedroom suites. Some shower baths, hair dryers, coffeemakers, microwaves, refrigerators, movies, video games, data ports, high-speed Internet access, voice mail, irons, ⊗. ⬚, roll-in showers, ⬚. **Recreation:** Pools, whirlpool, exercise rm, sports court. **Services:** Laundry, business services. **Dining:** Restaurant nearby.

HILTON GRAND VACATIONS CLUB
◆◆◆ Large Hotel

(702) 697-2900   *$129-449*
I-15 exit Flamingo Rd E, then N on The Strip; directly behind Flamingo Las Vegas; 3575 Las Vegas Blvd S.

4 pm check-in. 2-night minimum stay weekends. 3-day cancellation notice; fee. AX, CB, DC, DS, MC, VI. 17 stories; interior corridors. Gift shop. **Rooms:** 303; 112 2-bedroom units. Whirlpools, hair dryers, some efficiencies or kitchens, coffeemakers, microwaves, refrigerators, movies, VCRs, data ports, voice mail, irons, safes, some ⊗. ⬚, roll-in showers, ⬚. **Recreation:** Pool, wading pool, sauna, whirlpools, exercise rm. **Services:** Valet parking available, laundry, business services. **Dining:** Restaurant; 24-hr room service.

HILTON GRAND VACATIONS CLUB AT THE LAS VEGAS HILTON

◆◆◆ Large Hotel

(702) 946-9200   *$129-449*

At Paradise Rd, adj to Las Vegas Hilton; 455 Karen Ave.

4 pm check-in. 3-day cancellation notice. Senior discount. AX, CB, DC, DS, MC, VI. 16 stories; interior corridors. Gift shop, video library. **Rooms:** 405. Some shower baths, some whirlpools, hair dryers, coffeemakers, microwaves, refrigerators, VCRs, data ports, dual phone lines, voice mail, irons, safes, some ⊛. 🅰, roll-in showers. **Recreation:** Pool, whirlpools, exercise rm, jogging. **Services:** Laundry, business services. **Dining:** Restaurant.

HILTON GRAND VACATION CLUB ON THE LAS VEGAS STRIP

◆◆◆ Large Hotel

(702) 765-8300   *$129-449*

I-15 exit Sahara Ave E, ½ mi S on the Strip. 2650 Las Vegas Blvd S.

Parking fee. 2-night minimum stay weekends. 3-day cancellation notice; fee. AX, CB, DC, DS, MC, VI. 27 stories; interior corridors. Gift shop. **Rooms:** 506; 275 1- and 3 2-bedroom suites, some with kitchens and/or whirlpools. Some shower baths, hair dryers, coffeemakers, microwaves, refrigerators, movies, DVD players, CD players, data ports, dual phone lines, high-speed Internet access, voice mail, irons, safes, some ⊛. 🅰, roll-in showers. **Recreation:** 2 pools, whirlpool, exercise rm, game rm. **Services:** Laundry, business services. **Dining:** Restaurant; 24-hr room service.

HOLIDAY INN EXPRESS

◆◆◆ Small Hotel

(702) 736-0098   *$89-229*

I-15 exit Russell Rd, just W; 5760 Polaris Ave.

Expanded continental breakfast. Cancellation fee. Senior discount. AX, DC, DS, MC, VI. Pets, $100 extra charge. 4 stories; interior corridors. **Rooms:** 139. Some shower baths, hair dryers, coffeemakers, some microwaves, some refrigerators, movies, data ports, high-speed Internet access, voice mail, irons, some ⊛. 🅰, roll-in showers. **Recreation:** Pool, whirlpool, exercise rm. **Services:** Area transportation, laundry, business services.

HOLIDAY INN EXPRESS ⨂

◆◆◆ Motel

(702) 256-3766   *$79-169*

I-15 exit Sahara Ave, 6½ mi W; 8669 W Sahara Ave.

XP $10; ages 18 and younger, free. Expanded continental breakfast. 2-night minimum stay weekends. Senior discount. AX, DC, DS, MC, VI. Pets, $20 extra charge; in selected units. 3 stories, no elevator; interior corridors. Sundries shop. **Rooms:** 59. Some shower baths, some whirlpools, hair dryers, coffeemakers, some microwaves, some refrigerators, movies, data ports, voice mail, irons, some ⊛. Roll-in showers. **Recreation:** Pool, whirlpool. **Services:** Laundry, business services. **Dining:** Restaurant nearby.

HOLIDAY INN EXPRESS HOTEL & SUITES N LAS VEGAS

◆◆◆ Motel

(702) 649-3000   *$99-149*

I-15 exit W Craig Rd; 4540 Donovan Wy.

XP $10; ages 14 and younger, free. AX, DC, DS, MC, VI. Pets, $25 extra charge.

3 stories; interior corridors. Sundries shop. **Rooms:** 74. Some shower baths, some whirlpools, hair dryers, coffeemakers, some microwaves, some refrigerators, movies, data ports, dual phone lines, voice mail, irons, some ⊗. 🅰, roll-in showers. **Recreation:** Pool, whirlpool. **Services:** Laundry, business services.

HOMESTEAD STUDIO SUITES HOTEL-LAS VEGAS/MIDTOWN ◆◆ Motel
(702) 369-1414 $64-84
I-15 exit Sahara Ave E; 3045 S Maryland Pkwy.
XP $5; ages 18 and younger, free. Senior discount. AX, CB, DC, DS, JC, MC, VI. Pets, $25 extra charge. 3 stories; interior corridors. Sundries shop. **Rooms:** 123. Some shower baths, efficiencies, coffeemakers, microwaves, refrigerators, movies, some VCRs, data ports, voice mail, irons, some ⊗. 🅰, roll-in showers. **Recreation:** Health club nearby. **Services:** Laundry. **Dining:** Restaurant nearby.

HOWARD JOHNSON AIRPORT INN ◆ Motel
(702) 798-2777 $32-129
I-15 exit Tropicana Ave E; 1¾ mi to Paradise Rd, ⅓ mi S; 5100 Paradise Rd.
Senior discount. AX, CB, DC, DS, MC, VI. Pets, $100 extra charge, in selected units. 2 stories, no elevator; exterior corridors. **Rooms:** 327. Some shower baths, some hair dryers, some coffeemakers, some microwaves, some refrigerators, movies, some data ports, voice mail, some irons, some ⊗. Roll-in showers, 🆉. **Recreation:** 2 pools, health club nearby, game rm. **Services:** Area and airport transportation, laundry, business services. **Dining:** Restaurant; cocktails.

HOWARD JOHNSON LAS VEGAS STRIP ⏣ ◆◆ Motel
(702) 388-0301 $39-169
I-15 exit Sahara Ave, E to Las Vegas Blvd, then N; 1401 Las Vegas Blvd S.
XP $5; ages 16 and younger, free. Senior discount. Meal and breakfast plans available. AX, CB, DC, DS, MC, VI. Small pets, $10 extra charge. 2-3 stories; interior/exterior corridors. **Rooms:** 104. Hair dryers, coffeemakers, microwaves, refrigerators, movies, data ports, voice mail, irons, safes, some ⊗. **Recreation:** Pool, game rm. **Services:** Laundry, business services. **Dining:** Restaurant; 7 am-10 pm; wine/beer.

KEY LARGO CASINO & HOTEL AT THE QUALITY INN ◆◆ Motel
(702) 733-7777 $30-200
I-15 exit 38 at Flamingo Rd, E 4 blks to 377 E Flamingo Rd.
XP $10; ages 17 and younger, free. 2-night minimum stay weekends. 3-day cancellation notice; fee. Senior discount. AX, CB, DC, DS, JC, MC, VI. Casino, gift shop. 3 stories; interior/exterior corridors. **Rooms:** 316. Refrigerators, movies, data ports, some ⊗. 🆉 **Recreation:** Pool, whirlpool. **Services:** Area and airport transportation, laundry, business services. **Dining:** Restaurant, Coral Cafe, see separate listing; cocktails.

KOALA INN ⏣ ◆ Motel
(702) 384-8211 $40-125
I-15 exit E Charleston Blvd, ⅓ mi E to Casino Center Blvd, then ⁴⁄₁₀ mi N; 520 S Casino Center Blvd.
XP $10; ages 16 and younger, free. 2-night minimum stay weekends. Senior dis-

count. Weekly rates available. AX, CB, DC, DS, JC, MC, VI. 3 stories; interior corridors. **Rooms:** 48. Coffeemakers, some microwaves, refrigerators, movies, data ports, voice mail, some ⊛. **Services:** Laundry.

LA QUINTA INN & SUITES LAS VEGAS (SUMMERLIN TECH CENTER)
♦♦♦ Motel

(702) 360-1200   *$99-125*
US 95 exit 83, W Cheyenne Ave; 7101 Cascade Valley Ct.
XP $6; ages 18 and younger, free. Expanded continental breakfast plan available. AX, DC, DS, MC, VI. Pets. 5 stories; interior corridors. **Rooms:** 128; 5 1-bedroom suites. Some shower baths, hair dryers, coffeemakers, some microwaves, some refrigerators, movies, video games, data ports, high-speed Internet access, voice mail, irons, some ⊛. 🖰, roll-in showers. **Recreation:** Pool, whirlpool, exercise rm. **Services:** Laundry, business services. **Dining:** Restaurant nearby.

LA QUINTA INN & SUITES LAS VEGAS (WEST/LAKES) ⏺
♦♦♦ Motel

(702) 243-0356   *$79-309*
Just W of Fort Apache Rd; 9570 W Sahara Ave.
XP $10; ages 18 and younger, free. 2-night minimum stay weekends. AX, DC, DS, MC, VI. Small pets. 3 stories; interior corridors. **Rooms:** 75. Some shower baths, some whirlpools, hair dryers, coffeemakers, microwaves, refrigerators, movies, some VCRs, data ports, dual phone lines, voice mail, irons, some ⊛. 🖰, roll-in showers. **Recreation:** Pool, whirlpool, exercise rm. **Services:** Laundry, business services. **Dining:** Restaurant nearby.

LA QUINTA INN LAS VEGAS (CONVENTION CENTER)
♦♦♦ Motel

(702) 796-9000   *$99-159*
I-15 exit Flamingo Rd E; ¾ mi S of convention center, ½ mi E of The Strip; 3970 Paradise Rd.
XP $10; ages 18 and younger, free. 4 pm check-in. Expanded continental breakfast plan available. AX, DC, DS, MC, VI. Small pets. 3 stories; interior corridors. **Rooms:** 251; 30 2-bedroom units. Some shower baths, some whirlpools, hair dryers, coffeemakers, some microwaves, some refrigerators, movies, data ports, video games, voice mail, irons, some ⊛. Roll-in showers. **Recreation:** Pool, whirlpool, exercise rm. **Services:** Area and airport transportation, laundry, business services. **Dining:** Restaurant.

LA QUINTA INN LAS VEGAS (NELLIS)
♦♦♦ Motel

(702) 632-0229   *$89-199*
I-15 exit Craig Rd, E to Las Vegas Blvd N; 4288 N Nellis Blvd.
XP $10; ages 18 and younger, free. 3-day cancellation notice. AX, CB, DC, DS, MC, VI. Pets. 3 stories; interior corridors. **Rooms:** 59. Some shower baths, some whirlpools, hair dryers, coffeemakers, some microwaves, some refrigerators, movies, data ports, irons, some ⊛. 🖰, roll-in showers, ▦. **Recreation:** Pool, whirlpool, exercise rm. **Services:** Laundry, business services.

LA QUINTA INN LAS VEGAS (TROPICANA) ⏺
♦♦♦ Motel

(702) 798-7736   *$59-160*
I-15, exit Tropicana Ave W; 4975 S Valley View Blvd.

XP $10; ages 18 and younger, free. 2-night minimum stay in season. 14-day cancellation notice; fee and service charge. Pets. AX, CB, DC, DS, MC, VI. Gift shop. 3 stories, no elevator; interior corridors. **Rooms:** 59. Some shower baths, hair dryers, some kitchens, coffeemakers, some microwaves, some refrigerators, movies, data ports, irons, some ⊛. Ⓛ, roll-in showers. **Recreation:** Pool, whirlpool, exercise rm. **Services:** Laundry, business services.

LAS VEGAS HILTON ⏺
♦♦♦ Large Hotel

(702) 732-5111   *$65-1800*

I-15 exit Sahara Ave, 2 mi E; adj to convention center; 3000 Paradise Rd.

XP $30; ages 18 and younger, free. Senior discount. Package plans. AX, CB, DC, DS, JC, MC, VI. 30 stories; interior corridors. Casino, gift shop, entertainment, Star Trek: The Experience. **Rooms:** 3174; 150 1- and 75 2-bedroom suites, some with whirlpools. Some shower baths, some whirlpools, hair dryers, some refrigerators, movies, some VCRs, data ports, high-speed Internet access, voice mail, irons, safes, some ⊛. Ⓛ, roll-in showers, ⊠. **Recreation:** Pool, whirlpool, health club, massage, 6 lighted tennis courts, game rm. **Services:** Valet parking available, laundry, business services. **Dining:** 9 restaurants, including Andiamo, Hilton Steakhouse and Paradise Cafe, see separate listings; buffet, $9-13; 24 hrs; 24-hr room service; cocktails.

LUXOR LAS VEGAS
♦♦♦ Large Hotel

(702) 262-4000   *$79-399*

I-15 exit Tropicana Ave E, just S on The Strip; exit Russell Rd NB, E to The Strip, then just N; 3900 Las Vegas Blvd S.

XP $25; ages 12 and younger, free. AX, CB, DC, DS, JC, MC, VI. 30 stories; interior corridors. Casino, gift shop. **Rooms:** 4407; 372 1- and 35 2-bedroom suites, some with whirlpools, $179-799. Some shower baths, some whirlpools, hair dryers, some refrigerators, movies, video games, data ports, high-speed Internet access, voice mail, irons, some ⊛. Ⓛ, roll-in showers, ⊠. **Recreation:** 2 pools, wading pool, saunas, whirlpools, health club, massage, game rm. **Services:** Valet parking available, laundry, business services. **Dining:** Restaurants, including Luxor Steak House and Sacred Sea Room, see separate listings; 24-hr room service; cocktails.

MAIN STREET STATION
♦♦♦ Large Hotel

(702) 387-1896   *$40-200*

In downtown casino center; 200 N Main St.

XP $10; ages 12 and younger, free. 4 pm check-in. AX, CB, DC, DS, JC, MC, VI. 17 stories; interior corridors. Casino, gift shop. **Rooms:** 406. Some shower baths, movies, video games, data ports, voice mail, safes, some ⊛. Ⓛ, roll-in showers. **Dining:** Restaurant, Triple 7 Restaurant Brewery, see separate listing.

MANDALAY BAY RESORT & CASINO ⏺
♦♦♦♦ Large Hotel

(702) 632-7777   *Property failed to provide current rates*

I-15 exit Tropicana Ave, just E; 3950 Las Vegas Blvd S.

42 stories; interior corridors. Casino, gift shop, entertainment. **Rooms:** 3220; 114 1- and 93 2-bedroom suites with whirlpools. Some whirlpools, hair dryers, some refrigerators, movies, data ports, high-speed Internet access, dual phone lines,

voice mail, irons, safes, some ⊛. ♿, roll-in showers. **Recreation:** 6 pools, whirlpools, pool-side cabanas and bungalows, spa, health club, massage, jogging, golf. **Services:** Valet parking available, area transportation, laundry, business services. **Dining:** 9 restaurants, including Aureole, Border Grill, Shanghai Lilly and 3950 Restaurant, see separate listings; buffet, $12-25; 24 hrs; 24-hr room service; cocktails.

MARRIOT SUITES LAS VEGAS
◆◆◆ Large Hotel
(702) 650-2000
$139-399
Near convention center; at Paradise Rd; 325 Convention Center Dr.
Cancellation fee. Senior discount. AX, CB, DC, DS, JC, MC, VI. 17 stories; interior corridors. Sundries shop. **Rooms:** 278. Some shower baths, hair dryers, coffeemakers, refrigerators, honor bars, movies, some VCRs, data ports, high-speed Internet access, voice mail, irons, some ⊛. ♿, roll-in showers. **Services:** Laundry, business services. **Recreation:** Pool, whirlpool, exercise rm. **Dining:** Restaurant; 24-hr room service; cocktails.

MGM GRAND HOTEL & CASINO
◆◆◆ Large Hotel
(702) 891-1111
$89-399
I-15 exit Tropicana Ave, just E; 3799 Las Vegas Blvd S.
XP $30; ages 12 and younger, free. 14-30 stories; interior corridors. Casino, gift shop. **Rooms:** 5005; 679 1- and 73 2-bedroom suites, some with whirlpools. Some shower baths, hair dryers, some refrigerators, movies, video games, data ports, high-speed Internet access, some dual phone lines, voice mail, irons, safes, some ⊛. ♿, roll-in showers, 🔲. **Recreation:** 4 pools, whirlpools, health club, massage, game rm. **Services:** Valet parking available, area and airport transportation, laundry, business services. **Dining:** Restaurants, including Craftsteak, Emeril's New Orleans Fish House and NobHill, see separate listings; 24-hr room service; cocktails.

THE MIRAGE ⏣
◆◆◆◆ Large Hotel
(702) 791-7111
$89-599
I-15 exit Spring Mountain Rd, E to The Strip; 3400 Las Vegas Blvd S.
XP $30. Cancellation fee. AX, DC, DS, JC, MC, VI. 30 stories; interior corridors. Casino, gift shop, name entertainment. **Rooms:** 3044; 187 1-, 92 2- and 2 3-bedroom suites, $229-5000. Some shower baths, some whirlpools, hair dryers, some refrigerators, honor bars, movies, data ports, high-speed Internet access, dual phone lines, voice mail, irons, safes, some ⊛. ♿, roll-in showers, 🔲. **Recreation:** 2 pools, whirlpools, spa, health club, game rm. **Services:** Valet parking available, area transportation, laundry, childcare, business services. **Dining:** 8 restaurants, including Kokomos, Renoir and Samba Brazillian Steakhouse, see separate listings; buffet, $11-20; 24 hrs; 24-hr room service; cocktails.

MONTE CARLO RESORT & CASINO
◆◆◆ Large Hotel
(702) 730-7777
$59-399
On The Strip between Flamingo Rd and Tropicana Ave; 3770 Las Vegas Blvd S.
XP $25. Cancellation fee. AX, CB, DC, DS, JC, MC, VI. 32 stories; interior corridors. Casino, gift shop. **Rooms:** 3002; 28 1-bedroom suites, some with whirlpools, $149-489. Some shower baths, some whirlpools, hair dryers, movies,

data ports, high-speed Internet access, voice mail, irons, some ⊛. 🛇, roll-in showers, 🖿. **Recreation:** 3 pools, wading pool, sauna, whirlpool, health club, steam rm, massage, 3 lighted tennis courts, game rm. **Services:** Valet parking available, laundry, business services. **Dining:** Restaurants, including Blackstone's and The Cafe, see separate listings; 24-hr room service; cocktails.

MOTEL 6 BOULDER HIGHWAY
♦ Motel

(702) 457-8051 $36-100

Just S of Sahara Ave; 4125 Boulder Hwy.

XP $6; ages 17 and younger, free. Cancellation fee. AX, DC, DS, MC, VI. Small pets. 2 stories, no elevator; exterior corridors. Some shower baths, movies, data ports, some ⊛. **Rooms:** 161. Roll-in showers. **Recreation:** Pool. **Services:** Laundry. **Dining:** Restaurant nearby.

NEVADA PALACE
♦ Motel

(702) 458-8810 $35-80

½ mi N of Tropicana Ave; 5255 Boulder Hwy.

XP $10; ages 12 and younger, free. AX, CB, DC, DS, MC, VI. 3 stories; exterior corridors. Casino, gift shop. **Rooms:** 211. Movies, some ⊛. **Recreation:** Pool. **Services:** Business services. **Dining:** Restaurant.

NEW YORK-NEW YORK HOTEL & CASINO
♦♦♦ Large Hotel

(702) 740-6969 $80-400

I-15 exit Tropicana Ave, just E; 3790 Las Vegas Blvd S.

XP $30. 30-45 stories; interior corridors. Casino, gift shop. **Rooms:** 2024; 33 1-bedroom suites, with whirlpools. Some shower baths, some whirlpools, hair dryers, some refrigerators, movies, data ports, high-speed Internet access, voice mail, irons, safes, some ⊛. 🛇, roll-in showers. **Recreation:** Pools, whirlpool, health club, massage, game rm. **Services:** Valet parking available, laundry, business services. **Dining:** Restaurants, including America and Nine Fine Irishmen, see separate listings; 24-hr room service; cocktails.

THE ORLEANS ⏱
♦♦♦ Large Hotel

(702) 365-7111 $49-169

I-15 exit Tropicana Ave, 1 mi W; 4500 W Tropicana Ave.

XP $15; ages 15 and younger, free. Package plans. AX, CB, DC, DS, JC, MC, VI. 22 stories. Casino, gift shop, movie theaters, entertainment. **Rooms:** 1886; 28 1- and 30 2-bedroom suites, some with whirlpools, $250-1200. Some shower baths, hair dryers, some refrigerators, movies, data ports, high-speed Internet access, voice mail, irons, some ⊛. 🛇, roll-in showers. **Recreation:** Pool, wading pool, whirlpool, spa, health club, bowling, game rm. **Services:** Valet parking available, area transportation, laundry, childcare; business services. **Dining:** 6 restaurants, including Brendan's Irish Pub, Courtyard Cafe, Don Miguel's and Koji Sushi Bar & China Bistro, see separate listings; buffet, $6-12; 24 hrs; 24-hr room service; cocktails.

PALACE STATION HOTEL & CASINO ⏱
♦♦♦ Large Hotel

(702) 367-2411 $19-400

I-15 exit Sahara Ave W; SW corner of Sahara Ave and Rancho Dr; 2411 W Sahara Ave.

XP $20; ages 12 and younger, free. 2-night minimum stay weekends. Cancellation fee. $5 service charge. AX, CB, DC, DS, MC, VI. 2-21 stories; interior corridors. Casino, gift shop. **Rooms:** 1020; 24 1-bedroom suites with whirlpools. Some shower baths, some whirlpools, hair dryers, some coffeemakers, some refrigerators, movies, data ports, voice mail, irons, some safes, some ⊗. 🔲, roll-in showers, 🔳. **Recreation:** Pool, whirlpools, exercise rm, game rm. **Services:** Valet parking available, area and airport transportation, laundry, business services. **Dining:** 10 restaurants, including The Broiler and Palace Cafe, see separate listings; buffet, $6-16; 24 hrs; 24-hr room service; cocktails.

THE PALMS CASINO RESORT ◆◆◆ Large Hotel
(702) 942-7777 *Property failed to provide current rates*
I-15 exit Flamingo Rd W, ½ mi W; 4321 W Flamingo Rd.
43 stories; interior corridors. Casino, gift shop, movie theaters. **Rooms:** 424; 26 1- and 22 2-bedroom suites, some with whirlpools. Some shower baths, coffeemakers, movies, some CD players, data ports, dual phone lines, some ⊗. 🔲, roll-in showers. **Recreation:** Pool, whirlpool, exercise rm, massage, game rm. **Services:** Valet parking available, area and airport transportation, business services. **Dining:** Restaurant; 24-hr room service; cocktails.

PARIS LAS VEGAS ⊕ ◆◆◆◆ Large Hotel
(702) 946-7000 *$95-399*
I-15 exit Flamingo Rd E, S on The Strip; 3655 Las Vegas Blvd S.
XP $30; ages 18 and younger, free. Senior discount. Package plans. AX, CB, DC, DS, MC, VI. 33 stories; interior corridors. Casino, gift shop, entertainment. **Rooms:** 2916; 295 1-bedroom suites with whirlpools, $350-5000. Some shower baths, hair dryers, movies, data ports, high-speed Internet access, dual phone lines, voice mail, irons, safes, some ⊗. 🔲, roll-in showers. **Recreation:** Pool, whirlpools, health club, massage. **Services:** Valet parking available, area and airport transportation, laundry, childcare, business services. **Dining:** 8 restaurants, including Eiffel Tower Restaurant, Les Artistes Steakhouse, Mon Ami Gabi and Le Provencal, see separate listings; buffet, $14-29; 24 hrs; 24-hr room service; cocktails

PARK PLAZA LAS VEGAS LADY LUCK CASINO HOTEL ◆◆ Large Hotel
(702) 477-3000 *$45-65*
Downtown; in casino center; 206 N 3rd St.
XP $10; discounts for children. 2-night minimum stay weekends. Cancellation fee. Senior discount. Package plans. AX, DS, MC, VI. 17-25 stories; interior corridors. Casino, gift shop. **Rooms:** 754. Some shower baths, some whirlpools, refrigerators, movies, voice mail, some data ports, some ⊗. 🔲, roll-in showers. **Recreation:** Pool, exercise rm. **Services:** Valet parking available, business services. **Dining:** Restaurant, Burgandy Room, see separate listing; 24-hr room service.

RAMADA INN-SPEEDWAY CASINO ◆◆ Motel
(702) 399-3297 *Property failed to provide current rates*
I-15 exit 46 (Cheyenne Ave), just E; 3227 Civic Center Dr.
Casino. Small pets, $5 extra charge. 3 stories; interior corridors. Sundries shop. **Rooms:** 95. Some shower baths, data ports, voice mail, some ⊗. 🔲, roll-in showers. **Recreation:** Pool. **Services:** Area transportation, laundry. **Dining:** Restaurant, Rookies Bar & Grill, see separate listing; 24 hrs; cocktails.

RESIDENCE INN BY MARRIOTT LAS VEGAS SOUTH ◆◆◆ Motel

(702) 795-7378   *Property failed to provide current rates*
I-15 exit Russell Rd, just SW; 5875 Industrial Rd.
Pets, $150 extra charge. 4 stories; interior corridors. Sundries shop. **Rooms:** 160; 51 1- and 59 2-bedroom suites with kitchens. Some shower baths, hair dryers, some kitchens, coffeemakers, microwaves, refrigerators, movies, data ports, high-speed Internet access, voice mail, irons, some ⊛. ⓑ, roll-in showers. **Recreation:** Pool, whirlpool, exercise rm, sports court. **Services:** Area transportation, laundry, business services.

RESIDENCE INN-HUGHES CENTER ◆◆◆ Motel

(702) 650-0040   *$139-299*
I-15 exit Flamingo Rd E, at Paradise Rd; 370 Hughes Center Dr.
4 pm check-in. Complimentary evening beverages Mon-Thu. Cancellation fee. Senior discount. AX, DC, DS, MC, VI. Pets, $50 fee; $10 extra charge. Sundries shop. 11 stories; interior corridors. **Rooms:** 256; 71 1- and 41 2-bedroom suites with kitchens. Some shower baths, hair dryers, kitchens, coffeemakers, microwaves, refrigerators, movies, data ports, high-speed Internet access, voice mail, irons, some ⊛. ⓑ, roll-in showers. **Recreation:** Pool, whirlpool, exercise rm. **Services:** Laundry. **Dining:** Restaurant nearby.

RESIDENCE INN LAS VEGAS CONVENTION CENTER ◆◆◆ Motel

(702) 796-9300   *$139-349*
Opposite convention center; 3225 Paradise Rd.
Complimentary evening beverages Mon-Thu. 4 pm check-in. Cancellation fee. Senior discount. AX, CB, DC, DS, JC, MC, VI. Small pets, $50 fee; $10 extra charge. 2 stories, no elevator; exterior corridors. Sundries shop. **Rooms:** 192; 48 2-bedroom units with kitchens. Some shower baths, hair dryers, kitchens, coffeemakers, microwaves, refrigerators, movies, video games, data ports, some high-speed Internet access, voice mail, irons, some ⊛. ⓑ, roll-in showers. **Recreation:** Pool, whirlpool, sports court. **Services:** Laundry, business services. **Dining:** Restaurant nearby.

RIO SUITE HOTEL & CASINO ◆◆◆ Large Hotel

(702) 777-7777   *Property failed to provide current rates*
I-15 exit Flamingo Rd, ⅓ mi W; 3700 W Flamingo Rd.
4 pm check-in. 20-41 stories; interior corridors. Casino, gift shop. **Rooms:** 2548; 70 1- and 24 2-bedroom suites with whirlpools. Some shower baths, hair dryers, some coffeemakers, refrigerators, honor bars, movies, video games, data ports, high-speed Internet access, some dual phone lines, voice mail, irons, safes, some ⊛. ⓑ, roll-in showers, ▨. **Recreation:** 3 pools, whirlpools, health club, massage, 18 holes golf, game rm. **Services:** Valet parking available, area transportation, laundry, business services. **Dining:** Restaurants, including All American Bar & Grille and Tilted Kilt, see separate listings; 24-hr room service; cocktails.

RIVIERA HOTEL & CASINO ◆◆◆ Large Hotel

(702) 734-5110   *$59-139*
I-15 exit Sahara Ave E; 2901 Las Vegas Blvd S.
KP $20. 4 pm check-in. 2-night minimum stay weekends. Cancellation fee. AX,

CB, DC, DS, JC, MC, VI. 24 stories; interior corridors. Casino, gift shop. **Rooms**: 2073; 76 1-bedroom suites, some with whirlpools, $150-500. Some shower baths, some hair dryers, some refrigerators, movies, data ports, voice mail, some irons, safes, some ⊛. ⧉, roll-in showers, ⧉. **Recreation:** Pools, health club, massage, 2 lighted tennis courts. **Services:** Valet parking available, laundry, business services. **Dining:** Restaurant, Ristorante Italiano, see separate listing; 24-hr room service; cocktails.

ST. TROPEZ ALL SUITE HOTEL ⓐ
◆◆◆ Small Hotel
(702) 369-5400
$69-189
2 mi S of convention center, at Paradise Rd; 455 E Harmon Ave.
Continental breakfast. Senior discount. AX, CB, DC, DS, MC, VI. Pets, $250 deposit. 2 stories; interior/exterior corridors. **Rooms:** 149. Some shower baths, some whirlpools, hair dryers, coffeemakers, refrigerators, movies, VCRs, data ports, some dual phone lines, voice mail, irons, some ⊛. ⧉, roll-in showers, ⧉. **Recreation:** Pools, whirlpool, exercise rm. **Services:** Area and airport transportation, laundry, business services. **Dining:** Restaurant nearby.

SAM'S TOWN HOTEL & GAMBLING HALL ⓐ
◆◆◆ Large Hotel
(702) 456-7777
$29-225
1 mi E of I-515/SR 93 and 95, exit Flamingo Rd; 5111 Boulder Hwy.
XP $10; ages 16 and younger, free. $5 service charge. Senior discount. AX, CB, DC, DS, MC, VI. 9 stories; interior corridors. Casino, gift shop, movie theaters, entertainment. **Rooms:** 646; 33 1-bedroom suites, some with whirlpools, $119-275. Some shower baths, hair dryers, some refrigerators, movies, data ports, voice mail, irons, some ⊛. ⧉, roll-in showers, ⧉. **Recreation:** Pool, whirlpool, bowling, game rm. **Services:** Valet parking available, area transportation, laundry, business services. **Dining:** 6 restaurants, including Billy Bob's Steak House & Saloon, Fresh Harvest Cafe and Willy & Jose's Cantina, see separate listings; buffet, $6-15; 24 hrs; cocktails.

SANTA FE STATION HOTEL CASINO ⓐ
◆◆ Small Hotel
(702) 658-4900
$39-299
US 95 exit Ann Rd, just E; 4949 N Rancho Dr.
XP $15; ages 13 and younger, free. Senior discount. AX, DC, DS, MC, VI. 5 stories; interior corridors. Casino, gift shop. **Rooms:** 200. Some shower baths, hair dryers, some refrigerators, video games, data ports, voice mail, irons, some ⊛. ⧉, roll-in showers. **Recreation:** Pool, whirlpool, bowling, ice skating. **Services:** Valet parking available, laundry, business services. **Dining:** 3 restaurants, including Charcoal Room, see separate listing; 24 hrs; 24-hr room service.

SILVERTON HOTEL-CASINO
◆◆ Small Hotel
(702) 263-7777
$35-169
I-15 exit 33 (W Blue Diamond Rd), 3333 Blue Diamond Rd.
XP $10; ages 12 and younger, free. 2-night minimum stay in season and on weekends. 3-day cancellation notice, fee. Senior discount. AX, CB, DC, DS, MC, VI. 4 stories; interior corridors. Casino, gift shop. **Rooms:** 300; 14 1-bedroom suites with whirlpools, $200-350. Some shower baths, hair dryers, some coffeemakers, some refrigerators, honor bars, data ports, voice mail, some ⊛. Roll-in

showers, 🖵. **Recreation:** Pool, whirlpool. **Services:** Valet parking available, area transportation, laundry, business services. **Dining:** Restaurants, including Sundance Grill and Twin Creeks, see separate listings; 24-hr room service.

SOMERSET HOUSE MOTEL ⚌ ◆◆ Motel
(702) 735-4411 $35-55
Just E off The Strip; 1 blk W from convention center; 294 Convention Center Dr.
XP $5; ages 9 and younger, free. Senior discount. 3-day cancellation notice; fee. Weekly rates available. AX, CB, DC, MC, VI. 3 stories; interior/exterior corridors. **Rooms:** 104, Hair dryers, some kitchens. some microwaves, refrigerators, movies, data ports, some ⊗. 🖳, roll-in showers. **Recreation:** Pool. **Services:** Laundry, business services. **Dining:** Restaurant nearby.

STRATOSPHERE CASINO HOTEL & TOWER ◆◆◆ Large Hotel
(702) 380-7777 $39-209
Just N of Sahara Ave; 2000 Las Vegas Blvd S.
XP $15; ages 12 and younger, free. Senior discount. Cancellation fee. $5 service charge. AX, CB, DC, DS, JC, MC, VI. 9-24 stories; interior corridors. Casino, gift shop. **Rooms:** 2444; 33 1-bedroom suites, some with whirlpools, $139-450. Some shower baths, some whirlpools, hair dryers, some refrigerators, movies, data ports, voice mail, irons, some ⊗. 🖳, roll-in showers. **Recreation:** Pool, whirlpool, health club, massage. **Services:** Valet parking available, airport transportation, laundry, business services. **Dining:** Restaurants, including Roxy's Diner, see separate listing; 24-hr room service; cocktails.

SUMMER BAY RESORT LAS VEGAS Non-rated Motel (Under renovation)
Formerly Leisure Resorts Las Vegas
(702) 731-6100 $60-200
I-15 exit 38, E to Audrie St, just N; 100 Winnick Ave.
4 pm check-in. 2-night minimum stay. 3-day cancellation notice; fee. MC, VI. 3 stories; interior/exterior corridors. Gift shop. **Rooms:** 489; 100 2-bedroom units. Some shower baths, some whirlpools, hair dryers, coffeemaker, microwave, refrigerators, movies, VCRs, some data ports, voice mail, irons, safes, some ⊗. 🖳, roll-in showers, 🖵. **Recreation:** 7 pools, saunas, whirlpools, exercise rm, golf. **Services:** Area and airport transportation, laundry. **Dining:** Restaurant nearby.

SUNCOAST HOTEL & CASINO ⚌ ◆◆◆ Large Hotel
(702) 636-7111 $89-299
US 95 exit Summerlin Pkwy, to Rampart Blvd; 9090 Alta Dr.
XP $15; ages 16 and younger, free. AX, CB, DC, DS, JC, MC, VI. 2-night minimum stay weekends. 10 stories; interior corridors. Gift shop, movie theaters. **Rooms:** 427; 30 1- and 14 2-bedroom suites, some with whirlpools, $199-1000. Some shower baths, hair dryers, movies, data ports, dual phone lines, voice mail, irons, some ⊗. 🖳, roll-in showers. **Recreation:** Pool, whirlpool, exercise rm, bowling, game rm. **Services:** Valet parking available, area and airport transportation, laundry, childcare, business services. **Dining:** 3 restaurants, including Primo's—A Place for Steaks and Señor Miguel's, see separate listings; buffet, $5-12; 24 hrs; 24-hr room service; cocktails.

SUPER 8 AT NELLIS
◆ Motel

(702) 644-7878 $39-$99

I-15 exit Craig Rd, E 2⁷⁄₁₀ mi E to Las Vegas Blvd, then just N; 4435 Las Vegas Blvd N.

XP $5; ages 17 and younger, free. Senior discount. AX, DS, MC, VI. 2 stories, no elevator; exterior corridors. **Rooms:** 105. Some microwaves, some refrigerators, data ports, some ⊛. **Recreation:** Pool. **Services:** Laundry. **Dining:** Restaurant.

SUPER 8 MOTEL-BOULDER HWY ⏺
◆◆ Motel

(702) 435-8888 $44-108

At Harmon Ave; 5288 Boulder Hwy.

XP $5; ages 12 and younger, free. Cancellation fee. Senior discount. AX, CB, DC, DS, MC, VI. 4 stories; interior corridors. Gift shop. **Rooms:** 150. Movies, data ports, some ⊛. **Recreation:** Pool, whirlpool, exercise rm. **Services:** Laundry. **Dining:** Restaurant; 24 hrs.

SUPER 8 MOTEL LAS VEGAS STRIP
◆◆ Motel

(702) 794-0888 $56-150

I-15 exit Flamingo Rd E, S on Koval Ln; 4250 S Koval Ln.

Cancellation fee. Senior discount. AX, CB, DC, DS, MC, VI. Small pets, $15 extra charge, in selected units. 3 stories; interior corridors. **Rooms:** 288. Movies, data ports, some ⊛. ▣ **Recreation:** Pool, whirlpool. **Services:** Airport transportation, laundry, business services. **Dining:** Restaurant nearby.

TERRIBLE'S HOTEL & CASINO
◆◆ Small Hotel

(702) 733-7000 $39-59

I-15 exit Flamingo Rd, just E; 4100 S Paradise Rd.

XP $10; ages 12 and younger, free. Package plans available. AX, DC, DS, MC, VI. 3 stories; interior corridors. Casino, gift shop. **Rooms:** 371. Some shower baths, hair dryers, coffeemakers, movies, video games, data ports, voice mail, some irons, some ⊛. ⓑ, roll-in showers. **Recreation:** Pool, whirlpool, exercise rm. **Services:** Valet parking available, area and airport transportation, laundry. **Dining:** Restaurant, Bougainvillea Cafe, see separate listing; 24-hr room service.

TEXAS STATION GAMBLING HALL & HOTEL ⏺
◆◆◆ Small Hotel

(702) 631-1000 $59-149

Bus US 95; 3 mi N of downtown; 2101 Texas Star Ln.

XP $15; children stay free. AX, DC, DS, MC, VI. 6 stories; interior corridors. Casino, gift shop, movie theaters. **Rooms:** 200. Some shower baths, hair dryers, some coffeemakers, some refrigerators, movies, data ports, high-speed Internet access, voice mail, irons, safes, some ⊛. ⓑ, roll-in showers. **Recreation:** Pool, game rm, bowling, **Services:** Valet parking available, laundry, business services. **Dining:** 3 restaurants, including Austins, San Lorenzo and Texas Cafe, see separate listings; 24 hrs; buffet, $5-15; 24-hr room service; cocktails.

THEHOTEL AT MANDALAY BAY
◆◆◆◆ Large Hotel

(702) 632-7777 *Property failed to provide current rates*

I-15 NB exit Frank Sinatra Dr, just N; SB exit E Tropicana Ave, ⅓ mi E to Las Vega Blvd, then ⅓ mi S; 3950 Las Vegas Blvd S.

41 stories; interior corridors. Casino, gift shop. **Rooms:** 1117. Hair dryers, some refrigerators, honor bars, movies, DVD players, data ports, high-speed Internet access, dual phone lines, fax, voice mail, irons, safes, some ⊛. ⓑ, roll-in showers. **Recreation:** 5 pools, whirlpool, health club, spa, jogging. **Services:** Valet parking available, airport transportation, laundry, business services. **Dining:** Restaurant; 24-hr room service; cocktails.

TRAVELODGE LAS VEGAS STRIP

◆ Motel

(702) 735-4222

$49-150

I-15 exit Sahara Ave E; 2830 Las Vegas Blvd S.

3-day cancellation notice; service charge. Senior discount. AX, CB, DC, DS, JC, MC, VI. 2 stories; no elevator; exterior corridors. **Rooms:** 100. Some shower baths, hair dryers, coffeemakers, some refrigerators, movies, data ports, safes, some ⊛. **Recreation:** Pool. **Dining:** Restaurant nearby.

TREASURE ISLAND ⒶⒶⒶ

◆◆◆◆ Large Hotel

(702) 894-7444

$79-399

3½ mi S on The Strip; 3300 Las Vegas Blvd S.

XP $30. Cancellation fee. AX, CB, DC, DS, JC, MC, VI. 36 stories; interior corridors. Casino, gift shop, entertainment. **Rooms:** 2885; 20 1-bedroom suites with whirlpools, $129-1200. Some shower baths, some whirlpools, hair dryers, some refrigerators, movies, some VCRs, data ports, high-speed Internet access, voice mail, irons, safes, some ⊛. ⓑ, roll-in showers, ☒. **Recreation:** Pool, whirlpool, health club, massage, game rm. **Services:** Valet parking available, area transportation, laundry, business services. **Dining:** 8 restaurants, including Buccaneer Bay and Francesco's, see separate listings; buffet, $8-17; 24 hrs; 24-hr room service; cocktails.

TUSCANY HOTEL & CASINO

◆◆◆ Large Hotel

(702) 893-8933

$79-199

I-15 exit Flamingo Rd E, ½ mi; 255 E Flamingo Rd.

XP $20; ages 12 and younger, free. 3-day cancellation notice. Senior discount. AX, DS, MC, VI. Casino, gift shop. 3 stories; interior corridors. **Rooms:** 716; 4 2-bedroom suites. Hair dryers, some efficiencies (no utensils), coffeemakers, microwaves, some refrigerators, video games, data ports, voice mail, irons, safes, some ⊛. ⓑ, roll-in showers. **Recreation:** 2 pools, whirlpool, exercise rm. **Services:** Valet parking available, laundry, business services. **Dining:** Marilyn's Cafe and Steakhouse at Tuscany, see separate listings.

THE VENETIAN RESORT HOTEL CASINO

◆◆◆◆ Large Hotel

(702) 414-1000

$169-3500

On The Strip; 3355 Las Vegas Blvd S.

XP $35; ages 12 and younger, free. 3-day cancellation notice; cancellation fee. Package plans. AX, DC, DS, JC, MC, VI. 23-36 stories; interior corridors. Casino, gift shop. **Rooms:** 4027; 382 1- and 18 2-bedroom suites with whirlpools. Some shower baths, hair dryers, honor bars, movies, some CD players, data ports, high-speed Internet access, dual phone lines, fax, voice mail, irons, safes, some ⊛. ⓑ, roll-in showers. **Recreation:** 5 pools, whirlpools, health club, massage. **Services:** Valet parking available, airport transportation, laundry, business services. **Dining:**

Restaurants, including Bouchon at the Venetian, Delmonico Steakhouse, Lutece and Valentino Las Vegas, see separate listings; 24-hr room service; cocktails.

VILLA ROMA INN AT CONVENTION CENTER ⨁ ◆◆ Motel
(702) 735-4151 $35-209
Just E off the Strip; just W of convention center; 220 Convention Center Dr.
XP $10; ages 10 and younger, free. 2-night minimum stay weekends. Senior discount. AX, CB, DC, MC, VI. 2-3 stories; interior corridors. **Rooms:** 101. Some shower baths, hair dryers, movies, data ports, voice mail, irons, some ⊛. 🅐, roll-in showers. **Recreation:** Pool. **Services:** Business services. **Dining:** Restaurant nearby.

WELLESLY INN & SUITES (LAS VEGAS/EAST FLAMINGO) ⨁ ◆◆◆ Motel
(702) 731-3111 $99-149
I-15 exit Flamingo Rd, 2 mi E; 1550 E Flamingo Rd.
XP $10; ages 18 and younger, free. Cancellation fee. Senior discount. Weekly rates available. AX, CB, DC, DS, JC, MC, VI. Pets. 3 stories; interior corridors. **Rooms:** 125; 3 1-bedroom suites with efficiencies, $99-209. Some shower baths, hair dryers, efficiencies, coffeemakers, microwaves, refrigerators, movies, video games, data ports, voice mail, irons, safes, some ⊛. 🅐, roll-in showers, 🔳. **Recreation:** Pool, exercise rm. **Services:** Area and airport transportation, laundry, business services. **Dining:** Restaurant nearby.

WESTGATE FLAMINGO BAY ⨁ ◆◆◆ Condominium
(702) 251-3435 $89-219
I-15 exit Flamingo Rd W, just E of Jones Blvd; 5625 W Flamingo Rd.
7-day cancellation notice; fee. Senior discount. AX, DC, DS, MC, VI. 2 stories, no elevator; exterior corridors. **Rooms:** 208; 96 2-bedroom suites with kitchens and whirlpools. Hair dryers, coffeemakers, microwaves, refrigerators, VCRs, DVD players, data ports, voice mail, irons, safes, ⊛. 🅐, roll-in showers. **Recreation:** Pool, whirlpool, exercise rm, basketball, shuffleboard. **Services:** Laundry, business services.

THE WESTIN CASUARINA LAS VEGAS HOTEL & SPA ⨁ ◆◆◆ Hotel
(702) 836-9775 $139-299
I-15 exit Flamingo Rd E; 160 E Flamingo Rd.
XP $20; ages 17 and younger, free. 3-day cancellation notice; fee. Senior discount. AX, DC, DS, JC, MC, VI. Pets. 17 stories; interior corridors. Casino, gift shop, entertainment. **Rooms:** 825; 10 1-bedroom suites. Some shower baths, hair dryers, coffeemakers, honor bars, movies, data ports, high-speed Internet access, dual phone lines, voice mail, irons, safes, some ⊛. 🅐, roll-in showers. **Recreation:** Pool, whirlpool, health club, spa. **Services:** Valet parking available, laundry, business services. **Dining:** Restaurant; 24 hrs; 24-hr room service; cocktails.

Restaurants

AL DENTE ◆◆◆ Italian
(702) 967-7999 Dinner $14-36
On The Strip; at Bally's Las Vegas, 3645 Las Vegas Blvd S.
AX, CB, MC, VI. Open Fri-Tue 5:30-11 pm. Closed Wed-Thu. Dressy casual attire. ⊛ Cocktails. **Reservations:** Suggested. **Services:** Valet parking available.

ALL AMERICAN BAR & GRILLE
◆◆ Steakhouse
(702) 252-7777
Lunch $8-19, dinner $20-60
I-15 exit Flamingo Rd, ⅓ mi W; at Rio Suite Hotel & Casino, 3700 W Flamingo Rd.
AX, DC, DS, MC, VI. Open daily 11 am-11 pm, Fri-Sat to 1 am. Casual attire. ⊛
Cocktails. **Reservations:** Accepted. **Services:** Valet parking available. **Menu:**
Burgers, steaks and chops.

AMERICA
◆◆ American
(702) 740-6451
Lunch and dinner $8-23
*I-15 exit Tropicana Ave, just E; at New York-New York Hotel & Casino, 3790 Las
Vegas Blvd S.*
AX, CB, DC, DS, JC, MC, VI. Open 24 hrs. ⧉ Casual attire. ⊛ Cocktails.
Reservations: Accepted. **Services:** Valet parking available. **Menu:** Home-style
dishes.

ANDIAMO
◆◆◆ Regional Italian
(702) 732-5755
Dinner $31-70
*I-15 exit Sahara Ave, 2 mi E; adj to convention center; at Las Vegas Hilton, 3000
Paradise Rd.*
AX, CB, DC, DS, JC, MC, VI. Open daily 5-11 pm. Dressy casual attire. ⊛
Cocktails. **Reservations:** Suggested. **Services:** Valet parking available.

ANDRE'S FRENCH RESTAURANT
◆◆◆◆ French
(702) 385-5016
Dinner $22-36
At Lewis Ave, 401 S 6th St.
AX, CB, DC, MC, VI. Open Mon-Sat 6-11 pm. Closed Sun, major holidays and
Jul. ⧉ Dressy casual attire. ⊛ Cocktails. Entertainment. **Reservations:** Suggested.

A TASTE OF INDONESIA
◆◆ Indonesian
(702) 365-0888
Lunch and dinner $7-15
*I-15 exit Spring Mountain Rd 2½ mi W; between Decatur and Jones blvds; 5700 W
Spring Mountain Rd.*
DS, MC, VI. Open Mon-Sat 11 am-10 pm. Closed Sun. Casual attire. ⊛ Beer &
wine. **Reservations:** Accepted. **Menu:** Cuisine from across Indonesia.

AUREOLE
◆◆◆◆ American
(702) 632-7401
Dinner $69
*I-15 exit Tropicana Ave, just E; at Mandalay Bay Resort & Casino, 3950 Las Vegas
Blvd S.*
AX, CB, DC, MC, VI. Open daily 6-11 pm. Semiformal attire. ⊛ Cocktails.
Reservations: Required. **Services:** Valet parking available. **Menu:** Classic dishes
prepared by Chef Charlie Palmer.

AUSTINS
◆◆◆ Steakhouse
(702) 631-1033
Dinner $23-37
*Bus US 95; 3 mi N of downtown; at Texas Station Gambling Hall & Hotel, 2101
Texas Star Ln.*
AX, DC, DS, MC, VI. Open daily 5-10 pm, Fri-Sat to 11 pm. Dressy casual attire.
⊛ Cocktails. **Reservations:** Suggested. **Services:** Valet parking available.

BATTISTA'S HOLE IN THE WALL
♦♦ Italian

(702) 732-1424
Dinner $18-36

I-15 exit Flamingo Rd, ⅓ mi E, 1 blk E of The Strip, 4041 Audrie St.

AX, CB, DC, DS, MC, VI. Open daily 5-10:30 pm, Fri-Sat to 11 pm. Closed Thanksgiving, 12/24-25. Casual attire. ⊛ Cocktails. **Reservations:** Suggested. **Menu:** Dinners include house wine and cappuccino.

BIG MAMA'S RIB SHACK
♦ Barbecue

(702) 597-1616
Lunch $5-10, dinner $5-12

Near Rancho Dr; 2230 W Bonanza Rd.

Open Mon-Sat 10 am-9 pm, Fri-Sat to 10 pm, Sun noon-8 pm. Closed major holidays. Casual attire. ⊛ **Menu:** Daily specials and good-sized portions.

BILLY BOB'S STEAK HOUSE & SALOON
♦♦ Steakhouse

(702) 454-8031
Dinner $15-46

1 mi E of I-515/SR 93 and 95, exit Flamingo Rd; at Sam's Town Hotel & Gambling Hall, 5111 Boulder Hwy.

AX, DC, MC, VI. Open daily 5-10 pm. Fri-Sat to 11 pm. Casual attire. ⊛ Cocktails. **Reservations:** Suggested. **Services:** Valet parking available. **Menu:** Large portions of steak, seafood and chicken.

BLACKJACK LODGE
♦♦ American

(702) 876-0551
Lunch $5-10, dinner $5-17

I-215 exit Rainbow Blvd N; 6200 S Rainbow Blvd.

AX, MC, VI. Open 24 hrs. Casual attire. ⊛ Cocktails. **Menu:** Angus beef; sauces and dressings made in-house. Fish and chips is a popular entree.

BLACKSTONE'S
♦♦♦ Steakhouse

(702) 730-7777
Dinner $16-41

On The Strip between Flamingo Rd and Tropicana Ave; at Monte Carlo Resort & Casino, 3770 Las Vegas Blvd S.

AX, CB, DC, DS, MC, VI. Open daily 5-11 pm. Dressy casual attire. ⊛ Cocktails. **Reservations:** Suggested. **Services:** Valet parking available.

BLUE IGUANA
♦♦ Mexican

(702) 734-0410
Dinner $8-16

On The Strip; at Circus Circus Hotel, Casino & Themepark, 2880 Las Vegas Blvd S.

AX, CB, DC, DS, MC, VI. Open Fri-Tue 5-10 pm, Sat to 11:30 pm. Closed Wed-Thu. Casual attire. ⊛ Cocktails. **Services:** Valet parking available.

BOOTLEG BENNY'S
♦ American

(702) 450-4705
Lunch and dinner $8-15

Between Flamingo Rd and Tropicana Ave; 4705 S Durango Dr.

AX, MC, VI. Open 24 hrs. Casual attire. ⊛ Cocktails.

BORDER GRILL
♦♦♦ Mexican

(702) 632-7403
Lunch $11-18, dinner $16-31

I-15 exit Tropicana Ave, just E; at Mandalay Bay Resort & Casino, 3950 Las Vegas Blvd S.

AX, CB, DC, DS, MC, VI. Open daily 11:30 am-11 pm. Closed 12/25. Casual attire. Indoor and patio seating available. ⊛ Cocktails. **Reservations:** Suggested. **Services:** Valet parking available. **Menu:** Authentic Mexican cuisine.

BOUCHON AT THE VENETIAN
◆◆◆ French

(702) 414-6200   *Dinner $17-30*
On The Strip; at The Venetian Resort Hotel Casino, 3355 Las Vegas Blvd S.
AX, MC, VI. Open daily 6:30-10:30 am and 3-10:30 pm. Dressy casual attire. Patio seating available. ⊛ Cocktails. **Reservations:** Suggested. **Services:** Valet parking available. **Menu:** Chef Thomas Keller offers classic bistro dishes, items from the oyster bar and selections from a varied wine list.

BOUGAINVILLEA CAFE
◆ American

(702) 733-7000   *Lunch $6-10, dinner $8-15*
I-15 exit Flamingo Rd, just E; at Terrible's Hotel & Casino, 4100 S Paradise Rd.
AX, CB, DC, DS, JC, MC, VI. Open 24 hrs. Casual attire. ⊛ Cocktails. **Menu:** Varied menu and large portions.

BRADLEY OGDEN
◆◆◆ Continental

(702) 731-7731   *Dinner $39-54*
I-15 exit Flamingo Rd E; on The Strip; at Caesars Palace, 3570 Las Vegas Blvd S.
AX, CB, DC, DS, JC, MC, VI. Open daily 5:30-11 pm. Dressy casual attire. ⊛ Cocktails. **Reservations:** Suggested. **Services:** Valet parking available. **Menu:** "Farm-fresh" foods.

BRENDAN'S IRISH PUB
◆ Irish

(702) 365-7111   *Lunch and dinner $5-8*
I-15 exit Tropicana Ave, 1 mi W; at The Orleans, 4500 W Tropicana Ave.
AX, CB, DC, DS, JC, MC, VI. Open daily 11 am-midnight. Casual attire. ⊛ Cocktails. **Services:** Valet parking available. **Menu:** Limited menu but a good selection of beverages.

THE BROILER
◆◆ Steak & Seafood

(702) 367-2408   *Lunch $7-16, dinner $14-26*
I-15 exit Sahara Ave W; SW corner of Sahara Ave and Rancho Dr; at Palace Station Hotel & Casino, 2411 W Sahara Ave.
AX, MC, VI. Open daily 11 am-11 pm, Sat-Sun from noon. Casual attire. ⊛ Cocktails. **Reservations:** Accepted. **Services:** Valet parking available. **Menu:** The lunch menu emphasizes seafood; juicy steaks dominate the dinner menu.

BUCCANEER BAY
◆◆◆ Continental

(702) 894-7350   *Dinner $19-37*
3½ mi S on The Strip; at Treasure Island, 3300 Las Vegas Blvd S.
AX, CB, DC, DS, MC, VI. Open daily 5-11 pm. Dressy casual attire. ⊛ Cocktails. **Reservations:** Suggested. **Services:** Valet parking available. **Menu:** Contemporary continental gourmet cuisine.

BURGANDY ROOM ⊛
◆◆◆ American

(702) 477-3000   *Dinner $16-55*
Downtown in casino center; at Park Plaza Lady Luck Casino Hotel, 206 N 3rd St.
AX, DC, DS, MC, VI. Open daily 5-10 pm. Dressy casual attire. ⊛ Cocktails. **Reservations:** Suggested. **Services:** Valet parking available.

THE CAFE
♦♦ American

(702) 730-7777 — *Lunch and dinner $8-18*

On The Strip between Flamingo Rd and Tropicana Ave; at Monte Carlo Resort & Casino, 3770 Las Vegas Blvd S.

AX, CB, DC, DS, JC, MC, VI. Open 24 hrs. Casual attire. ⊗ Cocktails. **Services:** Valet parking available. **Menu:** Wide selection of well-made dishes.

CAFE LAGO
♦♦ American

(702) 731-7110 — *Lunch and dinner $9-29*

I-15 exit Flamingo Rd E; on The Strip; at Caesars Palace, 3570 Las Vegas Blvd S.

AX, CB, DC, DS, JC, MC, VI. Open 24 hrs. Casual attire. ⊗ Cocktails. **Services:** Valet parking available. **Menu:** Wide-ranging menu and buffet.

CARLUCCIO'S TIVOLI GARDENS
♦♦ Italian

(702) 795-3236 — *Dinner $10-14*

2½ mi E of Las Vegas Blvd S; at Spencer St, in Liberace Plaza, 1775 E Tropicana Ave.

AX, DS, MC, VI. Open Tue-Sun 4:30-10 pm. Closed Mon and major holidays. Casual attire. ⊗ Cocktails. **Menu:** Extensive menu of traditional Italian dishes.

CHARCOAL ROOM
♦♦ Steakhouse

(702) 515-4385 — *Dinner $22-68*

US 95 exit Ann Rd, just E; at Santa Fe Station Hotel Casino, 4949 N Rancho Dr.

AX, DC, DS, MC, VI. Open daily 5-9 pm, Fri-Sat to 10 pm. Dressy casual attire. ⊗ Cocktails. **Reservations:** Suggested. **Services:** Valet parking available. **Menu:** Beef, chicken and fish dishes.

CHARLIE PALMER STEAK
♦♦♦ Steakhouse

(702) 632-5120 — *Dinner $21-40*

I-15 exit Tropicana Ave E, S on The Strip; at Four Seasons Hotel Las Vegas, 3960 Las Vegas Blvd S.

AX, MC, VI. Open daily 5-10 pm. Closed 12/25. Dressy casual attire. ⊗ Cocktails. **Reservations:** Suggested. **Services:** Valet parking available. **Menu:** Great steaks plus fine appetizers, salads, desserts and a good selection of wine.

CHINA QUEEN
♦ Chinese

(702) 873-3288 — *Lunch $5-12, dinner $7-12*

I-15 exit Tropicana Ave W, just N on Rainbow Blvd; 4825 S Rainbow Blvd.

MC, VI. Open daily to 10 pm, Mon-Fri from 11 am, Sat-Sun from noon. Casual attire. ⊗

CHUCK WAGON
♦ American

(702) 435-9170 — *Lunch and dinner $5-14*

At Harmon Ave, adj to Super 8; 5288 Boulder Hwy.

MC, VI. Open 24 hrs. Casual attire. ⊗ Cocktails. **Menu:** Meals are filling.

COFFEE PUB
♦ California

(702) 367-1913 — *Lunch $7-10*

I-15 exit Sahara Ave, W ⅓ mi; 2800 W Sahara Ave.

AX, MC, VI. Open daily 6 am-2 pm. Casual attire. ⊗ Beer & wine. **Menu:** Breakfast and lunch choices may be accompanied by any of several hot and cold coffee specialty drinks.

CONRAD'S
◆◆◆ French

(702) 733-3502
Dinner $19-35

I-15 exit Flamingo Rd E, N on The Strip; at Flamingo Las Vegas, 3555 Las Vegas Blvd S.
AX, CB, DC, DS, MC, VI. Open daily 5:30-10:30 pm. Dressy casual attire. ⊛ Cocktails. **Reservations:** Suggested. **Services:** Valet parking available. **Menu:** French entrees and imaginative deserts.

CORAL CAFE
◆◆ American

(702) 733-7777
Lunch $4-7, dinner $5-14

I-15 exit 38 at Flamingo Rd, E 4 blks; at Key Largo Casino & Hotel at the Quality Inn, 377 E Flamingo Rd.
AX, CB, DC, DS, MC, VI. Open 24 hrs. Casual attire. ⊛ Cocktails. **Menu:** A popular menu offers lots of meal options.

COURTYARD CAFE
◆◆ American

(702) 365-7111
Lunch and dinner $5-22

I-15 exit Tropicana Ave, 1 mi W; at The Orleans, 4500 W Tropicana Ave.
AX, DC, DS, MC, VI. Open 24 hrs. Casual attire. ⊛ Cocktails. **Services:** Valet parking available. **Menu:** A wide and varied menu is augmented by a separate offering of Chinese food.

CRAFTSTEAK
◆◆◆ Steakhouse

(702) 891-7318
Dinner $24-42

I-15 exit Tropicana Ave, just E; at MGM Grand Hotel & Casino, 3799 Las Vegas Blvd S.
AX, CB, DC, DS, JC, MC, VI. Open daily 5:30-10:30 pm. Dressy casual attire. ⊛ Cocktails. **Reservations:** Suggested. **Services:** Valet parking available. **Menu:** Cooking emphasizes natural, pure ingredients. Signature dishes include porterhouse for two, beef short ribs and sea scallops.

DELMONICO STEAKHOUSE
◆◆◆ Steakhouse

(702) 414-3737
Lunch $14-44, dinner $27-44

On The Strip; at The Venetian Resort Hotel Casino, 3355 Las Vegas Blvd S.
AX, CB, DC, DS, MC, VI. Open daily 11:30 am-2 & 5:30-10:30 pm, Fri-Sun to 11 pm. Dressy casual attire. ⊛ Cocktails. Entertainment. **Reservations:** Required. **Services:** Valet parking available. **Menu:** Owner Chef Emeril Lagasse adds his influence to this American steakhouse.

DON MIGUEL'S
◆◆ Mexican

(702) 365-7111
Lunch $7-10, dinner $8-15

I-15 exit Tropicana Ave, 1 mi W; at The Orleans, 4500 W Tropicana Ave.
AX, DC, DS, MC, VI. Open daily 11 am-11 pm. Casual attire. ⊛ Cocktails. **Services:** Valet parking available. **Menu:** Traditional Mexican dishes.

EIFFEL TOWER RESTAURANT
◆◆◆◆ French

(702) 948-6937
Dinner $26-50

I-15 exit Flamingo Rd E, S on The Strip; at Paris Las Vegas, 3655 Las Vegas Blvd S.
AX, CB, DC, DS, MC, VI. Open daily 5:30-10 pm, Fri-Sat to 10:30 pm. Dressy casual attire. ⊛ Cocktails. Entertainment. **Reservations:** Suggested. **Services:** Valet parking available. **Menu:** Authentic gourmet French cuisine.

EMERIL'S NEW ORLEANS FISH HOUSE
◆◆◆ Creole

(702) 891-7374   *Lunch $14-26, dinner $20-37*

I-15 exit Tropicana Ave, just E; at MGM Grand Hotel & Casino, 3799 Las Vegas Blvd S.
AX, CB, DC, DS, MC, VI. Open daily 11 am-2:30 & 5:30-10:30 pm. Dressy casual attire. ⊛ Cocktails. **Reservations:** Suggested. **Services:** Valet parking available. **Menu:** Wide selection of Creole and Cajun dishes. Well-stocked wine selections.

EMPRESS COURT
◆◆◆ Chinese

(702) 731-7110   *Dinner $16-65*

I-15 exit Flamingo Rd E; on The Strip; at Caesars Palace, 3570 Las Vegas Blvd S.
AX, CB, DC, DS, MC, VI. Open Thu-Mon 6-10:30 pm. Closed Tue & Wed. Dressy casual attire. ⊛ Cocktails. **Reservations:** Suggested. **Menu:** Chinese delicacies.

FELLINI'S ITALIAN DINING
◆◆◆ Italian

(702) 870-9999   *Dinner $12-30*

4 mi W of The Strip; 5555 W Charleston Blvd.
AX, CB, DC, DS, MC, VI. Open daily 5-10 pm, Sat to 11 pm. Closed major holidays. Dressy casual attire. ⊛ Cocktails. Entertainment. **Reservations:** Suggested. **Menu:** Wide selection of Italian specialties and desserts.

FOWL PLAY
◆◆ American

(702) 655-4881   *Lunch $5-10, dinner $5-15*

I-15 exit Tropicana Ave W 6½ mi, then S; 5325 Fort Apache Rd.
AX, MC, VI. Open 24 hrs. Casual attire. ⊛ Cocktails.

FRANCESCO'S
◆◆◆ Italian

(702) 894-7348   *Dinner $25-75*

3½ mi S on The Strip; at Treasure Island, 3300 Las Vegas Blvd S.
AX, DC, MC, VI. Open daily 5-10:30 pm. Dressy casual attire. ⊛ Cocktails. **Reservations:** Suggested. **Services:** Valet parking available. **Menu:** Contemporary Italian cuisine prepared in an exhibition kitchen.

FRESH HARVEST CAFE
◆◆ American

(702) 456-7777   *Lunch and dinner $6-13*

1 mi E of I-515/SR 93 and 95, exit Flamingo Rd; at Sam's Town Hotel & Gambling Hall, 5111 Boulder Hwy.
AX, DC, MC, VI. Open 24 hrs, but Tue to 11 pm. Casual attire. ⊛ Cocktails. **Services:** Valet parking available. **Menu:** Breakfast and lunch offerings include a buffet in addition to an extensive menu.

GANDHI INDIA'S CUISINE ⓐⓐⓐ
◆◆ Indian

(702) 734-0094   *Lunch $9-11, dinner $13-23*

½ mi E of The Strip, just S of Flamingo Rd; 4080 Paradise Rd.
AX, DC, DS, MC, VI. Open daily 11 am-2:30 and 5-10:30 pm. Casual attire. ⊛ Cocktails. **Reservations:** Suggested. **Menu:** Flavorful dishes representing northern and southern India. Daily lunch buffet.

GARDEN ROOM
◆◆ American

(702) 369-5000   *Lunch and dinner $7-16*

I-15 exit E Flamingo Rd; at Harrah's Las Vegas Casino & Hotel, 3475 Las Vegas Blvd S.

AX, CB, DC, DS, JC, MC, VI. Open 24 hrs. Casual attire. ⊛ Cocktails. **Services:** Valet parking available.

GARDUNO'S OF MEXICO   ◆◆ Mexican
(702) 631-7000   *Lunch $7-15, dinner $8-20*
3 mi NW of downtown; at Fiesta Casino Hotel, 2400 N Rancho Dr.
AX, CB, DC, DS, MC, VI. Open daily 11 am-11 pm. Casual attire. ⊛ Cocktails. **Reservations:** Accepted. **Menu:** Order from the menu or go to the buffet.

GOLDEN STEER   ◆◆ Steakhouse
(702) 384-4470   *Dinner $23-60*
I-15 exit Sahara Ave E ⅓ mi; 1 blk W of The Strip, 308 W Sahara Ave.
AX, CB, DC, MC, VI. Open daily 5 pm-midnight. Closed 12/25. Dressy casual attire. ⊛ Cocktails. **Reservations:** Suggested. **Menu:** Italian specialties plus chicken, veal and seafood entrees.

GRAPE STREET CAFE   ◆◆◆ American
(702) 228-9463   *Lunch $7-10, dinner $10-26*
US 95 exit W Lake Mead Blvd, ½ mi W; 7501 W Lake Mead Blvd.
AX, MC, VI. Open Tue-Sat 11 am-10 pm, Fri-Sat to 11 pm. Closed Sun-Mon and major holidays. Dressy casual attire. Patio seating available. ⊛ Cocktails. **Reservations:** Suggested. **Menu:** An extensive wine list complements meal options.

GUADALAJARA BAR & GRILLE   ◆◆ Mexican
(702) 432-7777   *Lunch and dinner $6-15*
Just S of Sahara Ave; at Boulder Station Hotel Casino, 4111 Boulder Hwy.
AX, MC, VI. Open daily 11 am-10 pm, Fri-Sat to 11 pm. Casual attire. ⊛ Cocktails. **Reservations:** Accepted. **Services:** Valet parking available. **Menu:** Traditionally flavored dishes, salsa bar.

HILTON STEAKHOUSE   ◆◆◆ Steakhouse
(702) 732-5755   *Dinner $21-50*
I-15 exit Sahara Ave, 2 mi E; adj to convention center; at Las Vegas Hilton, 3000 Paradise Rd.
AX, CB, DC, DS, MC, VI. Open daily 5:30-11:30 pm. Dressy casual attire. ⊛ Cocktails. **Reservations:** Suggested. **Services:** Valet parking available. **Menu:** Mesquite-broiled steaks.

JOEY BISTRO & BAR   ◆◆◆ Italian
(702) 369-5639   *Lunch $5-10, dinner $9-18*
Just E off The Strip; at the Carriage House, 105 E Harmon Ave.
AX, MC, VI. Open daily 7 am-11 pm. Dressy casual attire. ⊛ Cocktails. **Reservations:** Suggested.

KOJI SUSHI BAR & CHINA BISTRO
♦♦ Asian

(702) 365-7111
Lunch and dinner $6-18

I-15 exit Tropicana Ave, 1 mi W; at The Orleans, 4500 W Tropicana Ave.
AX, CB, DC, DS, JC, MC, VI. Open daily 11 am-1 am, Sun from 2 pm. Casual attire. ⊛ Cocktails. **Reservations:** Accepted. **Services:** Valet parking available. **Menu:** Two menus list equally flavorful entrees.

KOKOMOS
♦♦♦ Steak & Seafood

(702) 791-7111
Dinner $17-50

I-15 exit Spring Mountain Rd, E to The Strip; at The Mirage, 3400 Las Vegas Blvd S.
AX, CB, DC, DS, MC, VI. Open daily 5-10:30 pm. Dressy casual attire. ⊛ Cocktails. **Reservations:** Suggested. **Services:** Valet parking available. **Menu:** Prime steaks, fresh seafood, lobster and chops.

LA SCALA ⓐⓐⓐ
♦♦♦ Italian

(702) 699-9980
Lunch $10-21, dinner $12-30

2 mi E of the Strip, in Mark I Tower; 1020 E Desert Inn Rd.
AX, DC, DS, MC, VI. Open Mon-Fri 11:30 am-2 and 5-10 pm, Sat-Sun 5-10 pm. Closed major holidays. Dressy casual attire. ⊛ Cocktails. **Reservations:** Suggested.

LAWRY'S THE PRIME RIB
♦♦♦ American

(702) 893-2223
Dinner $24-40

1 mi E of The Strip, just off Flamingo Rd; 4043 Howard Hughes Pkwy.
AX, CB, DC, DS, MC, VI. Open daily at 5 pm, Sun-Fri to 10 pm, Sat to 11 pm. Closed 12/25. Dressy casual attire. ⊛ Cocktails. **Reservations:** Suggested. **Services:** Valet parking. **Menu:** Roasted prime ribs of beef carved tableside.

LE CIRQUE
♦♦♦♦♦ French

(702) 693-8100
Dinner $85-95

I-15 exit E Flamingo Rd, on The Strip; at Bellagio, 3600 Las Vegas Blvd S.
AX, DC, DS, MC, VI. Open daily 5:30-10:30 pm. Semi-formal attire. ⊛ Cocktails. **Reservations:** Required. **Services:** Valet parking available. **Menu:** Classic French dishes.

LE PROVENCAL
♦♦♦ French

(702) 946-4656
Lunch and dinner $10-22

I-15 exit Flamingo Rd E, S on The Strip; at Paris Las Vegas, 3655 Las Vegas Blvd S.
AX, CB, DC, DS, JC, MC, VI. Open daily 11:30 am-10:30 pm. Dressy casual attire. ⊛ Cocktails. **Reservations:** Suggested. **Services:** Valet parking available. **Menu:** French and Italian dishes.

LES ARTISTES STEAKHOUSE
♦♦♦ French

(702) 967-7999
Dinner $20-36

I-15 exit Flamingo Rd E, S on The Strip; at Paris Las Vegas, 3655 Las Vegas Blvd S.
AX, CB, DC, DS, MC, VI. Open daily 5:30-11 pm. Dressy casual attire. ⊛ Cocktails. **Reservations:** Suggested. **Services:** Valet parking available. **Menu:** Slow-roasted fresh meats, poultry and fish are prepared in an open kitchen.

LILLIE LANGTRY'S ◆◆◆ Chinese
(702) 385-7111 *Dinner $13-50*
Downtown, casino center area; at The Golden Nugget, 129 E Fremont St.
AX, CB, DC, DS, MC, VI. Open Tue-Sat 5-10:30 pm. Closed Sun-Mon. Dressy casual attire. ⊛ Cocktails. **Reservations:** Suggested. **Services:** Valet parking available. **Menu:** Traditional Szechwan and Cantonese cuisine, and mesquite-broiled prime steaks.

LUTECE ◆◆◆ French
(702) 414-2220 *Dinner $28-46*
On The Strip; at The Venetian Resort Hotel Casino, 3355 Las Vegas Blvd S.
AX, CB, DC, DS, MC, VI. Open daily 5:30-10:30 pm. Dressy casual attire. ⊛ Cocktails. **Reservations:** Suggested. **Services:** Valet parking available. **Menu:** Modern French cuisine with classic influences.

LUXOR STEAK HOUSE ◆◆◆ Steakhouse
(702) 262-4778 *Dinner $25-52*
I-15 exit Tropicana Ave E, just S on The Strip; exit Russell Rd NB, E to The Strip, then just N; at Luxor Las Vegas, 3900 Las Vegas Blvd S.
AX, CB, DC, DS, JC, MC, VI. Open daily 5-11 pm. Dressy casual attire. ⊛ Cocktails. **Reservations:** Suggested. **Services:** Valet parking available. **Menu:** Steaks, seafood and chicken entrees.

MARILYN'S CAFE ◆◆ American
(702) 893-8933 *Lunch and dinner $5-13*
I-15 exit Flamingo Rd E, ½ mi; at Tuscany Hotel & Casino, 255 E Flamingo Rd.
AX, MC, VI. Open 24 hrs. Casual attire. ⊛ Cocktails. **Services:** Valet parking available.

McMULLAN'S IRISH PUB ◆◆ Irish
(702) 247-7000 *Lunch $6-15, dinner $8-16*
I-15 exit Tropicana Ave, 1¼ mi W; 4650 W Tropicana Ave.
AX, DC, DS, MC, VI. Open 24 hrs. Casual attire. ⊛ Cocktails. **Reservations:** Accepted.

MICHAELS ◆◆◆◆ Continental
(702) 737-7111 *Dinner $45-80*
On The Strip; at Barbary Coast Hotel, 3595 Las Vegas Blvd S.
AX, DC, DS, JC, MC, VI. Open daily 6-10 pm. Semi-formal attire. Cocktails. **Reservations:** Suggested. **Services:** Valet parking available.

MOLLY MALONE'S IRISH PUB ◆◆ American
(702) 837-0213 *Lunch $7-9, dinner $8-15*
I-15 exit 33 (Blue Diamond Rd) W to Decatur Blvd, then S; 11930 S Highlands Pkwy.
AX, DS, MC, VI. Open 24 hrs. Casual attire. ⊛ Cocktails. **Menu:** Plenty of choices of tasty, well-made fare.

MON AMI GABI
♦♦♦ French

(702) 944-4224 · *Lunch $10-29, dinner $20-29*
I-15 exit Flamingo Rd E, S on The Strip; at Paris Las Vegas, 3655 Las Vegas Blvd S.
AX, CB, DC, DS, MC, VI. Open daily 11:30 am-3:30 and 5-11 pm. Casual attire. Patio seating available. ⊗ Cocktails. **Reservations:** Suggested. **Services:** Valet parking available.

MONTEREY ROOM
♦♦ American

(702) 367-7111 · *Lunch $6-9, dinner $6-26*
I-15 exit Flamingo Rd W, just W; at Gold Coast Hotel, 4000 W Flamingo Rd.
AX, CB, DC, DS, JC, MC, VI. Open 24 hrs. Casual attire. ⊗ Cocktails. **Services:** Valet parking available. **Menu:** Chinese and American food menus.

NEROS
♦♦♦ Steak & Seafood

(702) 731-7110 · *Dinner $26-49*
I-15 exit Flamingo Rd E; on The Strip; at Caesars Palace, 3570 Las Vegas Blvd S.
AX, CB, DC, DS, MC, VI. Open daily 5:30-10:30 pm, Fri-Sat to 11 pm. Dressy casual attire. ⊗ Cocktails. **Reservations:** Suggested. **Services:** Valet parking available. **Menu:** Excellent choices of steak and seafood entrees.

NINE FINE IRISHMEN
♦♦♦ Irish

(702) 740-6463 · *Lunch $9-12, dinner $10-25*
I-15 exit Tropicana Ave, just E; at New York-New York Hotel & Casino, 3790 Las Vegas Blvd S.
AX, CB, DC, DS, JC, MC, VI. Open daily 6 am-10 pm. Casual attire. Patio seating available. ⊗ Cocktails. **Reservations:** Accepted. **Services:** Valet parking available.

NOBHILL
♦♦♦ Steak & Seafood

(702) 891-7337 · *Dinner $28-44*
I-15 exit Tropicana Ave, just E; at MGM Grand Hotel & Casino, 3799 Las Vegas Blvd S.
AX, CB, DC, DS, JC, MC, VI. Open daily 5:30-10:30 pm. Dressy casual attire. ⊗ Cocktails. **Reservations:** Suggested. **Services:** Valet parking available. **Menu:** Wide-ranging menu with a "San Francisco" feel.

OLIVES AT BELLAGIO
♦♦♦ Mediterranean

(702) 693-8181 · *Lunch $9-21, dinner $12-42*
I-15 exit E Flamingo Rd, on The Strip; at Bellagio, 3600 Las Vegas Blvd S.
AX, DC, DS, MC, VI. Open daily 11 am-2:30 and 5-10:30 pm. Casual attire. ⊗ Cocktails. **Reservations:** Suggested. **Services:** Valet parking available. **Menu:** Choose from an international list of wines.

PALACE CAFE
♦♦ American

(702) 367-2411 · *Lunch $6-12, dinner $8-20*
I-15 exit Sahara Ave W; SW corner of Sahara Ave and Rancho Dr; at Palace Station Hotel & Casino, 2411 W Sahara Ave.
AX, CB, DC, DS, JC, MC, VI. Open 24 hrs. Casual attire. ⊗ Cocktails. **Services:** Valet parking available. **Menu:** American and Chinese menus.

PARADISE CAFE
♦♦ American
(702) 732-5111
Lunch and dinner $7-16
I-15 exit Sahara Ave, 2 mi E; adj to convention center; at Las Vegas Hilton, 3000 Paradise Rd.
AX, CB, DC, DS, JC, MC, VI. Open 24 hrs. Casual attire. ⊛ Cocktails. **Services:** Valet parking available.

PASTA PALACE
♦♦ Italian
(702) 432-7559
Dinner $9-25
Just S of Sahara Ave; at Boulder Station Hotel Casino, 4111 Boulder Hwy.
AX, DC, DS, MC, VI. Open Mon-Sat 5 pm-10 pm, Fri-Sat to 11 pm; Sun 3-9 pm. Casual attire. ⊛ Cocktails. **Reservations:** Suggested. **Services:** Valet parking available. **Menu:** Fresh pasta, pizza and other traditional favorites.

PICASSO
♦♦♦♦♦ French
(702) 693-7111
Dinner $85-95
I-15 exit E Flamingo Rd, on The Strip; at Bellagio, 3600 Las Vegas Blvd S.
AX, CB, DC, DS, MC, VI. Open Wed-Mon 6-10 pm. Closed Tue. Semi-formal attire. ⊛ Cocktails. **Reservations:** Suggested. **Services:** Valet parking available. **Menu:** 2 prix fixe dinner options, prepared by award-winning chef Julian Serrano.

PICCOLI'S CUISINE
♦♦♦ Italian
(702) 791-5959
Lunch $8-15, dinner $9-19
On lower level of Citibank Park Plaza; 3900 Paradise Rd.
AX, CB, DC, DS, JC, MC, VI. Open Mon-Fri 11 am-2 and 5-10 pm, Sat-Sun 5-10 pm. Closed 12/25. Dressy casual attire. ⊛ Cocktails. **Reservations:** Suggested. **Menu:** Lamb and chicken kebabs are offered in addition to Italian food.

PIERO'S
♦♦♦ Italian
(702) 369-2305
Dinner $20-65
I-15 exit Sahara Ave, 2 mi E, ½ mi S on Paradise Rd; opposite convention center; 355 Convention Center Dr.
AX, CB, DC, DS, MC, VI. Open daily 5:30-10 pm, Sat to 10:30. Closed Thanksgiving, 12/24-25. Dressy casual attire. ⊛ Cocktails. Entertainment. **Reservations:** Suggested. **Services:** Valet parking. **Menu:** Osso Buco and fresh seafood dishes.

PING PANG PONG
♦♦ Chinese
(702) 247-8136
Dinner $10-29
I-15 exit Flamingo Rd W, just W; at Gold Coast Hotel, 4000 W Flamingo Rd.
AX, CB, DC, DS, MC, VI. Open daily 5 pm-3 am. Casual attire. ⊛ Cocktails. **Services:** Valet parking available. **Menu:** Many specialty dishes from various regions of China.

PRIME STEAKHOUSE
♦♦♦ Steakhouse
(702) 693-7111
Dinner $25-74
I-15 exit E Flamingo Rd, on The Strip; at Bellagio, 3600 Las Vegas Blvd S.
AX, CB, DC, DS, MC, VI. Open daily 5:30-10 pm. Dressy casual attire. ⊛ Cocktails. **Reservations:** Suggested. **Services:** Valet parking available. **Menu:** Prime meats, chops and seafood. Extensive wine list.

PRIMO'S—A PLACE FOR STEAKS
♦♦♦ Steakhouse
(702) 636-7111   *Dinner $13-40*
US 95 exit Summerlin Pkwy, to Rampart Blvd; at Suncoast Hotel & Casino, 9090 Alta Dr.
AX, CB, DC, DS, MC, VI. Open daily 4:30-9:30 pm. Dressy casual attire. ⊗ Cocktails. **Reservations:** Suggested. **Services:** Valet parking available. **Menu:** Steaks as well as seafood and chops.

RANGE STEAKHOUSE AT HARRAH'S
♦♦♦ Steakhouse
(702) 369-5084   *Dinner $23-54*
I-15 exit E Flamingo Rd; at Harrah's Las Vegas Casino & Hotel, 3475 Las Vegas Blvd S.
AX, DC, DS, MV, VI. Open daily 5:30-10:30 pm. Dressy casual attire. ⊗ Cocktails. Entertainment. **Reservations:** Suggested. **Services:** Valet parking available. **Menu:** Steaks, chops, fish and fowl.

RENOIR
♦♦♦♦♦ French
(702) 791-7353   *Dinner $85*
I-15 exit Spring Mountain Rd, E to The Strip; at The Mirage, 3400 Las Vegas Blvd S.
AX, CB, DC, DS, MC, VI. Open Tue-Sat 5:30-9:30 pm. Closed Sun-Mon. Semiformal attire. ⊗ Cocktails. **Reservations:** Suggested. **Services:** Valet parking available. **Menu:** Mediterranean-inspired French cuisine offered both a la carte and prix fixe, and an extensive wine list emphasizing French selections.

RISTORANTE ITALIANO
♦♦♦ Italian
(702) 794-9363   *Dinner $16-31*
I-15 exit Sahara Ave E; at Riviera Hotel & Casino, 2901 Las Vegas Blvd S.
AX, CB, DC, DS, MC, VI. Open Fri-Tue 5:30-11 pm. Closed Wed-Thu and 11/21-12/27. Dressy casual attire. ⊗ Cocktails. **Reservations:** Suggested. **Services:** Valet parking available.

ROOKIES BAR & GRILL
♦ American
(702) 399-3297   *Lunch $4-7, dinner $6-12*
I-15 exit 46 (Cheyenne Ave), just E; at Ramada Inn-Speedway Casino, 3227 Civic Center Dr.
AX, CB, DC, DS, JC, MC, VI. Open 24 hrs. Casual attire. ⊗ Cocktails.

ROSEMARY'S RESTAURANT
♦♦♦ American
(702) 869-2251   *Lunch $12-20, dinner $19-38*
I-15 exit Sahara Ave, 6 mi W; 8125 W Sahara Ave.
AX, CB, DC, DS, MC, VI. Open Mon-Fri 11:30 am-2:30 and 5:30-10:30 pm, Sat-Sun 5:30-10:30 pm. Closed major holidays. Dressy casual attire. ⊗ Cocktails. **Reservations:** Suggested. **Menu:** American fine dining with French influence.

ROXY'S DINER
♦♦ American
(702) 380-7777   *Lunch and dinner $5-15*
Just N of Sahara Ave; at Stratosphere Casino Hotel & Tower, 2000 Las Vegas Blvd S.
AX, CB, DC, DS, JC, MC, VI. Open daily 11 am-10 pm, Fri & Sat to 1 am. Casual attire. ⊗ Cocktails. **Services:** Valet parking available. **Menu:** All-American favorites with shakes or malts.

SACRED SEA ROOM
♦♦♦ Seafood

(702) 262-4772   *Dinner $20-52*

I-15 exit Tropicana Ave E, just S on The Strip; exit Russell Rd NB, E to The Strip, then just N; at Luxor Las Vegas, 3900 Las Vegas Blvd S.

AX, CB, DS, MC, VI. Open Thu-Mon 5-11 pm. Closed Tue-Wed. Dressy casual attire. ⊛ Cocktails. **Reservations:** Suggested. **Services:** Valet parking available. **Menu:** Fresh- and saltwater fish shipped in daily.

SAMBA BRAZILLIAN STEAKHOUSE
♦♦♦ Brazilian

(702) 791-7337   *Dinner $17-35*

I-15 exit Spring Mountain Rd, E to The Strip; at The Mirage, 3400 Las Vegas Blvd S.

AX, DC, DS, MC, VI. Open daily 5:30-10:30 pm. Casual attire. ⊛ Cocktails. **Reservations:** Suggested. **Services:** Valet parking available. **Menu:** "Churrascaria de rodizio" cooking-style meats, chicken and fish, skewered and carved tableside along with traditional South American side dishes.

SAN LORENZO
♦♦♦ Italian

(702) 631-1023   *Dinner $10-35*

Bus US 95; 3 mi N of downtown; at Texas Station Gambling Hall & Hotel, 2101 Texas Star Ln.

AX, CB, DC, DS, MC, VI. Open daily 4-9 pm, Fri-Sat to 10 pm. Casual attire. ⊛ Cocktails. **Reservations:** Suggested. **Services:** Valet parking available.

SEÑOR MIGUEL'S
♦♦ Mexican

(702) 636-7111   *Lunch $8-15, dinner $8-20*

US 95 exit Summerlin Pkwy, to Rampart Blvd; in Suncoast Hotel & Casino, 9090 Alta Dr.

AX, CB, DC, DS, MC, VI. Open daily 11 am-10 pm. Casual attire. ⊛ Cocktails. **Reservations:** Accepted. **Services:** Valet parking available.

SHANGHAI LILLY
♦♦♦ Chinese

(702) 632-7409   *Dinner $16-85*

I-15 exit Tropicana Ave, just E; at Mandalay Bay Resort & Casino, 3950 Las Vegas Blvd S.

AX, CB, DC, DS, JC, MC, VI. Open daily 5-11 pm. Dressy casual attire. ⊛ Cocktails. **Reservations:** Suggested. **Services:** Valet parking available. **Menu:** Imaginative Cantonese cuisine including selections of beef, seafood and pork.

SOURDOUGH CAFE
♦ American

(702) 258-5200   *Lunch $5-11, dinner $8-19*

US 95 exit Decatur Blvd, ¾ mi S at Evergreen Ave; at Arizona Charlie's Decatur, 740 S Decatur Blvd.

AX, DC, DS, MC, VI. Open 24 hrs. Casual attire. ⊛ Cocktails. **Services:** Valet parking available. **Menu:** Extensive menu, large portions.

THE STEAKHOUSE AT CAMELOT
◆◆◆ Steakhouse
(702) 597-7449   *Dinner $27-40*
I-15 exit Tropicana Ave E; at Excalibur Hotel & Casino, 3850 Las Vegas Blvd S.
AX, CB, DC, DS, MC, VI. Open daily 5-10 pm, Fri-Sat to 11 pm. Dressy casual attire. ⊛ Cocktails. **Reservations:** Suggested. **Services:** Valet parking available. **Menu:** Quality steaks, fine wines and delicious desserts.

STEAKHOUSE AT TUSCANY
◆◆◆ Steak & Seafood
(702) 893-8933   *Dinner $15-28*
I-15 exit Flamingo Rd E, ½ mi; at Tuscany Hotel & Casino, 255 E Flamingo Rd.
AX, DS, MC, VI. Open Tue-Sat 5-10:30 pm. Closed Sun-Mon. Dressy casual attire. ⊛ Cocktails. **Reservations:** Suggested. **Services:** Valet parking available. **Menu:** Wide selection of pasta, beef, chicken and fish dishes, plus specials.

STEFANO'S
◆◆◆ Italian
(702) 385-7111   *Dinner $14-35*
Downtown, casino center area; at The Golden Nugget, 129 E Fremont St.
AX, CB, DC, DS, MC, VI. Open Thu-Mon 5:30-10:30 pm. Closed Tue-Wed. Dressy casual attire. ⊛ Cocktails. **Reservations:** Suggested. **Services:** Valet parking available. **Menu:** Singing waiters serve creative, colorful dishes.

SUNDANCE GRILL
◆◆ American
(702) 263-7777   *Lunch and dinner $6-15*
I-15 exit 33 (W Blue Diamond Rd), at Silverton Hotel-Casino, 3333 Blue Diamond Rd.
AX, CB, DC, DS, JC, MC, VI. Open 24 hrs. Casual attire. ⊛ Cocktails. **Reservations:** Accepted. **Services:** Valet parking available.

TEXAS BBQ
◆ Barbecue
(702) 878-7319   *Lunch and dinner $5-11*
I-15 exit Sahara Ave W, 4 mi; 5781 W Sahara Ave.
MC, VI. Open Mon-Sat 11 am-8 pm. Closed Sun and major holidays. Casual attire. ⊛

TEXAS CAFE
◆◆ American
(702) 631-1000   *Lunch $6-12, dinner $6-20*
Bus US 95; 3 mi N of downtown; at Texas Station Gambling Hall & Hotel, 2101 Texas Star Ln.
AX, CB, DC, DS, JC, MC, VI. Open 24 hrs. Casual attire. ⊛ Cocktails. **Services:** Valet parking available.

3950 RESTAURANT
◆◆◆◆ Continental
(702) 632-7414   *Dinner $27-55*
I-15 exit Tropicana Ave, just E; at Mandalay Bay Resort & Casino, 3950 Las Vegas Blvd S.
AX, CB, DC, DS, MC, VI. Open daily 5:30-11 pm. Dressy casual attire. ⊛ Cocktails. **Reservations:** Suggested. **Services:** Valet parking available.

TILLERMAN
◆◆◆ Steak & Seafood
(702) 731-4036   *Dinner $21-55*
3½ mi E of Las Vegas Blvd S; 2245 E Flamingo Rd.

DC, DS, MC, VI. Open daily 5-10 pm. Closed major holidays. Dressy casual attire. ⊛ Cocktails. **Reservations:** Suggested. **Menu:** Fresh seafood and steak.

TILTED KILT
♦♦ American

(702) 777-2463   *Dinner $8-20*

I-15 exit Flamingo Rd, ⅓ mi W; at Rio Suite Hotel & Casino, 3700 W Flamingo Rd.

AX, CB, DC, DS, JC, MC, VI. Open daily 4 pm-midnight. Casual attire. ⊛ Cocktails. **Services:** Valet parking available. **Menu:** Irish-American fare.

TOWN HALL RESTAURANT
♦ American

(702) 731-2111   *Lunch $6-12, dinner $8-15*

Just E off The Strip, near Flamingo Rd; at Days Inn Town Hall Casino, 4155 Koval Ln.

AX, DC, DS, MC, VI. Open 24 hrs. Casual attire. ⊛ Cocktails.

TRIPLE 7 RESTAURANT BREWERY
♦♦ American

(702) 387-1896   *Lunch and dinner $6-16*

In downtown casino center; at Main Street Station, 200 N Main St.

AX, CB, DC, DS, MC, VI. Open daily 11 am-7 am. Casual attire. ⊛ Cocktails. **Services:** Valet parking available. **Menu:** A wide selection of brews complement plentiful food choices, including sushi and oysters.

TWIN CREEKS
♦♦♦ Steak & Seafood

(702) 914-8594   *Dinner $10-40*

I-15 exit 33 (W Blue Diamond Rd), at Silverton Hotel-Casino, 3333 Blue Diamond Rd.

AX, CB, DC, DS, JC, MC, VI. Open daily 5-10 pm, Fri-Sat to 11 pm. Dressy casual attire. ⊛ Cocktails. **Reservations:** Suggested. **Services:** Valet parking available. **Menu:** A good selection of steak, seafood and poultry, and some nice wines.

VALENTINO LAS VEGAS
♦♦♦ Italian

(702) 414-3000   *Dinner $16-42*

On The Strip; at The Venetian Resort Hotel Casino, 3355 Las Vegas Blvd S.

AX, DC, DS, MC, VI. Open daily 5:30-11 pm. Dressy casual attire. ⊛ Cocktails. **Reservations:** Suggested. **Services:** Valet parking available. **Menu:** Many ingredients imported directly from Italy are used in the restaurant's Italian specialties, which reflect a seasonally changing menu.

VENTUNO RISTORANTE
♦♦♦ Italian

(702) 733-3333   *Lunch $10-19, dinner $12-23*

I-15 exit Flamingo Rd E, N on The Strip; at Flamingo Las Vegas, 3555 Las Vegas Blvd S.

AX, CB, DC, DS, JC, MC, VI. Open daily 6 am-2 am. Dressy casual attire. ⊛ Cocktails. **Reservations:** Suggested. **Services:** Valet parking available.

VERANDAH
♦♦♦ California

(702) 632-5121   *Lunch $14-28, dinner $23-29*

I-15 exit Tropicana Ave E, S on The Strip; at Four Seasons Hotel Las Vegas, 3960 Las Vegas Blvd S.

Parking fee. AX, DC, DS, JC, MC, VI. Open daily 6:30 am-10 pm, Sat-Sun from 7 am. Dressy casual attire. ⊛ Cocktails. **Reservations:** Accepted.

VICTORIAN ROOM
◆◆ American

(702) 737-7111
Lunch & dinner $7-16
On The Strip; at Barbary Coast Hotel, 3595 Las Vegas Blvd S.
AX, CB, DC, DS, JC, MC, VI. Open 24 hrs. Casual attire. ⊛ Cocktails. **Reservations:** Accepted. **Services:** Valet parking available.

WAVERLY'S STEAK HOUSE
◆◆ Steakhouse

(702) 507-5700
Dinner $15-28
I-15 exit W Craig Rd, 1 mi; at Cannery Casino-Hotel, 2121 E Craig Rd.
AX, MC, VI. Open daily 5-10 pm. Dressy casual attire. ⊛ Cocktails. **Reservations:** Suggested. **Services:** Valet parking available. **Menu:** Filets and prime rib entree's in addition to pasta, chicken and fish choices. A nice selection of breads starts the meal. Several attractive and tasty desserts.

WILLY & JOSE'S CANTINA
◆ Mexican

(702) 456-7777
Dinner $8-15
1 mi E of I-515/SR 93 and 95, exit Flamingo Rd; in Sam's Town Hotel & Gambling Hall, 5111 Boulder Hwy.
AX, CB, DC, DS, MC, VI. Open Wed-Sun 5-10 pm, Fri-Sat to 11 pm. Closed Mon-Tue. Casual attire. ⊛ Cocktails. **Reservations:** Suggested. **Services:** Valet parking available.

YOLIE'S BRAZILIAN STEAK HOUSE
◆◆ Brazilian

(702) 794-0700
Lunch $10-15, dinner $16-30
On upper level, Citibank Park Plaza; 3900 Paradise Rd.
AX, DC, MC, VI. Open Mon-Fri 11 am-3 and daily 5-11 pm. Closed 12/25. Dressy casual attire. ⊛ Cocktails. **Reservations:** Suggested. **Menu:** Variety of meats served from a skewer, plus lamb, chicken and fish dishes.

YUKON GRILLE
◆◆◆ Steakhouse

(702) 258-5172
Dinner $15-25
US 95 exit Decatur Blvd, ¼ mi S at Evergreen Ave; at Arizona Charlie's Decatur, 740 S Decatur Blvd.
AX, DC, DS, MC, VI. Open Wed-Sun 5-10 pm. Closed Mon-Tue. Casual attire. ⊛ Cocktails. **Reservations:** Accepted. **Menu:** Steaks, seafood and chicken.

Laughlin

Lodging

COLORADO BELLE HOTEL & CASINO
◆◆ Large Hotel

(702) 298-4000
$26-90
3 mi S of Davis Dam; 2100 S Casino Dr.
XP $4; ages 12 and younger, free. Cancellation fee. AX, CB, DC, DS, MC, VI. Package plans. 6 stories; interior/exterior corridors. Casino, gift shop. **Rooms:** 1165; 24 1-bedroom suites, $125-175. Shower bath, some whirlpools, some hair dryers, some coffeemakers, some refrigerators, movies, some irons, safes, some ⊛, 🛗, roll-in showers, 🔲. **Recreation:** 2 pools, whirlpool, exercise rm, game rm. **Services:** Valet parking available, laundry, business services. **Dining:** Restaurant, Mississippi Lounge, see separate listing; cocktails.

DON LAUGHLIN'S RIVERSIDE RESORT HOTEL & CASINO   ◆◆◆ Large Hotel
(702) 298-2535 $39-199
2 mi S of Davis Dam; 1650 S Casino Dr.
2- to 3-night minimum stay in season and on weekends. 7-day cancellation
notice, fee. Package plans. AX, CB, DC, DS, MC, VI. Small pets, $100 deposit, $8
extra charge. 2-26 stories; interior corridors. Casino, gift shop. **Rooms:** 1404; 9
1-bedroom suites, some with whirlpools, $89-399. Some shower baths, some
whirlpools, coffeemakers, some refrigerators, movies, some ⊛. 🛆, roll-in showers,
🖉. **Recreation:** 2 pools, whirlpool, massage, game rm. **Services:** Valet parking
available, laundry, childcare, business services. **Dining:** Restaurant, The Gourmet
Room, see separate listing; cocktails.

EDGEWATER HOTEL/CASINO 🅰🅰   ◆◆◆ Large Hotel
(702) 298-2453 $39-350
2½ mi S of Davis Dam; 2020 S Casino Dr.
XP $4; ages 18 and younger, free. Cancellation fee. Package plans. AX, CB, DC,
DS, MC, VI. Pets, $100 deposit. 3-26 stories; interior corridors. Casino, gift shop,
entertainment. **Rooms:** 1419; 18 1-bedroom suites, some with whirlpools. Some
shower baths, some hair dryers, some coffeemakers, movies, some safes, some
⊛. 🛆, roll-in showers, 🖉. **Recreation:** Pool, whirlpool, game rm. **Services:** Valet
parking available, laundry, business services. **Dining:** 5 restaurants, including
Hickory Pit Steak House, see separate listing; buffet, $6-17; 24 hrs; cocktails.

FLAMINGO LAUGHLIN   ◆◆◆ Large Hotel
(702) 298-5111 $22-399
2 mi S of Davis Dam; 1900 S Casino Dr.
XP $5; ages 4 and younger, free. Senior discount. AX, CB, DC, DS, JC, MC, VI. 18
stories; interior corridors. Casino, gift shop. **Rooms:** 1907; 34 1- and 17 2-bed-
room suites. Some shower baths, some hair dryers, some coffeemakers, some
refrigerators, movies, video games, data ports, high-speed Internet access, voice
mail, some irons, some ⊛. Roll-in showers, 🖉. **Recreation:** Pool, exercise rm,
massage, 3 lighted tennis courts, game rm. **Services:** Valet parking available, airport transportation, laundry, business services. **Dining:** Restaurants, including
Alta Villa and Beef Barron, see separate listings; 24-hr room service; cocktails.

GOLDEN NUGGET LAUGHLIN   ◆◆◆ Small Hotel
(702) 298-7111 $29-189
3½ mi S of Davis Dam; 2300 S Casino Dr.
XP $7; ages 14 and younger, free. AX, DS, MC, VI. 4 stories; interior corridors.
Casino, gift shop. **Rooms:** 296; 4 1-bedroom suites, $129-229. Some shower
baths, hair dryers, coffeemakers, some refrigerators, movies, data ports, dual
phone lines, voice mail, some ⊛. 🛆, roll-in showers, 🖉. **Recreation:** Pool,
whirlpool, game rm. **Services:** Valet parking available, laundry. **Dining:**
Restaurants, including Jane's Grill and River Cafe, see separate listings; cocktails.

HARRAH'S CASINO HOTEL   ◆◆◆ Large Hotel
(702) 298-4600 $20-200
5 mi S of Davis Dam, on the river; 2900 S Casino Dr.
XP $10. 3-day cancellation notice; fee. AX, CB, DC, DS, MC, VI. 15-20 stories; exte-

rior corridors. Casino, gift shop. **Rooms:** 1600. Some shower baths, hair dryers, some coffeemakers, movies, data ports, voice mail, some ⊛. 🛇, roll-in showers. **Recreation:** Pools, whirlpools, health club, massage, game rm. **Services:** Valet parking available, laundry, business services. **Dining:** Restaurants, including Baja Blue and Range Steakhouse, see separate listings; 24-hr room service; cocktails.

RAMADA EXPRESS
◆◆◆ Large Hotel

(702) 298-4200 $27-199

3 mi S of Davis Dam; 2121 S Casino Dr.

XP $7. Cancellation fee. Package plans. Service charge. AX, CB, DC, DS, MC. 12-24 stories; interior corridors. Casino, gift shop. **Rooms:** 1501; 9 1-bedroom suites with whirlpools. Some shower baths, some whirlpools, some hair dryers, some coffeemakers, some refrigerators, movies, data ports, voice mail, some irons, some ⊛. 🛇, roll-in showers, 🖵. **Recreation:** Pool, whirlpool, game rm. **Services:** Valet parking available, laundry, business services. **Dining:** Restaurants; cocktails.

Restaurants

ALTA VILLA
◆◆◆ Steak & Seafood

(702) 298-8364 *Dinner $11-50*

2 mi S of Davis Dam; at Flamingo Laughlin, 1900 S Casino Dr.

AX, CB, DC, DS, JC, MC, VI. Open Sun-Tue and Fri 5-10 pm, Sat 5-11 pm. Closed Wed-Thu. Dressy casual attire. ⊛ Cocktails. **Reservations:** Suggested. **Services:** Valet parking available. **Menu:** Extensive.

BAJA BLUE
◆◆ Mexican

(702) 298-4600 *Dinner $7-17*

5 mi S of Davis Dam, on the river; at Harrah's Casino Hotel, 2900 S Casino Dr.

AX, DC, DS, MC, VI. Open daily 5-10 pm, Fri-Sat to 11 pm. 🛇 Casual attire. ⊛ Cocktails. **Services:** Valet parking available.

BEEF BARRON
◆◆ Steakhouse

(702) 298-5111 *Dinner $15-30*

2 mi S of Davis Dam; at Flamingo Laughlin, 1900 S Casino Dr.

AX, CB, DC, DS, MC, VI. Open daily 4-10 pm. 🛇 Casual attire. ⊛ Cocktails. **Services:** Valet parking available. **Menu:** Beef as well as a few entrees of fish and chicken.

FEATHERS CAFE
◆◆ American

(702) 535-5555 *Lunch & dinner $5-15*

9 mi S on Needles Hwy via Casino Dr; from I-40, exit W Broadway, 12 mi N; at Avi Hotel & Casino, 10000 Aha Macav Pkwy.

AX, DC, DS, MC, VI. Open 24 hrs. Casual attire. ⊛ Cocktails. **Services:** Valet parking available.

THE GOURMET ROOM
◆◆◆ Continental

(702) 298-2535 *Dinner $20-45*

2 mi S of Davis Dam; at Don Laughlin's Riverside Resort Hotel & Casino, 1650 S Casino Dr.

AX, CB, DC, DS, MC, VI. Open daily 5-10 pm, Sat to 11 pm. Casual attire. ⊛ Cocktails. **Reservations:** Suggested. **Services:** Valet parking available.

HICKORY PIT STEAK HOUSE
◆◆◆ Steakhouse

(702) 298-2453
Dinner $10-40

2⅓ mi S of Davis Dam; at Edgewater Hotel/Casino, 2020 S Casino Dr.

AX, DS, MC, VI. Open daily 4-9 pm, Fri-Sat to 10 pm. Casual attire. ⊗ Cocktails.
Reservations: Suggested. **Services:** Valet parking available.

JANE'S GRILL
◆◆ American

(702) 298-7111
Lunch & dinner $6-17

3½ mi S of Davis Dam; at Golden Nugget Laughlin, 2300 S Casino Dr.

AX, DS, MC, VI. Mon-Sat open 11 am-9 pm, Fri-Sat to 10 pm, Sun 9 am-1:30
and 4-9 pm. Casual attire. ⊗ Cocktails. **Services:** Valet parking available. **Menu:**
Choices range from pizzas, calzones and pastas to burgers and some nice salads.

MISSISSIPPI LOUNGE
◆◆ Seafood

(702) 298-4000
Lunch $4-10, dinner $6-12

3 mi S of Davis Dam; at Colorado Belle Hotel & Casino, 2100 S Casino Dr.

AX, CB, DC, DS, MC, VI. Open daily noon-10 pm. Casual attire. Cocktails.
Services: Valet parking available. **Menu:** Seafood specialties include peel-and-eat
shrimp.

RANGE STEAKHOUSE
◆◆◆ American

(702) 298-4600
Dinner $26-60

5 mi S of Davis Dam, on the river; at Harrah's Casino Hotel, 2900 S Casino Dr.

AX, DC, DS, MC, VI. Open daily 5-9 pm, Fri-Sat to 10 pm. Dressy casual attire. ⊗
Cocktails. **Reservations:** Suggested. **Services:** Valet parking available. **Menu:**
Varied.

RIVER CAFE
◆ American

(702) 298-7111
Lunch & dinner $5-33

3½ mi S of Davis Dam; at Golden Nugget Laughlin, 2300 S Casino Dr.

AX, DS, MC, VI. Open 24 hrs. Casual attire. ⊗ Cocktails. **Services:** Valet parking
available.

Overton

Lodging

BEST WESTERN NORTH SHORE INN AT LAKE MEAD
◆◆◆ Motel

(702) 397-6000
$59-79

I-15 exit 93, 10 mi NE on SR 169; 520 N Moapa Valley Blvd.

XP $5; ages 12 and younger, free. AX, CB, DC, DS, MC, VI. Senior discount.
Package plans. Small pets, $10 extra charge. Video library. 2 stories, no elevators;
interior corridors. **Rooms:** 43; 1 1-bedroom suite, $85-125. Hair dryers, cof-
feemakers, some microwaves, some refrigerators, movies, some VCRs, data ports,
irons, some ⊗. **Recreation:** Pool, whirlpool. **Services:** Laundry, business services.

Primm

Lodging

BUFFALO BILL'S RESORT & CASINO
◆◆ Large Hotel
(702) 382-1212
$34-120
45 mi S of Las Vegas via I-15, exit State Line; just E.
XP $5. Cancellation fee. Package plans. AX, CB, DC, DS, JC, MC, VI. Casino, gift shop. 16 stories; interior corridors. **Rooms:** 1240; 20 1-bedroom suites, some with whirlpools. Shower baths, coffeemakers, some refrigerators, movies, voice mail, some ⊛. ⬧, roll-in showers, ⬚. **Recreation:** Pool, whirlpool, golf. **Services:** Valet parking available, laundry, area transportation, business services. **Dining:** Restaurant; cocktails.

PRIMM VALLEY RESORT & CASINO
◆◆◆ Large Hotel
(702) 382-1212
$41-120
45 mi S of Las Vegas via I-15, exit State Line.
Cancellation fee. Package plans. AX, CB, DC, DS, JC, MC, VI. Casino, gift shop. 4 stories; interior corridors. **Rooms:** 623; 35 1-bedroom suites, some with whirlpools. Some shower baths, some hair dryers, coffeemakers, some refrigerators, movies, some irons, some ⊛. ⬧, roll-in showers, ⬚. **Recreation:** Pool, whirlpool, golf, playground, game rm. **Services:** Valet parking available, area transportation, laundry, business services. **Dining:** Restaurant, GP's Restaurant, see separate listing; 24-hr room service; cocktails.

WHISKEY PETE'S HOTEL & CASINO
◆◆ Large Hotel
(702) 382-1212
$25-120
45 mi S of Las Vegas, W of and adj to I-15; exit State Line.
Cancellation fee. Package plans. AX, CB, DC, DS, JC, MC, VI. Casino, gift shop. 2-19 stories; interior corridors. **Rooms:** 777; 10 1-bedroom suites, some with whirlpools. Some shower baths, coffeemakers, some refrigerators, movies, some ⊛. ⬧, roll-in showers, ⬚. **Recreation:** Pool, waterslide, whirlpool, golf, game room. **Services:** Valet parking available, area transportation, laundry, business services. **Dining:** Restaurants, including Trail's End, see separate listing.

Restaurants

GP'S RESTAURANT
◆◆◆ American
(702) 382-1212
Dinner $13-21
45 mi S of Las Vegas via I-15, exit State Line, at Primm Valley Resort & Casino.
AX, CB, DC, MC, VI. Open Wed-Sun 5-10 pm, Fri-Sat to 11 pm. Closed Mon-Tue. Dressy casual attire. ⊛ Cocktails. **Reservations:** Suggested. **Services:** Valet parking available. **Menu:** Specializes in prime rib and seafood, especially lobster.

TRAIL'S END
◆◆ American
(702) 382-1212
Lunch & dinner $5-20
45 mi S of Las Vegas, W of and adj to I-15; exit State Line; at Whiskey Pete's Hotel & Casino.
AX, CB, DC, MC, VI. Open 24 hrs. Casual attire. ⊛ Cocktails. **Services:** Valet parking available.

Bullhead City, Arizona

Lodging

BEST WESTERN BULLHEAD CITY INN 🅐🅐🅐   ♦♦♦ Small Hotel
(928) 754-3000   *$44-99*
1⁹⁄₁₀ mi S of Laughlin Bridge, then just E on 3rd St; 1126 Hwy 95.
XP $5; children free. Senior discount. AX, CB, DC, DS, JC, MC, VI. Pets, $10 extra charge. 2 stories, no elevator; exterior corridors. **Rooms:** 88. Hair dryers, some microwaves, refrigerators, movies, data ports, irons, safes, some ⊛. ▦. **Recreation:** Small pool, whirlpool. **Services:** Laundry, business services. **Dining:** Restaurant nearby.

Restaurants

BLACK BEAR DINER   ♦ American
(928) 763-2477   *Lunch $6-8, dinner $8-14*
3⁹⁄₁₀ mi S of Laughlin Bridge; 1751 W Hwy 95.
AX, DC, DS, MC, VI. Open daily 6 am-10 pm. Casual attire. ⊛ Beer & wine. **Menu:** Entrees such as meatloaf with mashed potatoes and chicken-fried steak are at the heart of the menu.

COLIANNO'S   ♦♦ Italian
(928) 758-7104   *Lunch $6-8, dinner $8-13*
4¹⁄₁₀ mi S of Laughlin Bridge; 1884 Hwy 95.
AX, DC, DS, MC, VI. Open daily 10 am-10 pm. Casual attire. ⊛ Cocktails. **Services:** Carryout. **Menu:** Steak, seafood and pasta dishes, as well as specialty pizza.

EL PALACIO   ♦♦ Mexican
(928) 763-2494   *Lunch $6-10, dinner $8-18*
4¹⁄₁₀ mi S of Laughlin Bridge; 1885 Hwy 95.
AX, MC, VI. Open daily 11 am-9:30 pm, Fri-Sat to 10 pm. Casual attire. ⊛ Cocktails. **Menu:** Assorted Mexican steak and seafood dishes, plus the more familiar enchiladas, burritos and tamales.

Campgrounds & Trailer Parks

*Warm weather, and nearby scenic and recreation areas attract thousands of campers to Las Vegas and Laughlin every year. Camping accommodations range from simple RV lots located close to the glitz and gambling action to more rugged settings in surrounding areas, including Bullhead City, Arizona. The campgrounds in this section are listed alphabetically by city or closest recreation area—**Boulder City**, **Lake Mead National Recreation Area** (Lake Mead and Lake Mohave), **Las Vegas**, **Primm**, **Red Rock Canyon National Conservation Area**, **Spring Mountains National Recreation Area**, **Valley of Fire State Park** and **Bullhead City, Arizona.** Unless otherwise noted, campgrounds are open all year.*

The following listings show the nightly camping fee for the number of people specified, including a recreational vehicle or automobile (with or without a trailer). Electricity, water and sewer RV hookups are indicated by the letters E, W and S, respectively.

Private campgrounds have been inspected by an Auto Club representative and meet AAA requirements for recommendation. Private campgrounds that did not meet the requirements for listing or that were not inspected have not been included in this book.

Public campgrounds typically allow a more natural experience or have fewer services, and as a result usually do not meet AAA requirements for recommendation; they are listed here as a service. Information for the public campgrounds was obtained from the administering government agency, which is shown with individual listings, i.e., National Forest (NF), National Park Service (NPS), Bureau of Land Management (BLM), State, County and Private.

RVing in Cottonwood

The ⒶⒶⒶ in a private campground listing identifies the establishment as a AAA Official Appointment; it indicates that the campground has expressed a particular interest in serving AAA members. In order to communicate this desire to the traveling public, these facilities have purchased the right to display the AAA emblem.

Bringing the family pet? Pets on leashes are welcome in most campgrounds. Leashes should be no longer than 6 feet. Be aware that some campgrounds charge a nominal fee for pets (these are noted).

For an additional fee, an RV towing and tire-change service option is available for motorhomes, campers and travel/camping trailers. Call (800) AAA-HELP; hearing impaired call (800) 955-4TDD.

RESERVATIONS

Most private campgrounds listed here accept reservations by phone. Those public campgrounds that are reservable include the appropriate contact information in the section head or individual campground listing. Otherwise, camping is "first come, first served."

Additional fees may be charged for some services and facilities, such as showers, laundry, and recreational activities or equipment. Swimming pools may or may not be heated.

Where accepted, major credit cards honored by the campgrounds appear in each listing and are abbreviated as follows:

AX=American Express   DS=Discover

CB=Carte Blanche   MC=MasterCard

DI=Diners Club   VI=Visa

All camping fees are subject to change.

Boulder City

BOULDER OAKS RV RESORT   Private
(702) 294-4425   *$30/4*
1010 Industrial Rd.
DS, MC, VI. Pets (limit 2). Some sites with view of distant Lake Mead. El 2507. 24 acres. **Sites:** 275 RV sites, EWS, 50 amps, phone and cable TV hookups. **Facilities:** Flush toilets. **Recreation:** Pool, sauna, whirlpool, recreation rm. **Services:** Laundry.

Lake Mead National Recreation Area

◄HEADQUARTERS
(702) 293-8990, 293-8907
25 mi SE of Las Vegas; 601 Nevada Hwy, Boulder City.
Unless noted otherwise, the maximum stay for camping in Lake Mead NRA is 30 consecutive days, with a cumulative total of 90 camping days in a consecutive 12-month period. All public campgrounds at lakes Mead and Mohave are first come, first served.

Lake Mead

BOULDER BEACH CAMPGROUND   NPS
6 mi NE of Boulder City via SR 166.   *$10/8*
Pets. **Sites:** 154 tent/RV sites (35-ft limit). **Facilities:** Disposal station, flush toilets, grills, picnic tables. **Recreation:** Boats, launch ramp. **Services:** Groceries, laundry.

CALLVILLE BAY RESORT & MARINA
NPS
22 mi NE of Henderson via SR 147 and Northshore Rd. $10/8
Pets. **Sites:** 80 tent/RV sites (35-ft limit). **Facilities:** Disposal station, piped water, flush toilets, showers, grills, picnic tables. **Recreation:** Boats, launch ramp. **Services:** Laundry.

ECHO BAY RESORT & MARINA
NPS
30 mi S of Overton on SR 167. $10/8
Pets. **Sites:** 166 tent/RV sites (35-ft limit). **Facilities:** Disposal station, water, flush toilets, showers, grills, picnic tables. **Recreation:** Boats, launch ramp. **Services:** Laundry.

LAS VEGAS BAY CAMPGROUND
NPS
9 mi NE of Henderson via Lake Mead Dr and Lakeshore Rd or 13 mi NW of Boulder City on SR 166. $10/8
Pets. **Sites:** 89 tent/RV sites (35-ft limit). **Facilities:** Disposal station, flush toilets, grills, picnic tables. **Recreation:** Boats, launch ramp.

TEMPLE BAR RESORT & MARINA
NPS
26 mi E of Boulder City via US 93, then 28 mi N via Temple Bar Rd. $10/8
Pets. **Sites:** 153 tent/RV sites (35-ft limit). **Facilities:** Disposal station, water, flush toilets, grills, picnic tables. **Recreation:** Marina, boats, launch ramp, boat and auto fuel. **Services:** Laundry, groceries.

Lake Mohave

COTTONWOOD COVE RESORT & MARINA
NPS
(702) 297-1464 $20-25/8
35 mi SE of Boulder City via US 95 and SR 164.
10 am check out. AX, DS, MC, VI. Pets. Desert landscape. **Sites:** 73 RV sites, EWS. **Facilities:** Disposal station, piped water, flush toilets, showers, air conditioning. **Recreation:** Beach, swimming, fishing, launch ramp, marina, houseboats, powerboats, personal watercraft, water-skiing and equipment. **Services:** Laundry, groceries, propane. **Dining:** Snack bar.

KATHERINE LANDING CAMPGROUND
NPS
(702) 293-8907, (928) 754-3272 $10/8
6 mi N of Bullhead City, off SRs 95 and 68.
Sites: 173 tent/RV sites (35-ft limit). **Facilities:** Disposal station, water, flush toilets, grills, picnic tables. **Recreation:** Boats, launch ramp, fishing, swimming. **Services:** Laundry.

Las Vegas

ARIZONA CHARLIE'S EAST RV PARK ⓐⓐⓐ
Private
(702) 951-5911 $19/2
4445 Boulder Hwy.
Weekly and monthly rates available. AX, DS, MC, VI. Small pets only. 11 acres. **Sites:** 239 RV sites, EWS, cable TV and phone hookups, 50 amps. **Facilities:** Flush toilets. **Recreation:** Pool, whirlpool, exercise rm, putting green, recreation rm, pool table. **Services:** Propane, area transportation, laundry.

BOULDER LAKES RV RESORT ⓐ Private
(702) 435-1157 *$22-24/2*
1 mi E of I-515/SR 93 and 95, exit Russell Rd, ⅓ mi N at Desert Horizons Rd; 6201 Boulder Hwy.
XP $3. Weekly and monthly rates available. MC, VI. Pets. Desert atmosphere, paved roads and pads. 10 acres. **Sites:** 417 level RV sites, no pull-thrus (50-ft limit); EWS; cable TV, phone hookups; 50 amps. **Facilities:** Flush toilets. **Recreation:** Pool, saunas, whirlpools. **Services:** Groceries, laundry.

LAS VEGAS KOA AT CIRCUS CIRCUS Private
(800) 562-7270 *$15-60*
I-15, exit Sahara Blvd, ¾ mi E, adj to Circus Circus Hotel, Casino & Theme Park; 500 Circus Circus Dr (enter off Industrial Rd).
Deposit required. AX, CB, DC, DS, JC, MC, VI. Pets. 35 acres. **Sites:** 399 paved RV sites, many pull-thrus; 378 EW, 365 S; 50 amps. **Facilities:** Dump station, flush toilets. **Recreation:** Pool, whirlpool, playground. **Services:** Groceries, laundry.

OASIS LAS VEGAS RV RESORT Private
(702) 260-2020 *$20-32*
Exit I-15 at Blue Diamond Rd (exit 33), 1½ mi E to Las Vegas Blvd, ½ mi S; 2711 W Windmill.
AX, DS, MC, VI. Small pets only. 46 acres. **Sites:** 702 RV sites, mostly pull-thrus; EWS; cable TV, phone hookups; 50 amps. **Facilities:** Dump station, flush toilets. **Recreation:** Pool, whirlpool, exercise rm, 18-hole putting course on natural turf greens, recreation rm. **Services:** Groceries, propane, laundry. **Dining:** Lounge.

Laughlin

AVI RV PARK Private
(702) 535-5555 *$17-50/4*
9 mi S on Needles Hwy via Casino Dr; from I-40, exit W Broadway, 12 mi N; 10000 Aha Macav Pkwy.
Deposit required; handling fee. Weekly and monthly rates available. AX, DS, MC, VI. Pets. On the Colorado River, adjacent to casino. No shade. 25 acres. **Sites:** 257 RV sites; gravel, level and some pull-thrus; EWS; 50 amps ($3); cable TV hookups. **Facilities:** Flush toilets, showers, lounge. **Recreation:** Beach, pool, whirlpool, swimming, boat ramp, marina, rental boats. **Services:** Groceries, propane, laundry.

Red Rock Canyon
NationalConservation Area

LAS VEGAS FIELD OFFICE
(702) 647-5000
4765 W Vegas Dr, Las Vegas.

Red Rock Canyon Visitor Center
(702) 363-1921
1000 Scenic Dr, Las Vegas.

13-Mile Campground
BLM

At the 13-mile marker on SR 159/W Charleston Blvd. $10

Maximum 14-consecutive-night stay in any 30-day period. First come, first served. Pets, $3. El 3100. **Sites:** 71 sites (14 tent, 57 tent/RV). **Facilities:** Primitive toilets, barbecue pits, picnic tables. **Services:** Visitor center 2 mi W of campground.

Spring Mountains National Recreation Area

HEADQUARTERS
(702) 515-5400
4701 N Torrey Pines Dr, Las Vegas.

Humboldt-Toiyabe National Forest
1200 Franklin Way, Sparks, NV.
35 mi NW of Las Vegas via US 95, turnoff at SR 157/Kyle Canyon Rd or SR 156/Lee Canyon Rd. Within Humboldt-Toiyabe National Forest.

Campgrounds open daily May through mid-Oct; early and late season may vary due to the weather. Maximum 14-consecutive-night stay in any 30-day period. Unless indicated otherwise, the maximum RV length is 30 ft.

For campsite reservations up to 240 days in advance, contact the National Recreation Reservation Service toll free at (877) 444-6777, (877) 833-6777 (TDD), or access their website at reserveusa.com. Reservation hours 10 am-7 pm EST. $9 non-refundable reservation fee; 3-night refund notice; $10 service fee for cancellations or changes; $20 no-show fee. AE, DS, MC and VI are accepted.

Dolomite
NF

43 mi from Las Vegas, on SR 156 in Lee Canyon. $13/family

$5 per additional vehicle. Pets. El 8400. **Sites:** 31 tent/RV. **Facilities:** Piped water, flush and primitive toilets, no showers; barbecues, fire rings, picnic tables. **Recreation:** Nature trails.

Fletcher View
NF

34½ mi from Las Vegas, on SR 157 in Kyle Canyon. $13/family

$5 per additional vehicle. First come, first served. El 7200. **Sites:** 12 tent/RV; (25-ft limit). **Facilities:** Piped water, primitive toilets, no showers; barbecues, fire rings, some picnic tables. **Recreation:** Riding stable within 1 mile.

Hilltop
NF

15 mi NW on US 95, 17 mi W on SR 157, 6 mi NW on SR 158. (Due to short parking spurs and a narrow approach road, this campground is not recommended for trailers and motorhomes.) $13/family

$5 per additional vehicle. El 8400. **Sites:** 31 tent/RV; 2 sites wheelchair accessible. **Facilities:** Piped water, flush toilets, showers, barbecues, fire rings, picnic tables. **Recreation:** Nature trails.

Kyle Canyon
NF

15 mi NW on US 95, 17½ mi W on SR 157. $13/family

$5 per additional vehicle. El 7000. **Sites:** 19 tent/RV sites; 9 sites wheelchair accessible. **Facilities:** Piped water, primitive toilets, no showers; barbecues, fire rings, picnic tables. **Recreation:** Riding stable within 1 mile.

McWilliams NF
In Lee Canyon, 43 mi from Las Vegas on SR 156. *$14/family*
$5 per additional vehicle. El 8400. **Sites:** 31 tent/RV; 2 sites wheelchair accessible. **Facilities:** Piped water, flush and primitive toilets, no showers; barbecues, fire rings, picnic tables. **Recreation:** Horseshoe pit.

Valley of Fire State Park

VALLEY OF FIRE STATE PARK VISITOR CENTER
(702) 397-2088
50 mi NE of Las Vegas via I-15 and SR 169.

Valley of Fire Campgrounds State
2 mi W of the visitor center. *$8/vehicle*
First-come, first-served. Pets. **Sites:** 51 sites (48 tent/RV, 3 tent); 2 wheelchair-accessible sites. **Facilities:** Piped water, flush and primitive toilets, showers, barbecues, fire rings, picnic tables. **Recreation:** Nature trails.

Bullhead City, Arizona

DAVIS CAMP COUNTY PARK County
(928) 754-7250 *$10-17*
1 mi N on SR 95; below Davis Dam.
Maximum 14-night stay, on beach. MC, VI. Pets. Hospital in town. 365 acres, on Colorado River. **Sites:** 140 RV sites (50-ft limit); 110 EWS, 30 EW; unlimited camping with full RV hookups. **Facilities:** Dump station, flush toilets. **Recreation:** Boating, fishing, swimming, boat ramp, dock. **Services:** Laundry, 24-hr attendant, visitor center.

SNOWBIRD RV RESORT Private
(928) 768-7141 *$20/2*
13¾ mi S of Laughlin Bridge on SR 95, then just E; 1600 Joy Ln.
XP $3. Pets, $1 extra charge. 15 acres. **Sites:** 135 (10 tent, 125 RV); 135 EW, 125 S; 50 amps ($3, 6/1-8/31), air conditioning ($3), washer/dryer hookup. **Facilities:** Flush toilets. **Recreation:** Pool, whirlpool golf, recreation rm. **Services:** Laundry.

Index

This index contains listings for points of interest, events and services.

H

I

J

K

L

M

N

T

U

V

W

X

Acknowledgments

Writer · **Jordan R. Young**

Cartographer · **Alyson Stanton**

GraphicDesigner · **Barbara Stanfield**

Editor · **Kristine Miller**

Photography

Mike Besack 82

David J. Brackney . 56, 60 (bottom), 65 (bottom), 68, 75, 85, 93, 95, 96, 97, 99, 166

Robert Brown 79

Todd Masinter . . . 6, 13, 34, 36, 38 (top), 47, 48, 61, 63, 64 (bottom), 70, 105

Jordan R. Young . . 15, 18, 22, 26, 38 (bottom), 41, 42, 57, 60 (top), 64, 66, 69

MGM Mirage 20

Cirque de Soleil/Tomasz Rossa. 45

Las Vegas News Bureau . . . . 4, 15, 39, 77, 96, 54, 55, 65 (top), 83

Scandia Family Fun Center 44

University of Nevada, Las Vegas/Special Collections . . . . 11, 12, back cover

The Venetian. 21

Notes